KIFTSGATE COURT GARDENS

KIFTSGATE COURT GARDENS
Three Generations of Women Gardeners

Vanessa Berridge

Photography by
Sabina Rüber

Foreword by
Robin Lane Fox

MERRELL
LONDON · NEW YORK

GARDEN KEY

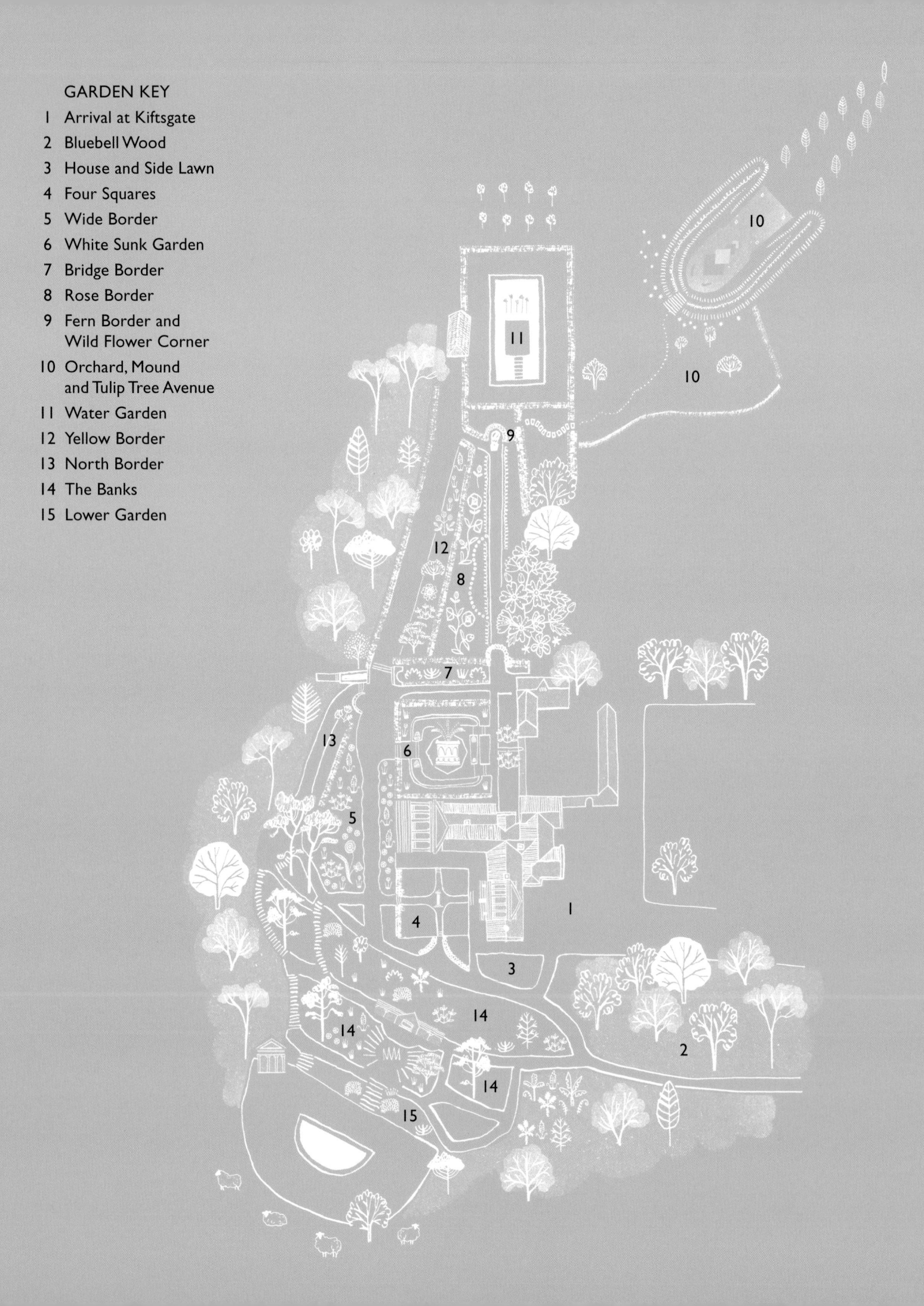

1. Arrival at Kiftsgate
2. Bluebell Wood
3. House and Side Lawn
4. Four Squares
5. Wide Border
6. White Sunk Garden
7. Bridge Border
8. Rose Border
9. Fern Border and Wild Flower Corner
10. Orchard, Mound and Tulip Tree Avenue
11. Water Garden
12. Yellow Border
13. North Border
14. The Banks
15. Lower Garden

Contents

6
Foreword
Robin Lane Fox

9
Introduction

The History

15
Early Kiftsgate

21
An Eye for Colour:
Heather Muir
(1888–1961)

33
A Practical Plantswoman:
Diany Binny
(1915–2006)

45
The Modernizing Spirit:
Anne Chambers
(b. 1951)

The Garden

56
Arrival at Kiftsgate

62
Bluebell Wood

69
House and Side Lawn

75
Four Squares

85
Wide Border

92
White Sunk Garden

103
Bridge Border

108
Rose Border

118
Fern Border and Wild Flower Corner

124
Orchard, Mound and Tulip Tree Avenue

132
Water Garden

141
Yellow Border

148
North Border

152
The Banks

163
Lower Garden

172
The 'Kiftsgate' Rose

174
Kiftsgate's Signature Plants

177
Afterword
Anne Chambers

178
Timeline of Kiftsgate's History
and Development

180
Select Bibliography

181
Acknowledgements
and Picture Credits

184
Index

Foreword
Robin Lane Fox

Kiftsgate's garden is an inspiring witness to artistry, horticultural skill, adventure and intelligent evolution. There is nowhere else in Britain that has such a family tradition of planting and dedication, now well into its third generation and, in 2019, its centenary year. Whenever anyone asks me which gardens to visit between April and late September, Kiftsgate is always in my top three or four suggestions. It has never been managed or made over by the National Trust. It is not run on a budget of managerial proportions, and yet it continues to outclass most 'heritage' gardens in public ownership. It is intimate but many-sided, evolving but with roots in a remarkable past.

Vanessa Berridge has based this excellent book on letters, records and hours of recollections by Anne and Johnny Chambers, full-time geniuses of the place for the past thirty years. As a result, Vanessa has been able to add much to the garden's early history, even finding a connection between its first planter, Heather Muir, and her early life among gardens in Herefordshire, including work by the king of Victorian formal parterres, W.A. Nesfield. Heather's own style was to be very different.

No other garden of such range and beauty can match Kiftsgate's claim to be an 'Englishwoman's garden'. It is not based on one woman's lifetime; it spans three. It is fascinating to follow its story from Heather Muir's beginnings in 1919 through the thirty-odd years of rule by her daughter the redoubtable Diany Binny, to the superb levels to which Anne, her granddaughter, has brought and maintained it since 1988. I have known it for more than fifty years, and each time I visit, I see new things, none more amazing than the Water Garden and its dripping and swaying gilded leaves, cleverly designed by Simon Allison in the late 1990s. I remember well its public opening, when I was asked at short notice to say a word or two about the 'new initiative'. I had assumed it would be a planting of summer-flowering campanulas. Instead, it was a major work of garden art, combining a dark pool, cleverly raised paving stones and the philodendron leaves in gilded bronze. Formerly the enclosed site had been a tennis court.

Anne and Johnny Chambers proudly display the 2003 Historic Houses Association/Christie's Garden of the Year Award, an accolade voted for by the visiting public.

KIFTSGATE COURT GARDENS
6

An aerial view of the Water Garden, added by Anne and Johnny, and regarded by Robin Lane Fox as 'a major work of garden art'.

There is far more to the garden's planting than its famous monster, the white rose 'Kiftsgate', which Heather bought, unawares, from the great rosarian E.A. Bunyard in the 1930s. Diany Binny even raised pterostyrax trees from seed, as few amateurs do, and planted them as a belt around the main car park, where their dangling chains of white flowers now confound keen visitors in late June. Anne and Johnny have transformed the steep bank, which used to descend to a swimming pool of incongruous blue. Brilliantly, they painted the pool black and then multiplied the planting before and above it with fine abutilons, the best hebes, magenta Madeiran geraniums and floriferous varieties of cistus. Like the Water Garden, it gives a new mood to the whole area, multiplying the garden's charms for visitors throughout the seasons.

Behind every famous Englishwoman's garden lurks an Englishman, or at least a naturalized Englishman. Heather's sights and skills were raised by her brilliant neighbour, a 'quiet American' personified, Lawrence Johnston at Hidcote, just up the road. Diany's husband, Tony, added notable tree peonies to the garden. When Anne returned from London to negotiate her mother and eventual control of the garden, few gave her, a Chelsea girl, much long-term chance of success. She surprised everyone, but she also had Johnny, who co-planned, worked and developed the nursery and plant stall for visitors. His skill at plant propagation has become an invaluable resource for the garden, which goes through losses and deaths as does every great collection. On its steep hill, there is nothing kind or forgiving about Kiftsgate's site and the soil on its Banks, making it even more inspiring to fellow gardeners.

At present, a successor is uncertain. However, Anne and Johnny's elder son, Robert, will be tipping the traditional gender balance only slightly when his turn eventually comes to put the male hand in charge. As he well realizes, it will be quite a legacy. From the early prunus to the last lace-cap hydrangeas and toad lilies (*Tricyrtis*), Kiftsgate is the joyful result of three generations. It glories in fine individual plants, excellently considered combinations and an inventiveness that has kept the design alive, enlarged and fresh. None of these attributes comes about by accident. This fascinating book sets each phase of the garden's history in contexts that will help visitors to notice even more in what they see.

KIFTSGATE COURT GARDENS

Introduction

Perched on the northern edge of the Cotswold Hills, Kiftsgate Court looks out to the west, towards Bredon Hill and the Malverns. To the left of the entrance, the ground sweeps gracefully away below a stone balustrade. On a bright early summer's morning, after rain, the mixed woodland along the slope is decked out in many shades of green. Weeping silver limes line the drive to the house, and below them are bluebell woods, a lake of blue in early May with interplantings of acers and prunus for spring and autumn colour.

This is just the curtain-raiser to a garden composed of many different scenes, representing the work of three generations of the same family. It was originally laid out in the 1920s and 1930s by Heather Muir, a woman with no horticultural training but gifted with rare imagination and an intuitive feeling for plants. In 1919 she and her husband, Jack, bought the Grecian-fronted Victorian house standing on a relatively narrow plateau from which a bank plunges 100 feet (30 m). This precipitous hillside is protected by soaring Scots pines planted in the 1750s on the advice of the farmer-poet William Shenstone. Here, Heather began to create what would become one of England's most exceptional gardens. Thanks to the microclimate, she would find that tender plants are hardy even towards the brow of the hill. The plateau garden benefits from a good loam soil and some clay, allowing the wide variety of planting that gives Kiftsgate its distinctive character.

Some elements of this garden are what one thinks of as traditionally English. Kiftsgate has a bluebell wood, clipped hedging and a rose garden, where the white *Rosa filipes* 'Kiftsgate' rears up into a copper beech like a vast billowing curtain. Yet this garden, made by Italian gardeners, is anything but standard English. There is no apron of lawn flanked by symmetrical herbaceous borders; instead, sinuous borders run across the top of the hillside, planted throughout with a mixture of perennials, rare and exotic shrubs, and roses. And if you make your way down the west-facing banks, you are in a world of Italianate planting and terracing, inspired originally by winters spent by the Muirs in the Mediterranean. Return to the plateau and you will walk into the twenty-first century through a cool, elegant water garden and, beyond that, over a mound and up an avenue of tulip trees leading to a stainless-steel leaf sculpture. Even the briefest of visits to Kiftsgate proves that this is a garden that never stands still.

Unlike National Trust-run gardens, which tend to be set in the aspic of one historical period, Kiftsgate has a sense of both continuity and gentle evolution. This is largely because the garden has belonged to the same family since its creation. Three women have tended Kiftsgate, each one its driving force for a third of a century, and each building on the legacy of the previous generation. Heather Muir gave Kiftsgate its structure, laying out the semi-formal gardens by the house, planting the Tapestry Hedge and Rose Border, and terracing the Banks. In 1954 Heather was succeeded by her daughter Diany Binny,

Heather Muir's Four Squares make a dramatic beginning for a garden visit, as the ebullient planting here is framed by the Georgian portico and the shelter belt of pine trees.

INTRODUCTION

who extended and developed her mother's planting, made more borders and paths, and refashioned the White Sunk Garden. Since the late 1980s, Diany's daughter Anne Chambers has been at the helm, further modernizing the garden and its planting, creating new areas of interest, and opening more often to the public.

Heather Muir started work at Kiftsgate in the aftermath of the First World War, a conflict that helped to change British gardening forever. Gardeners went off to fight, never to return, so armies of hands were no longer available to maintain the elaborate parterres of the Victorians. But, in fact, the reaction against Victorian formality had already set in before 1914. The social idealism of the Arts and Crafts movement, which had been founded by William Morris in the second half of the nineteenth century, laid far greater emphasis on the beauty of handmade local crafts, as opposed to factory mass production, replicated in gardening terms by industrial-scale carpet bedding.

The horticultural prophets of the Arts and Crafts movement were the garden writer William Robinson and the designer and writer Gertrude Jekyll. Robinson's books *The Wild Garden* (1870) and *The English Flower Garden* (1883) described an entirely new gardening aesthetic that emphasized individual, often perennial, plants chosen for their adaptability, rather than hot-housed exotics planted out in serried rows and artificial patterns. Jekyll, through hundreds of articles and a dozen books, promulgated the same message. She related plants to where they grew naturally, and planted them with others that thrived in similar conditions. 'It is not enough to cultivate plants well; they must be used well', she wrote in *Wood and Garden* (1899).

Whether or not Heather Muir had read Robinson and Jekyll, she was attuned to this style of gardening. She filled her borders with perennials and shrubs that would flourish in the prevailing conditions, and gave each border depth and character through her interest in foliage as much as through flower colour. A much younger contemporary of Jekyll, she effectively translated that great gardener's use of colour into something fresher and sharper for the twentieth century. Her instinctive understanding of which plants would combine well has helped to inspire those with smaller gardens. In its free-flowing associations, her style is light years away from static Victorian planting.

Heather was lucky with her timing. The interwar years were a golden era of English gardening, during which Lawrence Johnston consolidated his work at Hidcote Manor; Vita Sackville-West gardened at Long Barn and began the creation of Sissinghurst, both in Kent; Daisy Lloyd emulated William Robinson at Great Dixter in East Sussex; Gertrude Jekyll and William Robinson were still gardening; and Norah Lindsay set up as a society garden designer. Coton Manor garden in Northamptonshire was also started in the 1920s; unusually, as in the case of Kiftsgate, it remains in the same family almost a century later.

All these gardeners were known to Heather Muir; indeed, some were her personal friends. Lawrence Johnston was her next-door neighbour, and the fame of Hidcote Manor has somewhat obscured the Muir family's achievements at Kiftsgate. At the top of the hill leading from the village of Mickleton, visitors can pause to decide whether to turn right to Hidcote or left to Kiftsgate. David Wheeler, the editor of *Hortus* magazine, always goes to the left, as he wrote in his book *Over the Hills from Broadway* (1991): 'Gardening *cognoscenti*, confronted with open gates to vastly different worlds, today turn unhesitatingly to explore the exuberant, almost riotous, "living" garden tumbling down the escarpment towards the Vale of Evesham.'

Wheeler added, rightly, that comparisons between the two gardens arise only because of their proximity. Mostly these comparisons are not illuminating, although both gardens owe something of their original design to the Arts and Crafts movement, and Heather

Muir borrowed the idea of the Tapestry Hedge from Hidcote. But, in every other way, the gardens are different in aspect and conception. Hidcote is compartmentalized, with each 'room' tending to be devoted to particular plants. Kiftsgate, by contrast, is more open, a garden in which the various elements fit together seamlessly. The biggest difference, however, is that Hidcote, renowned in its own time, has had the muscle power of the National Trust since 1948 to keep it in the public eye as a monument to pre-Second World War gardening. Kiftsgate, conversely, is a 'living', constantly changing, garden.

The reason that Kiftsgate is less well known than many of its contemporaries has something to do with the character of its three gardeners. Heather Muir, Diany Binny and Anne Chambers have all been reserved women, concentrating their efforts on constantly enhancing their garden. For Heather and Diany, gardening was primarily a private activity, done simply because they enjoyed it. Anne, perhaps more than her mother and grandmother, has needed to put the garden on a business-like footing, yet she continues to garden daily with very little help.

These gardeners have not been writers: Vita Sackville-West's weekly column for *The Observer* put Sissinghurst on the garden-visiting map, and Christopher Lloyd's many books and four decades of *Country Life* articles did the same for Great Dixter. Not for the Muir women the speaking tours that introduced Beth Chatto and her garden to an international audience. None of them has sought the publicity that helped their fellow Gloucestershire gardener Rosemary Verey to become a familiar name well beyond gardening circles.

Although Heather Muir, Diany Binny and Anne Chambers have not written books, nor even kept a regular diary, two at least have maintained meticulous plant lists that provide an insight into the garden's evolution and, to an extent, changing fashions in planting. Their letters, too, and their gardening friends, all help us to understand how and why they have gardened.

I have been fortunate to have had exclusive access to the Kiftsgate Court Archive, containing letters to and from the various family members. The correspondence reveals something of the lives and motivations of these three remarkable women. Using other local documents and archives, I have delved behind the scenes at Kiftsgate to explore its history, which began more than 150 years before the Muirs arrived in 1919. But, most of all, I have been lucky enough to spend hours in the garden in the company of Anne Chambers, its present chatelaine. My account, illustrated by the glorious photography of Sabina Rüber, will, I hope, prove to readers that Kiftsgate is one of the great gardens of England.

Even in extreme old age, Diany still enjoyed spending time in the garden with her daughter Anne.

INTRODUCTION

The History

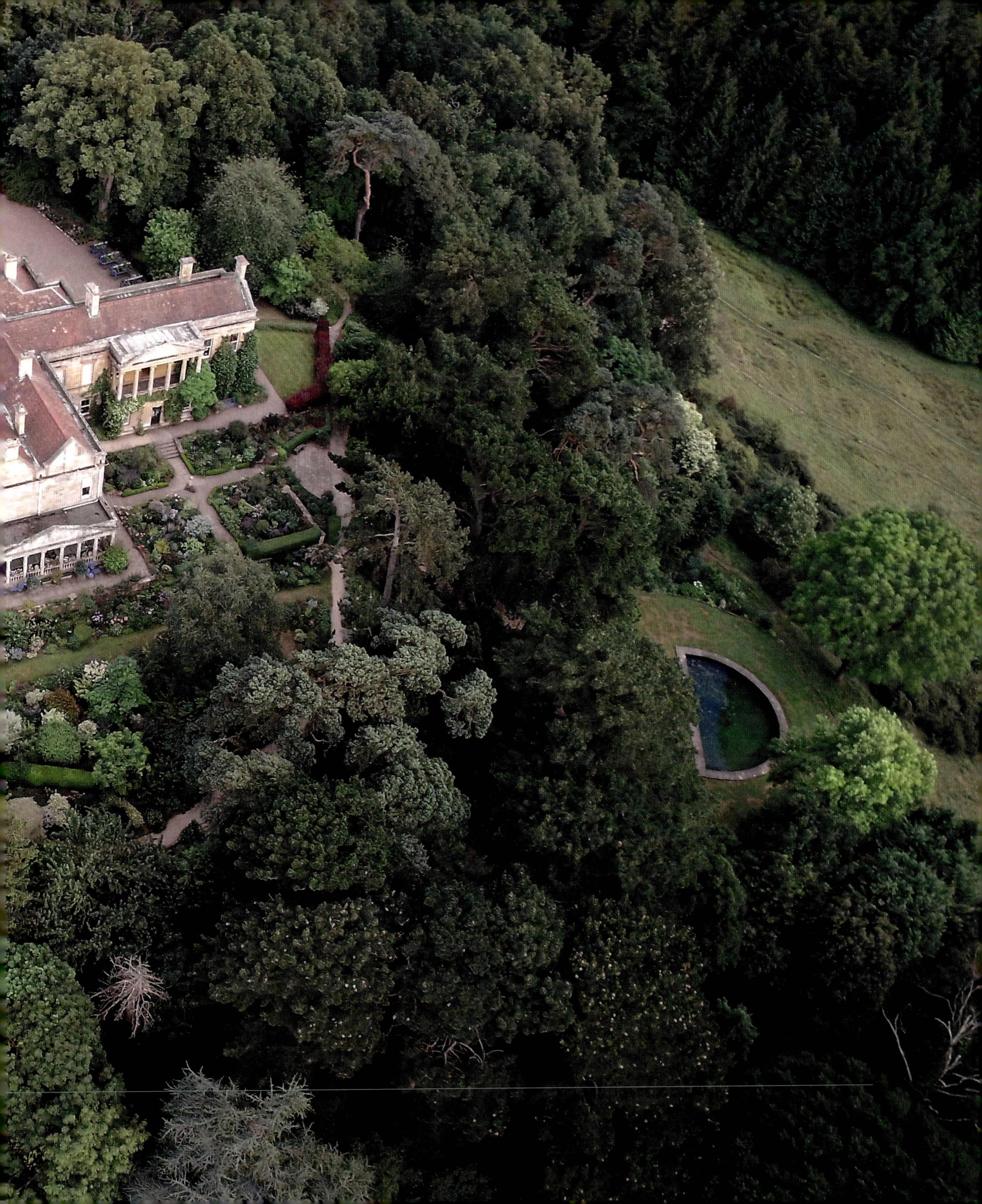

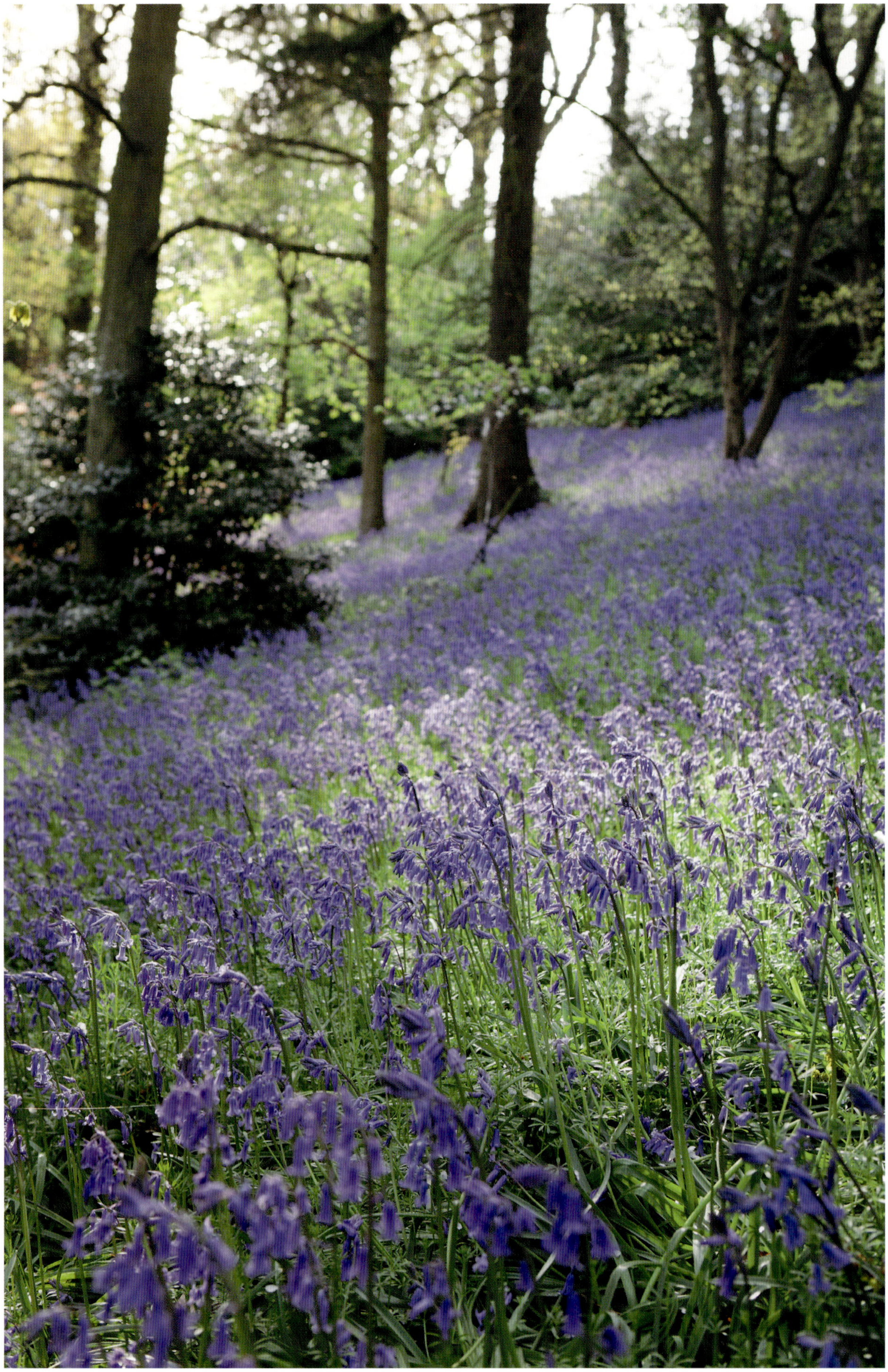

Early Kiftsgate

Kiftsgate Court stands on the top of Glyde Hill, above the village of Mickleton in Gloucestershire. Built at the end of the nineteenth century by Sidney Graves Hamilton, it is some centuries newer than the Graves family's seventeenth-century ancestral home, Mickleton Manor, which stands beside the village church. But the name chosen by Graves Hamilton for his new house was Anglo-Saxon, its origins dating back a millennium before even the manor was built.

'Kifts' probably derives either from the Old English *cyft*, meaning 'meeting' or 'conference', or from *cyþþ*, relating to 'kin' or 'native land' (as in 'kith'). 'Gate' is from *geat*, for 'gateway' or 'gap'. This compound name was given by the Anglo-Saxons to an ancient standing stone near Dover's Hill on the Cotswold Way. The Kiftsgate Stone marks a former 'moot' site, where the Anglo-Saxons would have met to discuss tribal matters. Perforations in the stone suggest that it may once have supported a gate, possibly explaining the 'gate' in 'Kiftsgate'. The stone continued to be used for local and national proclamations until the announcement of William IV's coronation in 1831.

Mickleton (from the Anglo-Saxon *mycclantune*, meaning 'large village') lies in the Hundred of Kiftsgate. A 'hundred' was a subdivision of a county or a shire that had its own court – one that presumably met, pre-Norman Conquest, at the Kiftsgate Stone. The word is more familiar now from the phrase 'taking the Chiltern Hundreds', which refers to the legal procedure by which an MP resigns from the House of Commons. So, although Kiftsgate Court itself is only some 130 years old, its name has a historic ring to it.

The Graves Family of Mickleton

The Graves family arrived in England with the Norman Conquest and settled originally in Yorkshire. The lawyer Richard Graves made a fortune during the Commonwealth years (1649–60), purchasing the Kiftsgate Hundred in 1654 and the manor of Mickleton in 1656. Some of his property may well have been sequestered from Sir Endymion Porter, who owned land around Mickleton and Aston-sub-Edge. A Catholic poet, art dealer and courtier of Charles I, Porter was painted by Anthony van Dyck on several occasions on his own and with the king. Porter chose the wrong side in the Civil

Opposite: The Bluebell Wood below the drive is at its glorious best in May.

Below: An ancient Anglo-Saxon meeting stone near Dover's Hill gives its name to Kiftsgate Court.

War, unlike Richard Graves, and was forced into exile, while the Graves family established themselves at Mickleton for three centuries. Mickleton Manor was finally sold by Mary Graves Hamilton in the 1950s.

Graves's grandson, also Richard, was a scholar and antiquarian whose particular area of interest was the Kiftsgate Hundred. His eldest son, Morgan (1708–1771), inherited Mickleton Manor, while his second son, another Richard (1715–1804), became a clergyman, poet, translator and novelist.

William Shenstone

When you drive towards Mickleton from Broadway today, you will see a line of Scots pines silhouetted against the sky between Kiftsgate and the Warwickshire border. These were planted in the 1750s at the suggestion of William Shenstone, who is described by Tim Richardson in his book *The Arcadian Friends* (2007) as a 'second-rank poet, failed farmer and superlative garden designer'. Born in 1714 at his father's farm, The Leasowes, at Halesowen, near Birmingham, Shenstone read avidly from an early age. One biographer, A.R. Humphreys, has recounted that 'if his parents forgot to purchase books at the country fairs they attended, his mother had to disguise a block of wood and carry it up to him in bed, to induce him, by this simple deception, to go to sleep, if not to awaken, in a state of contentment'.

In 1732 Shenstone went up to Pembroke College, Oxford, where he met Richard Graves, a friendship that Shenstone later said was 'the greatest happiness, and the greatest pride of my life'. Shenstone did not so much leave Oxford as fail to return, while Graves became a fellow of All Souls and was ordained. The two remained friendly until Shenstone's death in 1763, as Graves recalled in his *Recollection of Some Particulars in the Life of the Late William Shenstone, Esq.*, published in 1788: 'I enjoyed an intimacy, and carried on an occasional correspondence, with him [Shenstone], for thirty years.' This intimacy led to Shenstone's being invited in 1735 to visit Richard Graves's brother Morgan at the family home at Mickleton.

Shenstone was a reserved and indolent man, inclined to run to fat, and conscious that his background was less polished than that of some of his contemporaries. He seems to have held a candle for the sister of Morgan and Richard, and subsequently for a lady in Cheltenham, but his paltry £300 a year put marriage out of the question in the social circles in which he now moved.

The mid-eighteenth century was the heyday of the English landscape movement, and the time Shenstone spent with Morgan Graves at Mickleton Manor was a revelation to him. Landowners created naturalistic-seeming gardens and estates with sinewy walks and serpentine streams, all contrasting greatly with the rigid formalism of French gardens in fashion a generation earlier. Morgan Graves had been influenced by the *ferme ornée* created by the gentleman-farmer Philip Southcote at Woburn (or Wooburn) Farm, near Chertsey in Surrey. This 150-acre (60-ha) estate blurred the distinction between formal garden and pasture land in a self-consciously rustic way.

Morgan Graves improved his estate at Mickleton along similar lines. Like Southcote and indeed Shenstone, Graves was a farmer, so his landscape garden, dotted with follies, was surrounded by farmland, with cattle used ornamentally as well as for beef and dairy. As Richard Graves later recorded, it was at Mickleton that Shenstone 'seems to have conceived the first idea of attempting what proved the most fortunate … undertaking in which he was ever engaged'. An indifferent poet, like Vita Sackville-West two hundred years later, he appears to have realized that his true calling lay in gardening. He created a masterpiece of what he described as a 'landskip' at The Leasowes, embellishing his paternal estate, 'which his ancestors cultivated for a subsistence'.

The Leasowes comprised 150 acres (60 ha) of grazing and rolling farmland, with fields and planted valleys. Shenstone created lakes and cascades in the central valley, and planted groves of trees, hanging woods and avenues. In the spirit of pastoral poetry, he erected Gothic seats, arbours and alcoves, all with views over the surrounding countryside, and furnished the garden with memorial urns and statues. It was much admired by the gardening commentator Thomas Whately, who had also commended Southcote's Woburn Farm. In his *Observations on Modern Gardening* (1770), Whately wrote that The Leasowes 'is a perfect picture of [Shenstone's] mind, simple, elegant, and amiable; and will always suggest a doubt, whether the spot inspired his verse; or whether, in the scenes which he formed, he only realized the pastoral images which abound in his songs'.

Shenstone moved in literary circles, numbering among his friends the poets James Thomson, the author of *The Seasons* (1730), and Alexander Pope, whose villa, grotto and garden he admired at Twickenham. He would also have seen Lord Burlington's garden at Chiswick, designed by William Kent and regarded as the cradle of the English landscape movement. Other friends included his near neighbour Henrietta Knight, Lady Luxborough, exiled by her unpleasant husband as a result of her supposed dalliance with a young tutor. She, too, was a poet and a gardener; she planted an elm avenue at her Warwickshire estate, Barrells. All these connections influenced Shenstone's work at The Leasowes, which Samuel Johnson, another acquaintance, described in *Lives of the Poets* (1779–81) as 'the envy of the great, and the admiration of the skilful; a place to be visited by travellers, and copied by designers'. Despite his much smaller budget, Shenstone found that The Leasowes rivalled Lord Cobham's great landscape garden at Stowe as a visitor attraction.

Shenstone continued to visit his friends at Mickleton. In a letter to Richard Graves in July 1743, he wrote: 'I called yesterday at Mickleton; saw the portico, and snapped up a bit of mutton at your brother's.' The reference to what sounds like a new portico is intriguing, as it may have been the portico that now overlooks the Four Squares at Kiftsgate.

Having been inspired to dabble in landscape gardening at Mickleton, Shenstone returned the favour by influencing a future garden there. Framed views, eye-catchers and walks were all important features of eighteenth-century landscape gardens. In the 1750s Shenstone suggested running an elm avenue up from Mickleton Manor towards the summit of Glyde Hill. He also advocated planting Scots pines along the ridge: it is this line of trees that still shelters the garden at Kiftsgate Court. His third contribution was to suggest an avenue of limes, which would have led visitors to the boundary of Graves land. In creating these vistas through his friend's estate, Shenstone also composed the perfect site for a new house and a very different type of garden that would eventually be made

The garden designer William Shenstone, a friend of the Graves family at Mickleton, painted at The Leasowes, Halesowen, in 1760 by Edward Alcock.

EARLY KIFTSGATE

The view of Kiftsgate Court from Baker's Hill, above Mickleton, in pre-Muir days. William Shenstone's pines have been a feature of the escarpment for more than 250 years.

more than 150 years later. It is a curiosity that the romantic, Italianate garden at Kiftsgate owes its setting to the pre-Romantic English landscape movement, which emerged in the eighteenth century as a counterblast to continental influences.

The Building of Kiftsgate Court

In the late eighteenth century, Walwyn Graves (1744–1813), son of Morgan Graves and his wife, Anne Walwyn of Longford in Herefordshire, modernized his family's home in the Georgian style. Walwyn is believed to have added a Georgian front to Mickleton Manor, although Shenstone's reference to the portico in 1743 suggests that Morgan may previously have started updating the seventeenth-century house.

In 1879 Sidney Graves Hamilton (1855–1916), great-great-grandson of Morgan Graves, inherited Mickleton Manor through his mother after a series of deaths had wiped out a generation of the Graves family. Eight years later, this incomer from Torquay began work on a new house at the top of Glyde Hill. Influenced by having lived on the English Riviera, he perhaps preferred the more open aspect of the hilltop to the valley location of the manor. Like his ancestor Richard Graves, Graves Hamilton was an Oxford man, a classical scholar at Balliol and a fellow of Hertford College for many years.

In building Kiftsgate, Graves Hamilton removed the Grecian portico and the library wing from Mickleton Manor and transferred them to his new house on Glyde Hill. A light, horse-drawn railway was constructed up through the elm avenue to transport the building more or less intact to its new site. The Georgian portico and library were but a façade to a more substantial Victorian house with several wings and a large internal courtyard.

KIFTSGATE COURT GARDENS

A first-floor ballroom, its floor expensively sprung, was subsequently turned into bedrooms by the Muirs after they bought the house in 1919. Records show that it was 'all to be done in the best manner possible and none but the very best materials used'. These materials included stone from local quarries at Westington and Hidcote for the building and the paths, and English oak for all the woodwork in the house.

Sidney Graves Hamilton enjoyed his imposing new home for only fifteen years, although during that period he took an interest in its surroundings. He commissioned a range of greenhouses, 50 feet (15 m) long and 13 feet (4 m) wide, built out of 'good Red deal', and costing £114, according to the estimate from a builder in Chipping Campden. The Monterey pines along the Banks were almost certainly planted by Graves Hamilton, in another nod to his Devon years. A Victorian-style rose garden, with a pergola and disjointed rose beds, was created to one side of the house, and paving and lawns were laid in cruciform shape around a sundial in front of the Georgian portico.

In 1906 Graves Hamilton married Rosa Leah Pidgeon, and let both Mickleton Manor and Kiftsgate Court. The newly-weds moved to Malvern, where their only daughter, Mary Graves Hamilton, was born in the following year. Graves Hamilton died in 1916 and was buried in Mickleton churchyard, 'with gables of Mickleton Manor peering through the trees on one side, and Kiftsgate Court looking down from its lordly site on the other', according to an account by the local Women's Institute.

Sentiment, or perhaps financial constraints, meant that Rosa Graves Hamilton decided after the First World War to keep Mickleton Manor, and to sell her husband's larger and grander Kiftsgate Court. Jack and Heather Muir bought the property on 27 August 1919, paying £39,125 for the house and part of the estate, although the mineral and manorial rights were reserved to Mickleton Manor. An inventory records assets for which the Muirs paid a further £400. These included a range of loose boxes for horses (£60), a lean-to peach house (£25), two greenhouses, forcing pits and kitchen-garden lights (£60), a quantity of flower pots in the kitchen garden (£2 10s.), and an allowance for mature crops in the kitchen garden (£10). These details set the scene for the Muirs' future at Kiftsgate, a life that would combine riding and gardening, in Heather's case in equal measure.

Sidney Graves Hamilton laid out an uninspiring Victorian-style rose garden, which Heather Muir would replace with her dazzling Rose Border.

EARLY KIFTSGATE

KIFTSGATE COURT GARDENS

An Eye for Colour

Heather Muir
(1888–1961)

Opposite: Heather Muir planted the Tapestry Hedge to frame her Rose Border, which still features a thigh-high hedge of *Rosa gallica* 'Versicolor'.

Right: Heather Muir as a young married woman.

Below: Sir John Muir, the founder of the family's fortunes and father of Jack Buchanan Muir.

In 1919 Major John (Jack) Buchanan Muir and his wife, Heather, bought Kiftsgate Court, above Mickleton, in Gloucestershire. It has been suggested that Lawrence Johnston, the owner of Hidcote Manor and the Muirs' future next-door neighbour (see p. 26), first told them that the house was on the market, and it would certainly be Johnston who encouraged Heather as she set about making the garden more or less from scratch.

Both the Muirs enjoyed hunting, and they looked initially at an estate in Warwickshire with better stabling. Indeed, Jack Muir's initial reservations about the house are suggested by his letter in April 1919 to a Chipping Campden architect whom he was considering employing. 'From an architectural point of view the house is a nightmare', he wrote. The architect, perhaps injudiciously, agreed, but he also suggested that the house's architectural shortcomings were 'compensated for by its fine situation and surroundings'. Those compensations convinced Heather Muir that this was somewhere she could create a garden. Although it was an awkward-shaped site, she knew that on the plateau the soil was good and that the shelter belt of Scots pines, Monterey pines, Wellingtonias, oaks and chestnuts would protect her plantings from both north and west winds.

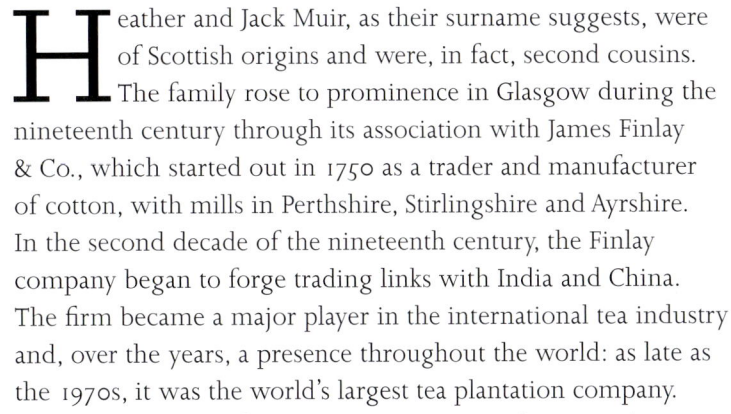

Heather and Jack Muir, as their surname suggests, were of Scottish origins and were, in fact, second cousins. The family rose to prominence in Glasgow during the nineteenth century through its association with James Finlay & Co., which started out in 1750 as a trader and manufacturer of cotton, with mills in Perthshire, Stirlingshire and Ayrshire. In the second decade of the nineteenth century, the Finlay company began to forge trading links with India and China. The firm became a major player in the international tea industry and, over the years, a presence throughout the world: as late as the 1970s, it was the world's largest tea plantation company.

Jack's father, the future Sir John Muir, was born in Glasgow in 1828, and by 1861 he was a junior partner in the Finlay company. He had also married Margaret Morrison Kay, from Cornhill, Lanarkshire, with whom he would have ten children. He steadily built up his interest in the business until, in 1883, he became the sole proprietary partner, employing some

AN EYE FOR COLOUR: HEATHER MUIR

90,000 people, mostly in the Indian subcontinent. The Indian business was known as Finlay Muir & Co. from 1870, when a branch was opened in Calcutta.

John Muir looked very much the Victorian patriarch; indeed, with his high-domed forehead, bushy white beard and voluminous, wavy hair, he slightly resembled his older contemporary Karl Marx. Unlike Marx, however, Muir was not interested in the overthrow of capitalism. He lived in a grand town house in Kelvingrove and had a country estate, Deanston House, at Doune in Perthshire. From 1889 to 1892, he was Lord Provost of Glasgow, for which he was rewarded by being made 1st Baronet Muir of Deanston. He was a Justice of the Peace for Lanarkshire and Perthshire, and Deputy Lieutenant of Lanarkshire. Many of his daughters married well, Jean entertaining Sir Winston Churchill regularly at her house in Hyde Park Gardens. Another, Elizabeth, married Thomas Moncreiffe of that Ilk. Family legend has it that, ignorant of the facts of life, she had to be calmed down in a cold bath on her wedding night.

Jack was John and Margaret Muir's ninth child and third son, born at Deanston House on 17 May 1876. He was educated at Fettes College, Edinburgh, and Trinity College, Cambridge. Sir John Muir died in August 1903, and, six years later, the business was incorporated as a private limited company. Jack was one of the directors, along with his three brothers, two older and one younger. He remained a director until 1945, although he did not play a very active part in the firm. There were long periods of absence when he was not even noted under apologies, and he attended no meetings after 1939. His older brothers were more involved: Alexander Kay Muir, who inherited the baronetcy, became chairman, and was succeeded by James Finlay Muir.

Jack and his cousin Agnes Heather Muir were married on 5 December 1911. Heather had been born on 13 August 1888 in Almeley in Herefordshire, the third daughter and fourth child of John Gardiner Muir, a first cousin of Sir John Muir, and his wife, Jessie Agnes Henderson Muir. Like his much older cousin, John Gardiner Muir was born in Glasgow, while Jessie was a farmer's daughter from Kirkwood Farm, Old Monkland, Lanarkshire. Money from the Muir–Finlay connection presumably came the couple's way, as, according to Heather's birth certificate, her father's occupation was 'gentleman'.

Heather Muir's parents, John Gardiner Muir and his wife, Jessie Agnes Henderson Muir.

The couple's home at the time of Heather's birth was Newport House, believed to have belonged to the Lollard martyr Sir John Oldcastle (d. 1417), the model for Shakespeare's Falstaff. The original medieval house was demolished by Lord Foley of Great Witley, who then, between 1712 and 1718, built the house in which Heather was born. A grandson of James Watt, a luminary of the Industrial Revolution and developer of the steam engine, bought Newport House in 1860. During his decade of ownership, Watt's grandson commissioned the leading Victorian landscaper William Andrews Nesfield to redesign the garden. Nesfield installed his trademark features, which included a stone tazza (vase) supported by lions (similar to one he installed in Regent's Park, London), and elaborate parterre beds. The garden was also extended down towards the lake with yew hedging and trees. Heather's parents were probably only tenants of Newport House, for they were peripatetic: their eldest daughter, Muriel (Milly), was born in Scotland in 1881, while the birth of their youngest child, Clara, was registered at Market Harborough in Leicestershire in 1891. The family later moved to Farming Woods Hall in Northamptonshire, and Heather's father became Deputy Lieutenant of the county.

The family lived in some style, as can be seen from a beautiful Victorian coromandel travelling vanity case sold at auction in Chiswick in 2017. The case, dating from 1874, probably belonged to Clara Turton Muir, an unmarried sister of John Gardiner Muir; she gave it to Clara Gardiner Muir, her youngest niece and namesake. The case contains silver-topped jars and scent bottles, grooming items with mother-of-pearl handles, and ivory brushes, mirrors and glove stretchers inscribed with the motto, crest and coat of arms of

A coromandel travelling vanity case of 1874 fitted with grooming items of sterling silver, ivory and mother-of-pearl. It belonged to Heather Muir's sister Clara Gardiner Muir.

Heather Muir (left) and her younger sister, Clara, on their ponies, probably at their childhood home of Farming Woods Hall in Northamptonshire.

AN EYE FOR COLOUR: HEATHER MUIR

the Muir family, all fitted in blue velvet trays. Documents found inside the case include a dance card from Eglinton Castle, North Ayrshire, dated 28 March 1883.

As girls, Heather and her sisters were often photographed in riding habits, and there would be keen horsewomen in all future generations. Heather would have been under three years old when the family left Newport House, so it is unlikely that the Nesfield parterre made much impression on her. But the fact that the Muirs chose to rent a house with so important a garden suggests that they were aware of horticultural fashion. This interest rubbed off on Heather, even if the garden she was to create would be the very antithesis of Nesfield's high Victorian formalism.

Jack Muir, photographed in the uniform of the Black Watch during the First World War.

Jack Buchanan Muir and Heather Muir during their engagement.

Although John Gardiner Muir and his family lived in England, they spent time in Scotland, as indicated by the dance card from Eglinton Castle. Heather and Jack may have met on one of these visits, and obviously fell, and remained, deeply in love. Congratulating Heather on her silver wedding in 1936, Jack's sister-in-law, Nada Muir, wrote, 'You will look back with joy on so many years of perfect married life, and the companionship of one to whom you mean <u>so much</u> (and who is not a man who would have been made happy by any other type of woman.)'

A charming story is told about a trip made by Jack and Heather to Paris during their engagement. They visited a glove shop, where Heather tried on but decided not to buy a pair of gloves. Later, she realized that she had lost her engagement ring, and failed to find it. After the First World War, the Muirs returned to the Paris glove shop. Heather picked up what turned out to be the same pair of gloves, and there, inside the fourth finger of the left hand, was her ring. She had unusually small hands and no one else had tried on the pair in the intervening years.

Tiny hands may not seem ideal for a gardener, but, by the time of her marriage, Heather must already have had in mind the creation of a garden. But first she bore three daughters: Marguerite Judith (Judy) in 1913; Diana Heather (Diany) in 1915; and Bettine Clara (Betsy) in 1917.

In October 1914 Jack was gazetted captain in the 6th (Perthshire) Battalion of the Black Watch, surviving the conflict

KIFTSGATE COURT GARDENS

24

Left: Kiftsgate Court shortly after the house was built by Sidney Graves Hamilton. The existing layout was retained by Heather Muir when she created the Four Squares.

Below: Heather Muir with her young daughters (from left to right), Diany, Betsy and Judy.

uninjured, while Heather spent the war years at Farming Woods. By 1919 the Muirs wanted their own home, and Kiftsgate had many attractions. Not the least was that it was less than 20 miles (32 km) from Postlip Hall, a medieval hall house just outside Winchcombe, also in Gloucestershire, and the home of Heather's younger sister, Clara Gardiner Muir. Clara had married Jack's younger brother, Matthew, in 1912, and their two children, Gillian, born 1914, and Ian Kay (Kim), born 1916, were close to their three cousins at Kiftsgate.

A pattern of family life established itself after the Muirs moved to Kiftsgate in 1919. Heather designed her garden primarily for spring and early summer, as high summer and early autumn were spent with Muir cousins in Perthshire. The Muirs tended to winter in the Mediterranean, as did their neighbour Lawrence Johnston, who in 1924 bought land in Menton on the Côte d'Azur, where he made his other garden, Serre de la Madone.

When the Muirs bought Kiftsgate, there was little in the way of garden, apart from paving and a flat lawn around a sundial in front of the Georgian portico, a formal but dilapidated Victorian-style rose garden on the other side of the house (now the site of the Rose Border), and the wooded banks below. One of Heather's first acts was to create a protecting framework of yew hedging around the top terrace. Inspired by Johnston at Hidcote, she also planted the Tapestry Hedge – a glossy mix of green and copper beech, yew, and plain and variegated holly – as a dramatic entrance to her Rose Border.

AN EYE FOR COLOUR: HEATHER MUIR

Heather kept the sundial and worked with the existing cruciform layout and Yorkstone paving by the portico. Instead of lawn, she planted box-edged beds to make what became known as the Four Squares. These beds were filled with the romantic and feminine mix of shrubs, roses and perennials that characterize the garden at Kiftsgate. The Wide Border and the Rose Border were also laid out in the 1920s, the latter filled with unusual rose varieties and cut through by a grass path, flanked by hedges of *Rosa gallica* 'Versicolor'. The Yellow Border, on the other side of a yew hedge from the Rose Border, also featured Heather's interest in the interplay of foliage and flower.

The interwar years were an exciting time in gardening, as the range of plants available had been increasing since the turn of the century, with such collectors as Reginald Farrer, George Forrest and the Chipping Campden-born Ernest Henry Wilson sending back garden-worthy plants from the Far East. Heather and Johnston put in joint orders for peonies that would take six months to arrive from Japan by ship. Some of these still flourish at Kiftsgate today.

Although Heather was encouraged and initially guided by Johnston, she quickly proved herself a formidable plantswoman in her own right. An early exponent of colour and textural contrast, she also had a natural understanding of plants and their requirements. 'It was her great sense of colour and love of plants that produced the final results in the garden', her daughter Diany wrote many years later. 'She must have been one of the first gardeners to keep borders to definite tones of colour as with the pink, crimson, lavender, purple and abundant greys of the Wide Border, then the dark mahogany foliage coupled with golden and sulphur yellows, splashed with vivid blues and mauves of the Yellow Border.' Heather's gift for colour was much admired by the eminent horticulturalist A.G.L. Hellyer, who described Kiftsgate as 'one of the loveliest rose gardens in England' in an article in *Country Life* in 1953. In an April 1954 issue of *Amateur Gardening*, he wrote

Lawrence Johnston and his gardeners in the Old Garden at Hidcote Manor in the early 1910s.

Lawrence Johnston (1871–1958)

The creator of the garden at Hidcote Manor, Kiftsgate's more famous next-door neighbour, was Lawrence Johnston. Born in Paris, he was the son of rich, nomadic Americans. He spent much of his childhood travelling round Europe, where he saw the grand Renaissance gardens that would in time influence the structure of his own garden. He became a British citizen in 1900, studied agriculture and served in the Second Boer War before moving to Gloucestershire in 1907, when his formidable mother, Gertrude Winthrop, bought the estate at Hidcote Bartrim.

Johnston began making the garden before the First World War. Initially, his chief influence was the Arts and Crafts movement, and in particular a book by Thomas Mawson, *The Art and Craft of Garden Making*, published in 1900. Inspired by Mawson, Johnston created avenues, vistas and rooms for the many different types of plants that he collected over the next few decades. He broke with the Arts and Crafts movement by creating structure not with local stone, but with gleaming tapestry hedges of beech, yew, box and holly, which would in turn influence Heather Muir at Kiftsgate.

Johnston returned from service in France, where he had almost died, to continue his great work just as Heather was starting out at Kiftsgate. In 1924 he began making the garden at Serre de la Madone in Menton, the terraced planting of which may have had an effect on Heather's Italianate Banks at Kiftsgate. Neither wrote articles, diaries or accounts of their gardens, nor did they like having their photographs taken, so there is no written or visual record of their association. But it is clear that Johnston encouraged Heather, and she in turn kept a weather eye on his great garden after he gave it to the National Trust in 1948.

KIFTSGATE COURT GARDENS

Left: Heather Muir with her three daughters, Judy, Betsy and Diany, in the Wide Border in its infancy.

Below: The Tapestry Hedge, between the Bridge Border and the Rose Border, was already well established by the time Judy Muir was photographed in the arch in the mid-1920s.

that Heather produced 'a series of pictures in colour that are rich but never glaring. They are the colours I associate with fine old tapestry.'

Heather kept neither a diary nor plant lists of her garden, as Diany did after she took over in the 1950s. Insight into Heather's thinking is provided, however, by a bill dated 11 March 1926 from the Exeter-based nursery Robert Veitch & Son. It shows that, less than six years after starting her garden, Heather had developed an impressive knowledge of rare shrubs and trees. Her order, which cost £5 15s. 3d. (about £250 today), included the Chilean *Lomatia ferruginea*; the Himalayan *Indigofera gerardiana*; a Chinese *Sophora viciifolia*; an uncommon pear, *Pyrus* 'Elise Rathe'; and three standard pears. Indigoferas remain important shrubs in the garden today.

In the 1930s Heather made a tennis court for her daughters, surrounding it with yew hedging. She cleared out the abundant ash from the Bluebell Wood (using dynamite, according to family myth), leaving the oaks and planting it with rare varieties of acer and rhododendrons grafted from *Rhododendron ponticum*. She also tackled the Banks below the Four Squares, using her team of Italian gardeners to make zigzag steps and paths from the caps and stalks of staddle stones. Heather designed and built a west-facing summer house, and planted the slopes with drought-tolerant cistus, rosemary, abutilons, spiky agaves and ceanothus. The style of planting here was prompted by her love of the Mediterranean, and possibly by the family's friendship with Aubrey and Lina Waterfield (see p. 35). The Waterfields owned the school attended for two years in their late teens by Diany and Betsy at Poggio Gherardo, within sight of Florence. On one visit to Kiftsgate, Aubrey sketched a plan for these terraces, which

AN EYE FOR COLOUR: HEATHER MUIR

may have helped to inspire Heather. Whatever her influences, she effectively created an Italianate garden on a Gloucestershire hillside, and produced a crescendo of interest in contrast to the ebullient rose and perennial garden above.

Another friendship, that with Lawrence Johnston and his mother, Gertrude Winthrop, played its part in the Muir family life. The grandchild-less Mrs Winthrop would take the three Muir girls to the theatre in Stratford-upon-Avon during their holidays from boarding at St James's, Malvern. After leaving school, Judy, the eldest, spent time in France, while Diany and Betsy went to Poggio Gherardo. The girls were prodigious correspondents, writing regularly to one another and to their parents when apart, their letters full of affection. They use various sobriquets: Judy is also Judells; Diany, Dumps and Di; Betsy, Becky. Their openings are florid, with many letters being addressed to 'Darlingest Darlings'. There is a sense that members of this rather reserved family found it easier to express themselves on paper than in person. This was also true of the Nicolsons at Sissinghurst, as Nigel Nicolson wrote in his memoir, *Long Life* (1997). The Nicolson relationships, like those of the Muirs, 'were created more by … letters than by conversation, for we all wrote avidly back and forth to each other, but were reticent when we met'.

In the mid-1930s Aubrey Waterfield visited Kiftsgate and painted a watercolour of his vision of a summer house that would match the style of Kiftsgate Court above.

Tragedy struck, however, in June 1936, when Judy, aged just twenty-three, took her life by throwing herself, blindfolded, from a maid's bedroom window into the yard below. Judy was more of a diary-keeper than her sisters, conveying a picture of the family's life with descriptions of hunting, point-to-points, parties, and Heather and Jack dining regularly with Johnston at Hidcote. The garden is barely mentioned ('There are three trees down', she writes in January 1930), but more apparent are her mood swings. She lists her faults, and wishes 'I could tell some body about it they might help me to be better.' Her relationship with her mother was troubled, as she describes in July 1930: 'I could never believe anyone could be so sweet to me as Mummy is she does everything in her power to make me happy & the worst of it is I seem to be constantly doing something that hurts her if only she was not so fond of me or so kind to me it wouldn't worry me half so much.'

The account of the inquest into Judy's death in the *Gloucestershire Echo* makes harrowing reading. According to Jack, she had been receiving medical attention for some unspecified emotional problems. The letters of sympathy that poured in to comfort the Muirs show them as belonging to a tight-knit social world. Their friends included the Countess Fortescue, granddaughter of the Marquess of Londonderry; Lady Anne Bridgeman, daughter of the Earl of Bradford; Richard Fleming, brother of Ian and Peter; and Helen Lees-Milne, mother of the diarist and country-house expert James. Significantly, many of their sympathizers were people with whom Heather shared a love of gardening: 'Johnny' Johnston cabled from Menton on the French Riviera, and his staff wrote from Hidcote. The garden designer Norah Lindsay (see opposite) commiserated from the

Diany Muir (later Binny), Heather Muir's middle daughter, learned to swim in Lawrence Johnston's pool at neighbouring Hidcote.

KIFTSGATE COURT GARDENS

Manor House at Sutton Courtenay in Oxfordshire, as did Cicely, wife of Mark Fenwick, the creator of the magnificent terraced garden at Abbotswood, near Stow-on-the-Wold. Another correspondent was Lady Bearsted, who with her husband, the 2nd Viscount, did so much to enhance the house and gardens of Upton House, near Banbury.

These friends offered solace at a time of unbearable sorrow, and Heather's granddaughter Anne believes that the garden became all the more important to her grandmother after Judy's death. By then, Heather had given Kiftsgate the structure and much of the planting that it retains in the twenty-first century. She continued her drive to find exceptional plants, not the least being the rose that would become synonymous with the garden. In 1938 she bought what she believed to be a *Rosa moschata*, a rambling musk rose, later identified as the more rampant *filipes* and given the cultivar name of 'Kiftsgate'. She planted it at the back of her Rose Border, where it proceeded to rocket upwards and sprawl out sideways like Sleeping Beauty's briar (see pp. 172–73).

In May 1938 Heather opened the garden for the first time for the National Garden Scheme, coincidentally the same month that Vita Sackville-West (see p. 31) admitted to Sissinghurst the people whom she and her husband, Harold Nicolson, snobbishly christened the 'shillingses'. The war years were difficult. Help was scarce, and Betsy and Diany were often away, Betsy driving for the Anglo-French Ambulance Corps in France. There were losses, too, of family and friends. Clara's son, Kim, a keen horseman, died in France in May 1940; a challenge cup race named after him is still run annually at the Cheltenham National Hunt Festival in March. In January 1943 Daisy Fortescue, who had commiserated with Heather on Judy's death, wrote, 'We have heard absolutely nothing of Peter – & it is 6 months to-day since he was reported missing.' Her only son, Viscount Ebrington, had been killed at the Battle of El Alamein.

There were four gardeners, plus kitchen gardeners, at Kiftsgate before the war, but thereafter the Muirs managed with just two, Heather herself putting in long hours. She was scolded by Betsy from France in May 1940: 'I got a letter from Pa saying you had been overdoing it gardening & were back in bad pain … you are naughty though you know, working away weeding scarcely 3 weeks after an op … Now will you please behave

Norah Lindsay with the Bloomsbury literati Sir Desmond MacCarthy (left) and Sir Edward Marsh, photographed by Lady Ottoline Morrell in 1925.

Norah Lindsay (1873–1948)

One of the letters that Heather Muir received on her daughter Judy's death in 1936 was from the garden designer and socialite Norah Lindsay. 'My dearest Heather,' sympathized Norah. 'This is only a few words of love, for I feel all your family are dear to me.' She wrote from the Manor House at Sutton Courtenay in Oxfordshire, where she lived after her marriage in 1895 to Harry Lindsay. There she created one of the most admired gardens in England, but, unlike Kiftsgate, it passed out of family hands: the house was bought by the Astor family in 1945, and David Astor lived there until his death in 2001.

The Lindsay marriage collapsed in 1924, leading Norah to take up garden design professionally, her trademark being a kind of inspired untidiness in which plants were given their heads. She numbered among her clients David Astor's mother, Nancy, at Cliveden, Buckinghamshire; Edward, Prince of Wales, at Fort Belvedere in Windsor Great Park; Nancy Lancaster at both Kelmarsh Hall in Northamptonshire and Ditchley Park in Oxfordshire; and Prince Otto von Bismarck at Friedrichsruh in northern Germany. She also designed for the Marquess of Lothian at Blickling Hall in Norfolk, where her parterre survives more or less intact.

Heather almost certainly met Norah through Lawrence Johnston, who inspired them both. A road trip round England with Johnston made a big impact on Norah, as she wrote to her mother: 'It has opened my eyes to the possibilities of gardens in other parts of England and was a great education.' Norah's letter to Heather suggests a close personal friendship and a likelihood that Heather would have been very aware of Norah's use of colour and slightly wayward planting.

AN EYE FOR COLOUR: HEATHER MUIR

yourself & leave the bloody garden alone for another 6 weeks … otherwise I shall return & put you under army discipline!'

Diany recalled that the clay tennis court, 'which required continual watering and upkeep, was allowed to become derelict and in 1955 there was a wonderful display of seedling roses, Scotch firs, etc. growing on it, which my mother was very grieved to see go when it was resurfaced'. Diany's developing interest in the garden comforted Heather, who missed Diany when she went to the Far East after the war. In April 1946 Heather wrote from 'Kiffy', as she called it, saying, 'I miss you so much walking round the garden. The Anemone blanda are perfectly lovely this year & I long for your comments – I can't stop gardening but it all seems rather useless these days & often wonder why I do it.' The next month, she was again describing the garden to Diany: 'The lower garden is looking perfectly lovely: tree paeonies, Haleasea [sic], Honesty & Clematis Rubra & large heath with the red maples in the evening sunlight with the fir trees looking up at home were really lovely, wish you'd been there, as I often do, as I know you love the beauty as much as I do.' More poignantly, she added, 'Ju's birthday today & I took a lovely bowl (the pink one) of lily of the valley (pink & white) down. It was lovely, so peaceful & the skimmias have berries ha! ha! miss.'

The garden soon recovered in the post-war years, as eulogies from many gardening friends, including Sybil Cholmondeley of Houghton Hall, Norfolk, testify. In July 1949 Lord Barrington, a considerable gardener himself at Nether Lypiatt Manor, near Stroud, wrote: 'This not just blarney … I think or rather am quite sure your garden is the best I have ever seen & yr taste is superb – every thing looks as tho' it thoroughly enjoyed growing & living at Kiftsgate.' The rosarian Graham Stuart Thomas (see p. 42) praised Kiftsgate above Sissinghurst, where 'the roses are trained up poles & tripods, making a fine show but lacking the luxuriant abandon of Kiftsgate. Congratulations on your magnificent artistry.'

Thomas helped to establish the garden's reputation among the general public with an article in the May 1951 issue of the *Journal of the Royal Horticultural Society*: 'I regard this as the finest piece of skilled colour work coupled with good cultivation and horticultural interest that it has been my pleasure to see.' Letters flooded in from grateful visitors, including from Vita Sackville-West, who wrote (in pencil) in July 1956 'to say how entranced I was by your beautiful garden. I came home totally disgruntled with mine – but at least it was a satisfaction to see that we had much the same tastes and that you liked the same things as I like. I took this as a great compliment and encouragement to myself!'

Heather Muir was respected throughout the gardening world, although, for the most part, she concentrated on her own garden rather than sitting in gatherings of the great and the good. But after Johnston gave Hidcote to the National Trust in 1948, she accepted an invitation to join a management committee formed by the Trust. Other members included the plantswoman Nancy Lindsay, daughter of the designer Norah, and 'Toty' de Navarro, son of the American actress Mary Anderson de Navarro, who had done so much to put the Cotswold village of Broadway on the American ex-pat map in the early twentieth century. In 1952 Heather suggested her gardening friend Graham Stuart Thomas as a possible curator for Hidcote; although her suggestion was not taken up, Thomas later became gardens adviser to the Trust. Nancy Lindsay was dropped from the committee, having antagonized its other members and Johnston himself. Jack Muir wrote about her to Diany when she was in the Far East: 'Nancy Lindsay was here for a night on Monday. She was very kind & brought quite a few things for the white garden, but my Lord how she talks, an endless stream. She mostly wears a red handkerchief over her head & looks like a witch.'

Heather played her full part in looking after the Trust's acquisition, as was recognized in a letter to her in 1953 from the American-born garden designer Lanning Roper, who also admired Hidcote: 'You have created a wonderful garden. There are so many features

Vita Sackville-West (1892–1962)

Vita Sackville-West was a great admirer of Heather's work at Kiftsgate and visited several times a garden that, she said, gave her 'a vision of such beauty and imagination'. Vita was born nearly four years after Heather, at Knole in Kent, a stately home that she loved but failed to inherit through the accident of having been born female.

Vita compensated for her loss by making two remarkable gardens, first at Long Barn, near Knole, and then from 1930 at Sissinghurst Castle, near Cranbrook in Kent. In the design of both she was assisted by her husband, the political diarist Harold Nicolson, who drew on his knowledge of Persian gardens from his time as a diplomat in Tehran. Harold gave Vita the structure of walls and yew hedging for her inspired plantsmanship; she shared with Heather an eye for colour and a willingness to mix roses, perennials and shrubs. In July 1956 Vita wrote to Heather, asking for information about plants seen at Kiftsgate: 'I wonder also if you could tell me the name of an extra-sweet-scented philadelphus. Tiny white flowers, but a huge bush. Stupid of me not to have noted exactly where it was. It wasn't Belle Étoile; a much smaller flower, and intensely strong scent all over the air.' (Johnny Chambers believes that this was probably *Philadelphus* 'Sybille', by the front door.)

Vita planted *Rosa filipes* 'Kiftsgate' in the orchard at Sissinghurst, and commended it in one of her *Observer* columns, which helped to make her name as a gardener: 'If you want something really alarming in its vigour, get *R. filipes*, but be sure to obtain the Kiftsgate variety. Anyone who has seen this in the lovely garden of Kiftsgate Court, Chipping Campden, where it originated and where it now spreads over a horizontal span of about 50 feet, must have gasped at the possibilities offered by such a rose.'

Vita Sackville-West stands on the steps of the tower at Sissinghurst Castle, Kent. Her characteristic costume of blouse and pearls, teamed with britches and high boots, has been described by her granddaughter Juliet Nicolson as 'Lady Chatterley above the waist, and Mellors below'.

which are outstanding, and so many plants of interest that we came away bewildered. It is miraculous what you have succeeded in doing at Hidcote in the last few years. As I said on Sunday, I see a marked improvement over last year.'

Heather continued to visit Johnston at Serre de la Madone in Menton until his death in 1958. In April 1956 she received a letter from the Vicomte de Noailles, one of the trustees of the Royal Horticultural Society (RHS): 'Freddo [Johnston's cook-valet] tells me that you looked in at the Serre de la Madone a few days ago ... Your advice both as to the looking after Johnnie and the running of the garden would have been very welcome. Perhaps if you come another year, you will be kind enough to let me know. And then, I would like to hear the latest news of the Kiftsgate garden and all its treasures.'

The latest news would have been that Jack had died some months earlier, in January 1956. A friend, writing to commiserate, described him as 'so absolutely straight & reliable, kind, generous, even tempered – & so very wise & far seeing and with all his virtues, such a good companion & sportsman, with such a sense of humour'. Even before Jack's death, Heather had decided to take a back seat at Kiftsgate garden, moving out to Front Lodge and handing over the reins and the big house to Diany, who in 1950 had married Tony Binny, a banker. As late as July 1960, just ten months before her death, Heather featured with Diany in an article on Kiftsgate in *Queen* magazine. 'Mrs Muir has a sure touch with colour', the feature reported. 'She likes shelter and generally hates to see plants and trees cut. Triumphs: the steep bank where large pale yellow, single roses (Frühlingsgold) are intermingled with tall bushes of blue ceanothus merging below with drifts of pale lavender abutilons ... a combination of *Rosa mundi* rose hedge and tall rose trees, flanked by yew hedge.'

AN EYE FOR COLOUR: HEATHER MUIR

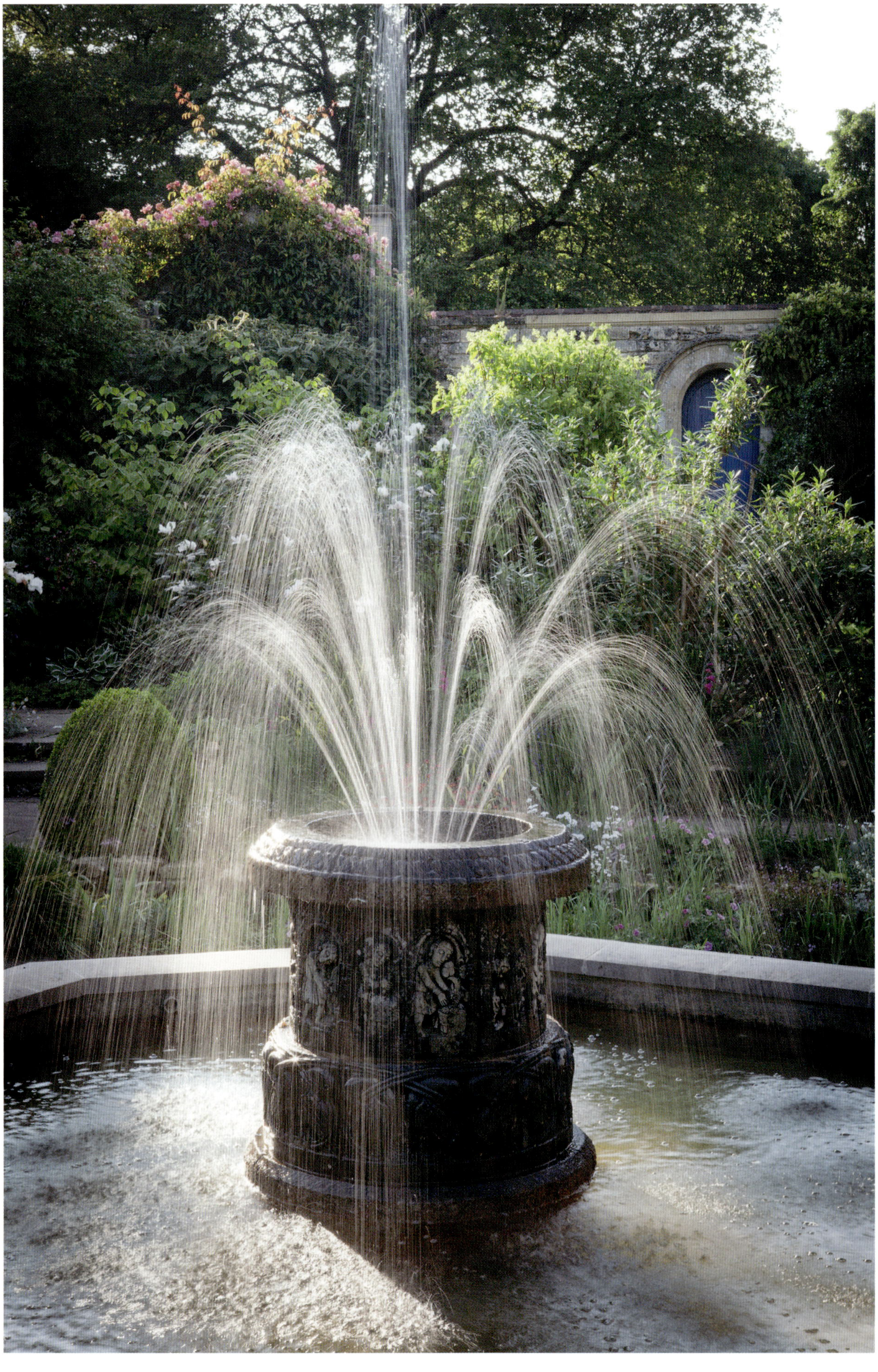

KIFTSGATE COURT GARDENS

A Practical Plantswoman

Diany Binny
(1915–2006)

Opposite: Diany made the White Sunk Garden her own, replacing her mother's lawn with a pool and a Pyrenean well-head fountain.

Right: Diany Muir before her marriage to Tony Binny.

Below: Heather Muir with Diany (left), Judy (centre) and Betsy (right). Judy was a less keen horsewoman than her sisters.

Diana Heather Muir, the second of Jack and Heather Muir's three daughters, was born on 12 March 1915, coincidentally the day on which she died ninety-one years later, having outlived her younger sister, Betsy, by a year. Always known as Diany (apart from the family sobriquet 'Dumps'), she was a keen horsewoman, often photographed dressed in riding clothes, with her sisters and mother.

Diany was educated at St James's, Malvern, before spending two years at a school in Florence run by Aubrey and Lina Waterfield. The Waterfields described the establishment at their castellated villa of Poggio Gherardo as a 'beginning' rather than a finishing school, where British girls learned Italian and were taught about Italian history, art and cooking. Aubrey, an artist, gave drawing and painting lessons, and excursions were arranged to Arezzo, Siena, Assisi, Perugia and Venice. Sending her sheltered daughter abroad worried Heather, as you can hear in a relieved early letter to Diany: 'The Waterfields sound too kind for words.' For Diany, her time at Poggio Gherardo was transformative, inculcating a love of Italy and its gardens that always remained with her; she bought Italian art whenever she could afford it.

A letter from Betsy in the mid-1930s, on her arrival in Florence after Diany had left, gives a flavour of the sisters' experiences. On the first morning, Betsy was taken by Lina and her daughter, Kinta, into the city to see the Palazzo Vecchio and the equestrian statue of Cosimo I de' Medici in the Piazza della Signoria, and to have doughnuts and lemonade in a corner shop. Betsy slept in Diany's pink-painted bedroom with an 'absolutely heavenly view' over Florence: 'It is your old room with me alone, except for your ghost which haunts it!'

Diany became close to the Waterfield family, and Aubrey's and Lina's letters to her make it clear that they thought of her as a much-loved niece and appreciated her receptiveness as a reader. It was to Diany that Kinta confided news of her engagement in 1933: 'Well if you swear on all that's Holy …

The view of Florence from the terrace at Poggio Gherardo in the 1930s, at the time both Diany and Betsy Muir attended the Waterfields' school there.

I will tell you something … But my God you must not tell a word to a soul. I am engaged!!! To some-one called Jack Beevor – I didn't want a soul to know & I haven't told anyone, as it is all so sudden.' (One of the couple's sons is the military historian Sir Antony Beevor.)

A painting by Aubrey Waterfield of Diany arranging flowers is now in a bedroom at Kiftsgate. He also painted several panels for her family home, sending painstaking instructions to Diany in June 1936. With the instructions was a sketch of the staircase showing how the panels should be hung, and revealing that the Waterfields had stayed at Kiftsgate. 'In your work room,' Aubrey wrote, 'there was a linoleum floor covering. Any really <u>flat</u> floor will do. Lay quantities of old newspaper on the floor & then unroll the decoration face downwards very carefully & pin it out with drawing pins as flat as ever you can, you will want at least 3 or 4 boxes of drawing pins.' The panels still hang in the hallways and the drawing room.

Aubrey Waterfield's instructions would have arrived just after the death of Diany's older sister, Judy. Lina's condolences followed four days later: 'Few hours pass in the day that my thoughts do not fly to Kiftsgate … If Aubrey & I feel sad and bewildered what must your feelings be like.' Even before Judy's death, there is a sense from Diany's letters that she, too, was sometimes at odds with herself. She wrote from Florence to 'Judells Darlingest', saying, 'You know Darling I do wish I understood people better. I suppose it must be that I am not really in sympathy with them, & so I never see their really genuin [sic] side.' She signs herself 'Frumpty dumpty, wumpty Dump'.

Emma, Diany's younger daughter, believes the shyer Diany was overshadowed by her high-spirited, popular older sister, and that Judy's aura continued after her death. Unsurprisingly, Judy's tragedy triggered a crisis. Diany joined an evangelical Christian organization called the Oxford Group, founded by an American missionary, Frank Buchman. He believed all problems were rooted in fear and selfishness, and that the solution was to hand oneself over to God's plan. Fellow members Joan, Nan and Sally wrote often to Diany in the late 1930s, describing their feelings about God. All, however,

A wall hanging of magnolias, painted for Kiftsgate Court by Aubrey Waterfield in the mid-1930s, remains in the drawing room there.

KIFTSGATE COURT GARDENS

Aubrey Waterfield (1874–1944) and Lina Waterfield (1874–1964)

The ideals and interests of Aubrey and Lina Waterfield had a powerful effect on the young Diany Muir. Her two years at Poggio Gherardo, above Florence, ensured that Kiftsgate's Italianate beginnings would be reinforced when she in turn came to tend the garden.

Aubrey Waterfield met Lina (Caroline) Duff Gordon when he was an undergraduate at New College, Oxford. Lina had been brought up at Poggio Gherardo by her paternal aunt, the writer Janet Ross, a friend of Mark Twain, Bernard Berenson and G.F. Watts, the last of whom painted the youthful Lina. Lina and Aubrey married in 1902 and bought a near-ruined castle at Aulla, 16 miles (26 km) from La Spezia in Italy. Aubrey, a reclusive painter, created a remarkable garden on the castle's rooftop. Lina wrote books about Italy, took a leading role in founding the British Institute of Florence in 1917, and for many years was the Italy correspondent for *The Observer* newspaper.

After leaving Poggio Gherardo, Diany corresponded frequently with both Aubrey and Lina, who covered a wide range of subjects in their letters. In one, Aubrey recalled a visit to Aulla by D.H. and Frieda Lawrence. 'The real Lorenzo', he wrote, 'was an enchanting companion because he adored life & nature & enjoyed every minute utterly unconscious of himself in anything while he was so.' Lawrence returned the Waterfields' hospitality by dismissing Aubrey as no more than a gentleman painter.

Aubrey also wrote about the difficult political situation in Italy, as Mussolini became increasingly authoritarian. Lina left *The Observer* when its editor, J.L. Garvin, wanted her to follow a more propitiatory approach to the dictator. 'Between you & me,' Aubrey told Diany, 'he wrote Lina the letter of an absolute cad.'

The Waterfields were eventually forced to leave Italy virtually penniless. Aubrey spent time as a translator for Italian prisoners of war in a camp at Sudeley Castle, not far from Kiftsgate at Winchcombe. But the British authorities soon decided that this was a luxury on which they could economize, and he was laid off. Aubrey's health broke down and he died in July 1944. Lina continued to write to Diany until her death twenty years later.

Above, left: A self-portrait drawing of Aubrey Waterfield in the 1910s.

Above, right: Lina Waterfield at Poggio Gherardo in the 1930s, drawn by her husband.

A portrait of Diany Muir, painted by Aubrey Waterfield during her time at the Poggio Gherardo school, hangs in a bedroom at Kiftsgate Court. Diany's arm was in a sling as she had broken her collarbone while point-to-pointing.

were cagey about professing openly their membership of the Oxford Group. 'You don't ever need to mention the Oxford Group at home or among your friends – Probably lots better not to', wrote Joan, while Nan noted Diany's reserve and reassured her by saying, 'People will soon know you are leading a different life.'

Other friends and Diany's family were aghast. Her first cousin Robin Muir wrote from the Turf Club in November 1936: 'Were you tight when you wrote that letter abt your "Oxford Group"? … There's quite enough hypocrisy & stuntery in the usual religions without starting a new stunt.'

Diany, it seems, was searching for intellectual or spiritual fulfilment. She corresponded with a literary critic based in Stratford-upon-Avon, Martin Gilkes, the author of *On Poetry* (1933). In his letters, he guided Diany's reading, contrasting Tolstoy and Dostoevsky, and, 'if you want poetry', urging her to read Gerard Manley Hopkins, 'an account of how Eliot came out of the French symbolists', W.B. Yeats, and 'Auden, Spender & that lot'. For prose, he suggested Ibsen, George Moore, Proust, Gertrude Stein and James Joyce. A meaty reading list.

Despite her religious and literary enthusiasms, Diany still rode to hounds; a letter from one of her religious friends wished her luck in a point-to-point. And, in a diary entry from February 1938, Diany recorded that her future husband, Tony Binny, had dined at Kiftsgate.

Although they would not marry until 1950, Tony wrote to Diany throughout the war: from Bulford Camp in Wiltshire; with the British Expeditionary Force in France; and from India and Burma. She sent him books. In one letter from France on his birthday, 13 December 1939, Tony wrote: 'You simply have to become a fatalist out here and

A PRACTICAL PLANTSWOMAN: DIANY BINNY

The Muir girls were all taught to ride side-saddle. In the 1930s Betsy (left) continued the custom in an elegant riding skirt; Diany, however, chose to hunt astride.

live from one minute to the next making the most of everything, its [sic] a ghastly mistake to start thinking as you then very soon begin to realise the futility of it all.'

The war provided a focus for both Diany and Betsy. Betsy drove for the Anglo-French Ambulance Corps, for which she was awarded a Croix de Guerre and was commended by both the British and the French. Her French commanding officer wrote, 'Les missions ont été accompliés dans les circonstances parfois penibles, souvent périlleuses' (The missions were carried out in circumstances that were sometimes painful and often perilous).

Diany joined the Red Cross Society in July 1939 and began training as a nurse at St Thomas's Hospital in London. Her medical training was cut short, probably by a life-threatening attack of mastoiditis, but she remained with the Red Cross in Warwickshire until December 1941, when she was discharged 'by reason of her undertaking other work of national importance'.

For the next two years or so, that work was helping Betsy to run her farm at Burmington, near Shipston-on-Stour, Warwickshire. Farming was not the sisters' forte: they kept chickens but could not bear to wring their necks. Diany allegedly threw the birds from an upstairs window as Betsy shot at them from below. The sisters also spent wartime autumns staying in primitive bothies and stalking on the Blair Atholl estate in Scotland. With so many men away on active service, their help was needed for the annual cull to balance deer numbers.

Diany's interest in the garden was emerging by the outbreak of war. In January 1940 she wrote lyrically about winter at Kiftsgate in her diary: 'The ice on the trees, hedges, & even blades of grass sticking through the snow is quite unbelievable, the twigs have about six times their thickness of ice sticking to them & you cannot shake it off, if you pull it it just makes a sort of jingling noise & is absolutely stiff, it makes the trees look really lovely although it is breaking a frightful lot of branches with the weight.' This sharp observation and attention to detail would serve Diany well when she took over from her mother in 1954.

At the end of November 1944, Diany was appointed as a temporary clerk in the Foreign Office, where she remained for the rest of the war. Like many women whose youth had been overshadowed, she had conflicting emotions on VE Day, which found her alone in London: 'I feel depressed & full of self pity, a flat blank feeling – & looking back on little achieved or done, & blank feeling because I am not celebrating in the streets.' Tony Binny was still abroad on active service, so, in late 1945, Diany decided to go to the Far East.

Diany spent a year working in Singapore in welfare for the Women's Voluntary Services. She moved in medical circles: her application to join the Singapore Swimming Club was proposed by a Mr A.F. Caldwell from the College of Medicine. After spending some time in Hong Kong, she sailed home on the *Queen of Bermuda* in March 1947, travelling six to a cabin meant for one: 'As usual when getting on to a troop ship I was unutterably depressed by the sight of so much humanity (there are over 3,000 aboard!).' Diany's unwillingness to speak to other passengers meant that she 'missed the boat over getting some bridge as everyone is now fixed up'. Bridge was another lifelong passion.

Betsy and Heather wrote regularly to Diany during her eighteen-month absence. In the late 1940s Betsy spent long periods in Ireland with her first cousin Gill, the daughter

KIFTSGATE COURT GARDENS

of Heather's sister Clara. Gill and her husband, Evan Williams, a former jockey, managed Knockainey Stud at Hospital, County Limerick. A letter from Heather to Diany, written at Braco, Perthshire, in September 1946, discloses Heather's concern about Betsy's nervous state – an understandable worry, given Judy's tragedy. Heather was unhappy about what she saw as the rackety existence at Knockainey. 'The trouble is that when she goes to Gill,' Heather wrote to Diany, 'she is in the centre of drink & sexual life & undoubtedly it excites that part of her nervous system … the atmosphere at Gill's couldn't be worse for her … there is of course no doubt that her health would be best served by marriage but I doubt Betsy with her sensitive nature would be anything but miserable with a man who she just lived with. She's not <u>hard</u> enough to do it.'

Betsy never married. Diany's daughters, Anne and Emma, remember their aunt as a well-dressed woman who turned up in a succession of smart cars, once a Bristol, to take them out from school. Diany, however, finally became engaged to Tony Binny in late 1949. A friend, Richard Fleming (brother of the James Bond creator, Ian), commented, 'I simply can't think why you both couldn't have made up your minds long ago, you silly asses.' The widowed Lina Waterfield, back at Poggio Gherardo, also congratulated her, observing rather archly, 'It is a piece of news that I had looked for in vain but always felt must come – only Diany is a very critical young woman & so I knew it would take some time to find the right man.' A disappointed suitor wrote sadly from the British Army of the Rhine: 'Staying away after you became engaged was possibly the best thing.'

John Anthony Francis Binny, the son of Lieutenant Colonel Stewart Scott Binny, DSO, was born at Sandhurst in 1911. Lt Col. Binny was killed near Ypres in March 1916, leaving his wife, son and daughter with little money. Tony left Wellington College in Berkshire at the age of fifteen and took a job loading bananas. In 1936 he joined the supplementary reserve of officers of the 15th/19th The King's Royal Hussars, and served with distinction throughout the Second World War. After being demobbed, he was introduced into the City by Paul Hamlyn, becoming the youngest main board director of the National Westminster Bank.

Diany and Tony were married in April 1950 at St Peter's, Eaton Square, and moved into a flat nearby. Anne Heather was born in November 1951, inheriting her grandmother's and mother's middle name, and eventually the mantle of the garden. (Katherine) Emma followed two years later, in November 1953. In 1954, as Heather found it increasingly hard to manage the garden, Diany decided to base herself at Kiftsgate with the girls, while Tony spent weekdays in London.

Jack and Heather Muir moved out to Front Lodge, dividing their time between there and London until Jack's death in 1956 and Heather's in 1961. The Binnys' first act was to reduce Kiftsgate Court to a more manageable size by demolishing three sides of the front courtyard – a total of sixteen rooms. Diany then turned her attention to the garden, finding there the personal fulfilment that she had sought through religion in the 1930s.

Diany applied herself as methodically as she had twenty years earlier to her literary studies. Untrained horticulturally, like her mother, she wanted to understand plants and their relationships with one another, and took pains to extend her knowledge. Emma remembers Diany

Both Anne Chambers and her sister, Emma, remember their Aunt Betsy (second from right) as a stylish society woman, as can be seen in this photograph taken in the 1950s.

A PRACTICAL PLANTSWOMAN: DIANY BINNY

wedging scraps of paper with the names of new plants into her dressing-table mirror in order to help her to memorize them. On one scrap, for instance, she listed forty-five wild flowers under three columns, headed 'English', 'Latin' and 'Family'. Among the flowers are 'common daisy – bellis perennis – Compositae' and 'greater stitchwort – stellaria Holostea – Caryophyllaceae'. Diany used large hardback, alphabetized notebooks for detailed descriptions of plants and accounts of where she had seen them. In one, she wrote about myosotis, also known as 'Mouse-ear' and 'Scorpion-grass': 'Stalked radical & sessile cauline leaves; calyx 5-cleft; corolla salver-shaped with blunt scales. Name signifying a mouse's ear from the shape of the leaf.' She recalled having seen 'Myosotis palustris (forget-me-not) at Lynes House, Wilts, on Oct 6th 1939'.

In another book, plants are listed alphabetically under the subheadings 'Herbacious' (*sic*; Diany's spelling was erratic), 'Roses', 'Climbers', 'Shrubs and Trees' and 'Bulbs'. There is a column for notes, which are sometimes dismissive but always descriptive. 'Alyssum' is a 'horrible white edging plant'; 'Aralia' is 'like a Shumach [sumac] without fur'; and 'Daphne Mezereum' is 'sweet smelling'. Diany also noted each plant's colour, its season of interest and where she had seen it. For example, 'Godetia' is 'annual, pink, Scotland'.

Diany underpinned an innate understanding of the requirements of plants with close observation. She had little taste for gardening books, believing that the best way to learn about gardening was actually to do it. Latterly, she was even more scornful of television gardening programmes, regarding them, according to the garden designer Timothy Leese, 'as so much nonsense'.

A later notebook recorded gardens and nurseries visited, some of the latter having since moved or changed name. In 1978, for example, Diany went to The Knoll, Dorset; Beth Chatto, Essex; Hillier Gardens, Hampshire; Spetchley Park, Worcestershire; Scott's, Somerset; and Bressingham Gardens, Norfolk. In 1979 she bought plants from Fibrex Nurseries at Evesham, Ballards Nursery at Malvern and Stone House Cottage Nursery, near Kidderminster. Plants are listed from her excursions: in August 1978 at Spetchley Park, she admired and was given a cutting of 'Calycanthus occidentalis (all spice), thought it was a magnolia with smallish orange red flowers V.P.' (her shorthand for 'very pretty'). At the Oxford Botanic Garden, she noted, 'Daphne gentiana <u>very</u> pretty lilac before leaves, get if possible.'

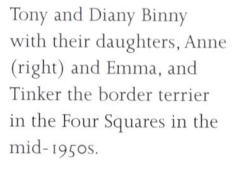

Tony and Diany Binny with their daughters, Anne (right) and Emma, and Tinker the border terrier in the Four Squares in the mid-1950s.

Hilda Murrell (1906–1984)

As an environmental activist and a campaigner against nuclear power and weapons, Hilda Murrell may appear to have been an unlikely friend for the fox-hunting Diany Binny. But Hilda was also an accomplished rose grower who had written to Heather Muir in 1956, exclaiming, 'It is an honour to supply roses to the creator of one of the really lovely and famous gardens of this country.' Over the following decade, Heather's daughter and Hilda became close, visiting gardens together and sharing a mutual passion for roses.

The elder of two daughters, Hilda Murrell was born in Shrewsbury into a family of nurserymen, seedsmen and florists whose original business was established in 1837. She won a scholarship to Newnham College, Cambridge, to study modern and medieval languages, before joining the family business. In 1937 she became the first woman to run a rose nursery at a time when the Royal National Rose Society did not allow female members. Thanks to her outstanding horticultural and business skills, Hilda presided over Edwin Murrell Ltd's golden years, supplying notable gardens throughout Britain. She helped Vita Sackville-West to design the White Garden at Sissinghurst.

This brilliant rosarian was conscious that there is always more to be learned and more plants to be discovered. Not only did she supply Kiftsgate with roses, but also Diany gave her cuttings in return, as is revealed in a letter of July 1967. 'The cuttings are all in & so far look fine', Hilda wrote to Diany. 'The roses are budded. Damascena bifera is of course the same as Quatre Saisons! I have ordered budding eyes of Francis E Lester & R. macrantha so hope to get these going.' Hilda goes on to thank Diany for 'tearing around so many wonderful places … I like Kiftsgate best … Your colour is glorious … Rosa macrantha is the picture that stays with me. It was <u>exquisite</u>.'

In 1970, when Hilda sold the nursery to Duncan Murphy and Percy Thrower (the original presenter of *Gardeners' World*), Diany was one of the first she told: 'I want particularly to thank you [for] the trouble you took to continue my horticultural education. All the main additions to this in recent years have come from or through you.'

In 1946 Hilda had been a founder member of the Soil Association. In her retirement, she was very active in the Shropshire branch of the Council for the Protection of Rural England; her acutely observed nature diaries were edited and published in 1987, after her death, by her nephew, Robert Green. She also became increasingly concerned about the threat from nuclear power to the British landscape and environment. In 1983 she wrote a prophetic critique of the government's policy on radioactive waste management. She was preparing to testify at the Sizewell B Inquiry into a planned nuclear power plant in Suffolk when she was found murdered near her Shrewsbury home in March 1984. This led to a flurry of conspiracy theories and an allegation by the Labour MP Tam Dalyell that she had been silenced for her opposition by the British security services; but in 2005 a petty thief was convicted of her murder when a cold-case review linked him to the crime scene through DNA. Whatever the motive, it was a sad end to a life devoted to beauty and peace.

Each year saw a daunting catalogue of jobs to be tackled: in 1979 Diany had sixteen replanting projects for the Banks, the Wide Border and the Yellow Border, and all but two were carried out. These projects included putting 'berberidopsis [given to her by Louisa Arbuthnott of Stone House Cottage Nursery] between purple pittosporum & acacia below summer house' and using 'convolvulus mauritanicus & campanula isophylla on little borders below summer house'.

Diany became an accomplished, practical plantswoman, with a feeling for the unusual. She had a well-developed colour sense, yet knew when to allow a splash of vulgarity. The advantage of inheriting a mature garden was offset by having her mother living barely 600 yards (550 metres) away at Front Lodge. She constantly felt Heather's presence, later writing, 'It was difficult to change things and in fact it took me four years to pluck up enough self-confidence to alter my mother's plans but realized finally that gardens, like time, do not stand still and once I had started to implant my own idea, there was no turning back.' By 1972 Lionel Fortescue, the creator of the renowned 10-acre (4-ha) garden at The Garden House, Buckland Monachorum in Devon, was complimenting Diany on what she had achieved: 'Among medium-sized gardens in this country I feel sure Kiftsgate has no rival.'

Diany's first big project, in the early 1960s, was the creation of the half-moon swimming pool on the lawn of the Lower Garden. A natural stone edge, without diving boards or steps, helped to fit the pool seamlessly into the garden. The apparently flat lawn proved anything but, so the ground was levelled and a ha-ha made

Betsy Muir prunes a rose on the terrace, while Diany and their mother sit beside the lawn of the White Sunk Garden in the early 1950s. Diany later replaced the lawn with a pool and fountain.

between the garden and the fields beyond. At the same time, a second, more accessible, path was laid down through the Banks to the Lower Garden, with individual paviours rather than the staddle stones used by Heather.

The first of William Shenstone's limes fell in 1924, and when two more followed in 1957 and 1962, Diany began filling the gaps with weeping silver limes (*Tilia tomentosa* 'Petiolaris'). Between 1972 and 1976, Shenstone's elm avenue, leading up Glyde Hill from Mickleton Manor below, was destroyed by Dutch elm disease, but this avenue, unlike the drive, was not replanted.

Diany's favourite place, where she continued to garden even in old age, was the White Sunk Garden. She changed it dramatically from her mother's creation by taking up the lawn and laying paving instead. At its centre she put a pool with a Pyrenean well-head fountain, which she had found at the Chelsea Flower Show.

Diany created the North Border from a grassy slope behind the Wide Border, with a low retaining wall built by the Italian gardener (Heather and Diany always had Italian gardeners). The soil, however, turned out to be yellow clay, probably dumped there when the house was built, and entirely unsuitable for the grey foliage plants that Diany had intended for the border. She persevered, planting, among other things, eucalyptus and junipers, and the border came into its own in the drought of 1976, when the rest of the garden suffered badly.

A world war had divided Heather Muir's creation of the garden from Diany's taking the helm in 1954. Yet, in some ways, little had changed. There may have been fewer gardeners in the 1950s than in the mid-war years, and Diany was more hands-on than her mother, but there was still a large kitchen garden, with box-edged beds and its own gardener, Mr Jones. In the mid-1940s, when Diany was in the Far East, both Betsy and Heather wrote to tell her about Heather's and Jack's problems with an unsatisfactory butler. A decade later, Diany still had a butler, Mr Wormesley, whose wife was the cook. When the Binnys decamped in the late summer of each year to stalk in the Scottish Highlands, the Wormesleys were taken along, in Victorian fashion, to cook and wait.

The rhythm of the seasons in the 1960s was similar to that in the 1930s: summer was devoted to the garden when the horses were put out to pasture, but in winter the house was still geared to hunting. Social life remained formal. Timothy Leese, a friend of Emma Mackenzie, Diany's younger daughter, spent weekends at Kiftsgate in the early 1970s: 'We would arrive on Friday nights and have a drink with Tony and Diany in their dark, sombre drawing room full of Chinese porcelain that Diany

Diany's dedication to pruning the roses herself earned the admiration of gardening friends, such as Lionel Fortescue.

KIFTSGATE COURT GARDENS

had collected in the Far East in the 1940s. But we would then be shuffled off to the girls' quarters at the other end of the house.'

A few peonies in the Wide Border are virtually Tony's only legacy to the garden. He lived increasingly in London, where he was chairman of Blue Circle and Tube Investments. Prolonged separation took its toll on the Binnys' marriage, and they divorced in 1974, when Emma was twenty-one.

The divorce was acrimonious, with money an issue. Diany moved to Front Lodge, leaving Kiftsgate Court itself empty for almost a decade. As she noted in the script for an article (we do not know where, when or if it was published), she even considered removing the roof:

> How exciting to have a ruin – a grand ruin complete with Palladian portico in the middle of the garden. It would be so easy to take the roof off Kiftsgate, allowing the yellow Banksia rose to weep over the top and perhaps meet up with the Wisteria. No longer would one have to cut the huge leaved Magnolia Delavayi away from the windows, and perhaps … the Kiftsgate rose would seize its chance to overpower all around and make it the ramparts of a Sleeping Beauty Palace. I know I will never do it as it still means too much to me. There are too many happy memories, both of my own childhood and those spent with my family, for me to destroy it.

Although she could no longer afford to live in Kiftsgate Court, Tony's departure fuelled Diany's determination to maintain its garden to the very highest standard, and she fearlessly removed plants not earning their keep. As it had been for Heather after Judy's death, so the garden was solace for Diany after her divorce. 'I spend many happy and contented hours gardening on my own,' she wrote, 'stopping now and then to relax with a cigarella.' Inspired by the work of the sculptor Simon Verity at Rosemary Verey's Barnsley House, near Cirencester, Diany commissioned him to make two statues: one of a mother and child for a belvedere on the Top Banks; the other a seated woman, carved from derelict tombstones found by Diany in a churchyard. The latter was erected against yew hedging at the end of the Rose Border, framed by a sorbus arch and a semicircle of yew, and surrounded by a deciduous fern border.

Simon Verity, who sculpted the statue of a seated woman for Diany Binny, also painted this watercolour cartoon. Diany is shown, as so often, in trousers and with a cheroot in hand.

Always close, Diany and Betsy became even more devoted, sharing a passion for gardening. Betsy had sold the Burmington farm and bought a house, Hidcote Vale, at Hidcote Boyce, less than a mile from Kiftsgate. There, she made a garden, which she also opened to the public, and the two sisters swapped plants. In August 1980 Diany's 'cuttings from Bet' included *Hebe recurva*, *H. rakaiensis*, *Chaenomeles speciosa* 'Moerloosei' and *Ozothamnus ledifolius*. Betsy's immaculate, regimented garden was much admired: each plant had its place, as she did not like them growing into one another.

After Diany's divorce, the sisters and their cousin Beryl Hobson became an inseparable trio, meeting for supper every Thursday. Diany and Betsy would often play Scrabble or bezique, while, with Beryl, they would look for a fourth for a mean game of bridge. Beryl, who lived a few miles away at Paxford and was godmother to Diany's daughter Emma, was the widow of a Muir cousin, Sir John Hobson, Attorney General at the time of the Profumo case. She was an adept propagator, a skill acquired earning holiday money on the production line at her family's pottery in Staffordshire. She also helped the sisters with their openings and gave the less numerate Diany financial advice. In 1982 Beryl made detailed comparisons between plant sales and visitor numbers for the previous year, and wrote two pages of 'COMMENTS – which I intend to be helpful & not critical'. She pointed out that 'there is no accounting for how many plants are sold', adding, 'I think it advisable to do more free advertising.' All in all, though, Beryl admitted, 'You have done another GOOD job!'

Diany, Betsy and Beryl visited gardens together at home and abroad, with Diany and Betsy leading and Beryl following on behind, taking notes. On a visit to Prince Peter Wolkonsky's gardens of Kerdalo, their travelling companion was Beryl's niece Gina Price, the creator of Pettifers Garden, near Banbury. Wolkonsky began designing his 45-acre (18-ha), multifaceted garden on the north coast of Brittany in 1965; Diany regarded it as the best garden made in Europe since the Second World War. Gina says that it was at Kerdalo, in the company of Diany, that she suddenly realized what gardening was all about. In a notebook, Diany jotted down shrubs acquired on a visit there in 1983: a spring-flowering, unusual rose-family member, *Rhaphiolepis* × *delacourii* 'Kerdalo'; *Hoheria lyallii*; and *Exochorda* × *macrantha* 'The Bride' – all still at Kiftsgate.

Diany's encouragement was important not only to Gina, but also to other younger gardeners, including Victoria Wakefield, Louisa Arbuthnott and the designer Timothy Leese. All pay tribute to Diany's plantsmanship and her ability to recognize and nurture a good garden plant. 'You can't be very happy with that border', Diany told Gina when she was a neophyte. Undaunted, Gina credits Diany with teaching her about colour and structure. 'Diany was a strong woman, wonderful and so funny', recalls Louisa Arbuthnott, whose Stone House Cottage Nursery was a source of rare plants for Diany: 'She and Betsy used to come here with Beryl. Beryl was slightly more mainstream in that she didn't always wear men's clothes and smoke cheroots. Diany would come here and bark at plants she didn't like.'

Graham Stuart Thomas, photographed by Tessa Traeger in 2001.

Graham Stuart Thomas (1909–2003)

In 1951 the rosarian Graham Stuart Thomas identified Heather Muir's supposed *Rosa moschata* as a particularly vigorous cultivar of *Rosa filipes* and gave it the name 'Kiftsgate'. In the same year, an article of his in the RHS journal helped to raise Kiftsgate's profile among garden visitors. Heather returned the favour, recommending her friend in 1952 as a possible curator for Hidcote. Her advice was not heeded in this instance, but three years later, thanks in part to Heather's intervention, Thomas was appointed gardens adviser to the National Trust. Over the course of more than two decades, he supervised the restoration of many important Trust gardens. One of his major achievements was the design of the rose garden in the former walled kitchen garden at Mottisfont Abbey in Hampshire, where he mixed perennials with roses in subtle balances of colour and form. He was also responsible for the recultivation of many old roses, following in the footsteps of E.A. Bunyard. A prolific author, Thomas wrote a notable trilogy on roses: *The Old Shrub Roses* (1955), *Shrub Roses of Today* (1962) and *Climbing Roses Old and New* (1965). The last two were illustrated with his own detailed drawings and paintings.

Thomas was born in Cambridge into a keen gardening family. He studied at the Cambridge University Botanic Garden, then worked for the alpine specialist Clarence Elliott at Six Hills Nursery in Stevenage (the nursery that gave its name to the popular nepeta). In 1931 he became foreman at a wholesale nursery near Chobham, Surrey, and later ran Sunningdale Nurseries in partnership with Jim Russell. While at Chobham, he would cycle over to Munstead Wood to learn about colour, design, herbaceous perennials and roses from the aged Gertrude Jekyll.

Thomas became as friendly with Heather's daughters, Diany and Betsy, as he had been with their mother. They visited one another regularly and corresponded, their letters peppered with discussions and recommendations about plants. Under 'Names (from Graham)', Diany noted in 1980, 'Aster amellus var. not Mönch' and 'Phygelius white is P. aequalis Yellow Trumpet.' In 1994, when Thomas was well into his eighties, he wrote that he was 'doing a book of short essays on a wide variety of subjects, one of which is entitled "Climbers in Trees". Of course your "Kiftsgate" rose is mentioned … People have no idea what it can do unless they have seen it.' Unmarried and living alone, he wrote in another letter that 'old friends are very valuable these days'. He died in 2003.

KIFTSGATE COURT GARDENS

While her garden remained an intensely personal place, Diany recognized that she had to open Kiftsgate more often and to sell the plants she grew and propagated there. She was ably assisted by her head gardener, David Weller, who subsequently worked at Knightshayes, the Heathcoat Amorys' hillside garden in Devon. The walled kitchen garden was gradually turned over to propagation, and part of the forecourt was made into a car park, edged on one side by an arboretum of specimen trees. To raise funds, in 1980 Diany allowed Kiftsgate to be used as a location for *Sir Henry at Rawlinson End*, an eccentric British film that later achieved cult status. In 1984 Roy Lancaster and Graham Rose filmed Kiftsgate for *Gardeners' World*, and in January 1988 Diany wrote hopefully to the programme's executive producer, John Kenyon, asking whether he would be interested in filming ten-minute weekly shots, charting the garden's progress throughout the summer. Kenyon replied that the idea was currently 'on the back burner', although television cameras would return to Kiftsgate in the following decade.

Seeking publicity for the garden did not come easily to the naturally diffident Diany, whose manner could be austere. On open days, she sold tickets at a card table by the front door, cross-questioning unsuspecting visitors considering buying a 'Kiftsgate' rose. 'Your garden won't be nearly big enough for it', she would say smartly. 'Put it back.' Her reaction would make the potential purchaser all the more eager to buy. Another visitor, looking for her purse, revealed a handbag full of cuttings. 'Shall we call that £10?', flashed Diany.

Diany's friends, such as Louisa Arbuthnott, also recall her kindness and generosity: 'Diany invited us to come and take cuttings at Kiftsgate, helping us to start our nursery.' Diany herself would later buy unusual plants from Louisa when Stone House Cottage Nursery became established.

In her final years, Diany suffered from dementia, but she showed flashes of her old feistiness and interest in the garden until shortly before her death in March 2006.

Diany was a woman of decided opinions. She hated ivy, annuals and bulbs, sneakily cutting the heads off Anne's tulips when her daughter introduced them into the garden. She believed that ground cover was lazy gardening, and that clematis should never be run up into roses. She had no sense of smell yet recognized its importance and chose such fragrant shrubs as *Osmanthus delavayi*. Her favourite plants included *Rosa × odorata* 'Mutabilis', *Hebe hulkeana*, *Carpenteria californica* and *Deutzia setchuenensis* var. *corymbiflora*, all of which flourish in the garden today. She was in the vanguard of fashion by planting trilliums, again still a feature of the spring at Kiftsgate. Her individuality, her disdain for fashion (she continued to plant kniphofias when they were completely out of vogue) and her superb plantsmanship have left a permanent mark on Kiftsgate Court Gardens.

Beryl Hobson (left) often accompanied her cousins Betsy (right) and Diany on garden visits, and helped to sell plants on their open days.

Muir sisters and cousins gather at Kiftsgate Court to wave off Anne and Johnny Chambers on their honeymoon in January 1983. From left, Betsy Muir; Anne's godmother, 'Chou' (Margaret) Hayes (née Muir); Diany Binny; and Beryl Hobson.

A PRACTICAL PLANTSWOMAN: DIANY BINNY

KIFTSGATE COURT GARDENS

The Modernizing Spirit

Anne Chambers
(b. 1951)

Opposite: Outlined by early-morning light, the Chambers' latest innovation is the filigree leaf sculpture by Pete Moorhouse at the end of the Tulip Tree Avenue.

Right: Anne Chambers stands by *Clematis armandii*, which flowers in late winter around the pool on the Banks.

Emma (left) and Anne as small girls, wearing the smocked dresses and buttoned shoes that were so fashionable in the 1950s.

Kiftsgate, like all gardens, has been a barometer of social change. Diany had run house and garden along much the same lines as Heather had done, and her two daughters, Anne and Emma, experienced a childhood similar to that of Diany, Judy and Betsy.

When Anne and her husband, Johnny Chambers, moved to Kiftsgate in 1988, they faced a very different world and a more challenging prospect. Anne had some help in the house and with her three children, but certainly had no butler or cook. The spiralling inflation of the 1970s and 1980s caused upheaval and meant that the Chambers, like the owners of other country houses and gardens, had to put their home on a much more business-like and professional footing in order to preserve it. Heather and Diany had essentially gardened mainly for spring and summer, but the Chambers family wanted a year-round garden, not just for their visitors but also for themselves. They would not be hunting or disappearing to the South of France in winter. Even when Kiftsgate was closed between October and the end of March, they would be on hand most of the time during those months to prepare the garden for more than 20,000 visitors a year. Opening hours lengthened. In 1988 the public were admitted only three afternoons a week in high summer; by 2018 Kiftsgate was open five days a week from May to the end of August, and three afternoons a week in April and September.

Nevertheless, for Anne, Kiftsgate has remained a personal family garden, which she cares for in the spirit of her grandmother and mother: 'We have very much made it our life, which revolves around our being here. We have only two gardeners and occasional help, because if you employ more people you begin to lose that direct contact with the garden and it's not yours anymore. We take all the day-to-day decisions.'

Anne Heather Binny was born at Queen Charlotte's Hospital in London on 30 November 1951. Her sister, (Katherine) Emma, was born there two years later. The sisters remember an almost Victorian childhood, during which they were looked after by nannies and governesses. After tea, they would be dressed up and brought downstairs to meet their mother, although seldom their father, who was mostly in London. Once a week, they were taken to Front Lodge for tea with their grandmother – an event that Anne, shyer than her bigger and bolder younger sister, often found an ordeal.

THE MODERNIZING SPIRIT: ANNE CHAMBERS

Holidays were spent with the girls' nanny at Frinton-on-Sea in Essex, where they had a beach hut, or with a strict governess, Miss Reed, at Bembridge on the Isle of Wight, staying in a guest house run by a landlady with a glass eye. Their first family holiday was to Majorca when Anne was fifteen years old; it was not a success because Anne was taken ill.

According to Emma, Diany was mostly oblivious to what her children were doing, although she would take them to London in the school holidays for dentist and hairdresser appointments and for clothes shopping. Otherwise, Diany was gardening, hunting or stalking. Although Anne never cared much for riding, stalking was a passion that she and Emma both shared with their mother. In the late summer of each year, the Binnys took a lodge, Ben Alder, near Dalwhinnie in the Highlands, where Anne learned to shoot. She and Emma continued to rent the lodge for stalking holidays even after their parents' divorce.

When the Binnys were at home, the house was often full of guests who had come to see the garden. 'That was part of our family life', says Anne. When there were no visitors, the garden was the girls' playground, offering dozens of places for hide and seek, such as the tunnel beneath the Bridge Border, leading to what in Heather's time had been the laundry cottage on the hillside below. They would wander through the kitchen garden, prohibited from picking the peaches and figs until Friday night. Mischievously, Emma would open the protective fruit cages erected by Mr Jones and let in the birds.

Neither Anne nor Emma showed much interest in gardening as children. 'It was never thrust down our throats,' Anne recalls, 'because my mother knew it would put us off.' They did, however, have small borders in the backyard, where Anne planted lily of the valley.

Emma remembers the day her grandmother died in 1961 because, unusually, Diany, rather than the butler, fetched her from school. Diany also gave Emma an unappetizing supper: no domestic goddess, she was unaware that kippers need to be cooked.

By then, Anne was already a weekly boarder. Later, she and Emma went to Lawnside in Great Malvern. Anne's school reports show her to have been a diligent

Anne (left) and Emma, holding Tinker, seated by the sundial in the centre of the Four Squares. Behind, the door leads into what was their mother's drawing room, now the tearoom for garden visitors.

The garden was often full of visiting parties during the sisters' childhood. Here, the Binnys host a group of Tony's colleagues from the National Westminster Bank.

KIFTSGATE COURT GARDENS

pupil, with a particular interest in languages and the history of art. She left school before taking her A levels, with Tony wanting to send her to finishing school in Switzerland. Diany was determined, however, that Anne should go to Italy, and thoroughly researched the options. Anne spent six months with five other English girls in a flat in Florence with a Signora Rosselli, following a similar programme to her mother's. Like her, Anne was blissfully happy, and developed a taste for travel.

Anne also took a Cordon Bleu course, and entertained with her parents at home. At the back of one of Diany's hardback notebooks are lists drawn up in Anne's handwriting for cocktail, dinner and weekend parties held in the late 1960s/early 1970s, before the Binnys' divorce changed the shape of life at Kiftsgate. In essence, the tone is similar to that of Judy's diaries of social events forty years earlier. Anne's party lists included Robin Lane Fox, the Oxford classicist and *Financial Times* gardening correspondent; the biographer Lucy Hughes-Hallett; and the future Conservative minister David Heathcoat Amory, then at Christ Church, Oxford.

Anne Binny as a teenager, while a pupil at Lawnside in Great Malvern, Worcestershire.

On her return from Italy, Anne took a year's secretarial course at Queen's College in South Kensington. She shared a flat with Emma in nearby Roland Gardens and worked for periods to save up before going travelling. In 1971 she spent six months in the United States, working for two months as a nanny in Maryland and then zigzagging by Greyhound bus across the country with a friend.

After Emma's marriage in January 1976, Anne bought a house in Clapham, battling with its tiny garden and difficult soil; she started to comb local nurseries for special plants. In April 1978 she married David Child, a man of big ambitions who thought that they should renovate Kiftsgate Court and move there. The house, having stood empty for several years, needed to be completely rewired and have damp treatment throughout. A flat was created for Anne and her husband in the stables while work was in progress. The Childs' marriage lasted for less than two years, but, had it not been for David, Anne might never have begun the restoration of Kiftsgate. Thanks to money from a family trust, the house was made habitable again by the time of Anne's marriage to Jonathan (Johnny) Chambers in January 1983.

Johnny first visited Kiftsgate in 1979, when he was staying nearby at Foxcote for a mutual friend's wedding. He was shown round the house and garden, but little thought that, within a few years, he would be sharing the responsibility for their upkeep. Unlike the husbands of his wife's predecessors, he has played an active role in the garden: Anne and Johnny's stewardship of Kiftsgate has been a joint enterprise.

Jonathan Guy Chambers was born in London in 1949, the son of an ophthalmologist and an obstetrician and gynaecologist. He was educated at the University of Southampton, where he studied engineering. A postgraduate course at Cambridge helped him to put his academic studies into a business context. He worked for two engineering companies, with an international trade role that involved him in lengthy trips to the Middle East, Africa and Eastern Europe. His visits to gardens in Iran while on business there after the revolution of 1979 partly inspired the Mound and the leaf sculpture at the end of the Tulip Tree Avenue at Kiftsgate.

The Chambers' first child, Robert, was born in 1983, followed by Clare in 1985 and Patrick in 1988. In the children's early years, the family split their time between their home in Battersea and weekends at Kiftsgate. As Anne's interest in gardens grew, she took soil, plants and jam jars of weedkiller back to London on Sunday evenings. With decisions about

THE MODERNIZING SPIRIT: ANNE CHAMBERS

schools on the horizon, Johnny gave up his job in 1988 and the family moved full-time to Kiftsgate. Diany was in her early seventies by then, and welcomed the support of her elder daughter and her husband.

Anne admits that when she joined her mother, her gardening knowledge was limited: 'It was daunting at first. I had small children and very little time; it seemed as though I would never get a proper handle on what had to be done.' She did have a nanny for the children, and they eventually went off to boarding school, so she was able to work with her mother and gradually learn about the garden. Although she was starting from scratch, she was brought up with the garden, and the vocabulary was familiar to her. Diany's motto was 'The art of gardening is to notice', and during their long rambles together round the garden, Anne trained her eye.

Diany, by all accounts, was less possessive than Heather, and her relationship with Anne was easier. She encouraged Anne to watch her prune the roses, a job in which she had always taken particular pride. 'How you manage to do all the training and pruning of so many roses, a scratchy unpleasant task, I cannot imagine', Lionel Fortescue had written to Diany many years earlier. Anne continues to prune many of the roses herself, particularly the older ones planted by her mother and grandmother.

Anne and Johnny began their gardening on what Diany once described as 'the desperately steep, pine needled covered banks'. As Diany's health and agility declined, the Banks became the preserve of the Chambers, and one of their first acts was to reterrace and replant them. Their restoration work kept the original structure laid down by Heather, and the planting was refreshed but not necessarily changed. The Banks still capture the essence of the Mediterranean on a Cotswold escarpment, with ceanothus, indigofera, abutilons, cistus and pencil cypress coping happily with the bone-dry ground and the shade from the towering pines.

Diany had battled with a series of cold winters in the 1960s, losing many tender plants on the Banks. Since the beginning of the twenty-first century, winters have become milder: Heather's original *Abutilon vitifolium* have multiplied up the Banks, and Anne has been able to introduce to the Lower Garden tender plants such as crinodendron (which she spotted in the Logan Botanic Garden in Scotland), echiums (which Diany thought would never survive), and *Trachelospermum asiaticum* to cover a wall near the top of the Banks. The Chambers also opened up woodland on the right-hand side of the Banks and called the area Tresco, furnishing it with plants from the Scilly Isles, where they holidayed with their children.

Over the years that Anne has been chatelaine at Kiftsgate, work has continued on the Banks: health and safety are now more of an issue, so handrails have been installed to help visitors to negotiate precipitous steps and narrow paths. In the early 1990s the Chambers painted black the elliptic-shaped pool on the lawn of the Lower Garden to reflect the branches of the trees above; it now looks more ornamental and even less like a swimming pool. A whole section of the Top Banks needed replanting and reterracing after a mighty *Arbutus unedo* (from Heather's time) was felled by heavy snow in early 2018.

Greater footfall has taken its toll on the garden, so in the early 1990s Anne and Johnny paved the grass path that runs through the Rose Border with blue bricks from the stable yard – a move applauded by Diany's gardening friend Prince Peter Wolkonsky.

The Chambers have made two significant extensions to the garden. When the surface of Heather's clay tennis court began to break up, they designed a Water Garden within the surrounding yew hedges, inspired by Sir Geoffrey Jellicoe's garden for Sutton Place, near Guildford in Surrey. The rectangular pond now covers the area of the doubles court, with white paving stones leading to the central island of grass. In the pond stands a sculpture by Simon Allison, its twenty-four gilded bronze leaves moulded from a philodendron. The Water Garden is unlike any other part of the garden, acting as a welcome hiatus from the dense planting elsewhere. Anne's mother and aunt were split on this innovation. Diany broadly welcomed it, but Betsy – a precise and old-fashioned plantswoman, a stickler for correct plant names and a demon pruner – declared trenchantly, 'This isn't proper gardening.'

The spoil from making the pool led to a second, even bigger, project: the creation of the Mound and the Avenue, opened to the public in 2017 and lying beyond the Wild Flower Corner and Orchard, which Anne and Johnny have also planted. A mown path leads through the Orchard to a flight of steps up a semicircular mound made from thousands of tons of soil excavated from the Water Garden. The banks are planted with hedges of rugosa roses, purply-red 'Roseraie de l'Haÿ' and white 'Blanche Double de Coubert'. From the Mound, the eye is drawn through an avenue of tulip trees (*Liriodendron tulipifera*), planted in 2007, to a stainless-steel leaf sculpture, designed by Pete Moorhouse.

With these two new creations, Anne and Johnny have made Kiftsgate a garden for the twenty-first century. The clean lines and simplicity, and the delicate sculptures, contrast with the rich array of roses, perennials and shrubs elsewhere, and turn the garden into a place of different moods. These were bold moves, but the Water Garden met with general approval, and in 2003 Kiftsgate won the annual Historic Houses Association/Christie's Garden of the Year Award, voted for by the visiting public.

Heather had opened just once or twice a year for the National Garden Scheme. Diany did so more frequently, and was more systematic, keeping accounts and improving public access by making and landscaping a car park. She turned the walled kitchen garden into a plant nursery and began selling divisions and seedlings. The Chambers, however, professionalized the whole operation. They transformed what had been Diany's drawing room into a shop and tearoom, which serves lunches in summer. Even more significantly, they revolutionized the plant-selling aspect, as a result of Johnny's observation on an open Sunday afternoon that cuttings of *Weigela florida* 'Foliis Purpureis' from the Wide Border were selling like hot cakes. 'It made me realize', he says, 'that we should be growing more of our own plants and stepping up this side of the business.'

As Anne followed her mother round the garden, learning about pruning and plant associations, Johnny learned about plant propagation by watching the gardeners handling cuttings and seedlings. He installed irrigation and polytunnels in the nursery, and on open days today the stands are loaded with plants propagated from those growing in the garden. There were few plant fairs and specialist nurseries in the 1980s, so Kiftsgate provided an uncommon selection for keen gardeners. Much of the delight in buying a plant at Kiftsgate is that, in most cases, you can actually see it growing in the garden, and get ideas about soil, aspect and companion planting.

Unlike her mother and grandmother, Anne has been fortunate in that her husband, Johnny, has been as much involved in the garden as she is.

THE MODERNIZING SPIRIT: ANNE CHAMBERS

The propagation nerve centre is also the main source of young plants for the garden itself. A major challenge for Anne has been to maintain older planting, including roses, hydrangeas, abutilons and many trees that have been in the garden since her grandmother's time. Diany scarcely touched the structure of the garden, apart from making the swimming pool in the Lower Garden, but she added greatly to the garden's plant store, introducing more roses, hebes, deutzias, dictamnus, cornus, peonies and – a favourite – *Carpenteria californica*. She also planted the arboretum by the drive and filled the White Sunk Garden with a host of small treasures. The colour combinations and plant associations that Diany inherited from Heather are still a feature, but many of the plants creating these effects have grown old and need replacing. Occasionally, this has meant plucking up courage to take out a long-cherished treasure. A case in point was a bright-red single rose, Scarlet Fire, planted by Heather but becoming increasingly ragged eighty years on. Anne has always had to strike a balance between keeping faith with her predecessors and finding new cultivars and plants for the garden and to sell.

Like her mother before her, Anne has done this largely by making frequent visits to other people's gardens and by seeking out specialist nurseries. In her early days, Anne was given an unusual schizostylis by Graham Stuart Thomas and rarities by the former Sissinghurst head gardeners Pamela Schwerdt and Sibylle Kreutzberger from their new Gloucestershire garden. An exceptional source is Crûg Farm Plants, a nursery established in North Wales in 1991 by Bleddyn and Sue Wynn-Jones. The Wynn-Joneses have discovered many rare plants on expeditions to Jordan, East Asia, Central and North America, and Europe. From them, Anne has bought *Schizophragma hydrangeoides* 'Moonlight', which she has planted in the Bridge Border. Other nurseries regularly visited include Pan-Global Plants at Frampton-on-Severn and Stone House Cottage Nursery in Worcestershire, owned by Louisa Arbuthnott, who was encouraged by Diany when she started out. John Coke's perennial nursery at Bury Court in Surrey once regularly supplied the garden, as increasingly does the perennials and grasses nursery Dove Cottage, near Halifax in West Yorkshire.

Anne learned to swim at Sezincote, the Anglo-Indian garden at Moreton-in-Marsh originally designed with the help of Humphry Repton, so it has always been important

Johnny Chambers has revolutionized the nursery side of the business at Kiftsgate. He has introduced new polytunnels, but the old Victorian greenhouses, built for Sidney Graves Hamilton and housing an ancient fig, are still in use.

Philip Vincent, Lead Gardener

Philip Vincent has been at Kiftsgate since May 1993. Gardening was an early passion for him, so he built up experience in a garden centre and later a nursery, and also studied amenity horticulture at Pershore College of Horticulture. He spent four years in the Parks Department of Cheltenham Borough Council, before working at Daylesford House, first for Baron Thyssen and subsequently for the Bamford family when they bought the estate.

Although Anne and Johnny Chambers were already living at Kiftsgate when Philip started there, Diany Binny was still playing a major role in the garden. Philip worked closely with her, and she taught him how to prune the deutzias and philadelphus. 'She showed me what she liked and I learned from her', he recalls. 'I learned to cut the flowering wood out and train the shrubs, especially the *Deutzia × rosea*, the way it had always been done at Kiftsgate.' He continues to be in charge of shrub pruning, as well as pruning the roses in the Rose Border. Anne and Johnny tend to take on the roses in the White Sunk Garden and the Four Squares and on the house.

The four of them were successful as a team. Philip says that Anne carried on her mother's work, and much of the maintenance of the garden is today still done along the same lines. In particular, Philip is glad to have had the link through Diany to the garden's creator, Heather Muir. He came to love the garden, which was already three-quarters of a century old when he arrived, and feels immense responsibility for maintaining it to the standard that both the family and visitors expect. A feature that he especially likes is the bold and largely unfashionable use of shrubs through beds such as the Wide Border. 'So many gardens we visit seem to be mainly herbaceous', he says. 'Having shrubs is a must because they give a lovely structure, even in winter.'

Philip has also enjoyed seeing the new developments at Kiftsgate over the quarter of a century that he has gardened there: 'I like being able, as a gardener, to respond to different ideas. The Water Garden on the old tennis court, the Mound and Tresco are all very successful.' He appreciates, too, the introduction to the garden of striking new plants such as the claret-coloured *Calycanthus × raulstonii* 'Hartlage Wine' in the Four Squares and the black pepper plant *Zanthoxylum piperitum* on the Top Banks. New cultivars of existing plants have come into the garden, among them *Euphorbia × pasteurii* 'John Phillips' and *E. × p.* 'Phrampton Phatty'. The latter was a hybrid found in the garden by the owner of Pan-Global Plants at Frampton-on-Severn. All this adds to the multilayered experience of gardening at Kiftsgate.

Philip spends most of his time actually in the garden, helping with potting-up only on rainy days. The chief propagator is Tom Coleman, who has worked at Kiftsgate since 2014. Tom is in the nursery throughout the spring and summer, and has credited Philip with being 'a guiding hand', able, through his huge experience, to show Tom what he should be looking for. Tom, Anne and Johnny all visit rare plant fairs and nurseries to find unusual plants for the garden. One of the biggest challenges is to source different plants that will cope with the dry shade of the Banks. New plants have to be positioned in a deep hole and watered by hand, with earth banked around the plant to stop the moisture draining away down the slope.

Sometimes Tom is propagating a plant in the nursery that has been lost from the garden; it will be missing for a season, but then will make its way back into the garden. It is a good way of keeping the older, interesting plants going. Eighty per cent of the plants sold can be seen in the garden. Geraniums and roses are always popular with visitors, according to Philip. 'But', he adds, 'things go through fashions. Some years you get stuff you can't produce enough of and then the next year, you can't sell it. At the moment, grasses and *Dianthus carthusianorum*, *knappii* and *cruentus* are all selling well.'

Philip begins cutting the box in the Four Squares in July or August, and then starts on the yew and other hedges, finishing around the end of October. Once the visiting season ends, Tom joins Philip in the garden, and they go round together, pruning, forking over and mulching. They also have to tackle what Philip describes as 'the dreaded Banks': they must rake all the pine needles down from the top to the bottom, bag them up and burn them.

During the summer, another part-time helper is employed, but otherwise all the gardening is done by Anne and Johnny with the help of Philip and Tom. 'It's certainly full on', Philip admits. 'You're never lost for something to do.' But he is filled with pride when he considers what is achieved by such a small team: 'I go to other big gardens where you know they've got quite a few gardeners, and there are weeds and they're untidy. I think we do a marvellous job here.'

Buying plants raised in the garden is one of the pleasures of a visit to Kiftsgate. Here, the view towards the plant stalls is framed by the spring-flowering *Cornus* 'Kenwyn Clapp'.

to her. Its climate and soil are similar to those of Kiftsgate, and its tree-covered slopes and mix of perennials and shrubs strike a chord with her, as do the south-facing terraces of Powis Castle, on the border between England and Wales. There are more salvias now at Kiftsgate thanks to visits to Wollerton Old Hall Garden in Shropshire, while advice from Ursula Cholmeley at Easton Walled Gardens in Lincolnshire has been followed in the Orchard. Anne also relates very much to work done by Ian and Susie Pasley-Tyler at Coton Manor in Northamptonshire, for they, too, are the third generation to tend a garden laid out in the 1920s.

Anne's correspondence reveals that she has never rested on her laurels. In 1990 she exchanged letters about peonies – in particular, her *Paeonia rockii* – with Sir Peter Smithers, whose garden in Switzerland had been much admired by Diany and Betsy. Smithers recommended to her the French peony nursery Pivoines Rivière, which took scions from his own plants and was the 'only one good supplier' in Europe. As her mother's peonies are beginning to fail, Anne adds annually to her stock from Pivoines Rivière's catalogue, choosing ones with such delicious names as 'Étoile des Neiges', 'Guardian of the Monastery', 'Souvenir de Maxime Cornu' and 'L'Espérance'. Many have been grown from Smithers's peonies, reinforcing the link between Anne's garden and her mother's time.

Every other year, the Chambers meticulously update the published list of plants for garden visitors. Adding new plants and deleting those that have been changed or have died is an immense task: for example, some 180 different species or cultivars are listed in the Lower Garden alone.

Although Diany Binny had tried to interest *Gardeners' World* in running regular features on Kiftsgate, she otherwise took little interest in publicizing the garden. Anne, running it as a business, knew that she needed to raise its profile, and encouraged articles in magazines and newspapers. She also appeared on television in 1995 in the BBC series *The English Country Garden*. Walking round in conversation with Rosemary Verey, Anne announced staunchly, 'We have never been followers of fashion throughout this garden', while flagging up that Diany had been 'ahead of the game with trilliums'. In her turn, Verey admired the Yellow Border: 'The mixture of shrubs and herbaceous plants is one of the reasons why this border is so good.'

Anne has written little herself, but she gives talks to gardening clubs and leads tours round gardens in Italy and the South of France. In Menton, she has taken groups to Serre de la Madone, the French home of Heather's gardening neighbour Lawrence Johnston, and to Le Clos du Peyronnet, home to three generations of the Waterfield family – again a connection with Diany. As the fame of Kiftsgate spread, garden-design days run by a company called Border Lines were held there, with a lecture, lunch and a tour of the garden. Lecturers included Robin Lane Fox, the bulb expert Christine Skelmersdale, the rosarian Hazel Le Rougetel, the former Sissinghurst gardeners Pamela Schwerdt and Sibylle Kreutzberger, and the leading Irish gardener and plantswoman Helen Dillon. Anne would sit at the back during the lectures, picking up tips from the visiting experts.

Anne's life has become deeply embedded in Gloucestershire. From 2009 to 2010, she was High Sheriff, the Queen's representative on law and order in the county, a largely ceremonial role; she was the first Lady Warden of the Honourable Company of Gloucestershire from 2015 to 2016; and she is also President of the Gloucestershire Federation of Gardening Societies. She is a trustee of the Ernest Wilson Memorial Garden in Chipping Campden, created in memory of the plant hunter who was born in the town in 1876. Among the plants he brought home from his expeditions to the Far East was *Magnolia delavayi*, planted by Heather Muir beside the Grecian portico above the Four Squares at Kiftsgate.

In the spring of 2018, an aptly named *Magnolia wilsonii* was planted in the North Border, presented in honour of Kiftsgate's opening for eighty years under the National Garden Scheme. The year 2019 marked the centenary of the Muirs' arrival at Kiftsgate. Three generations of Muir women have each devoted more than thirty years of their lives to its garden. Anne's years in charge have been a collaboration with her husband, Johnny, and together they have kept in good heart this great Gloucestershire treasure.

Anne in her ceremonial costume of High Sheriff of Gloucestershire, a role she assumed from 2009 to 2010. With her on the terrace are Johnny and the couple's three children, Clare, Patrick and Robert.

THE MODERNIZING SPIRIT: ANNE CHAMBERS

The Garden

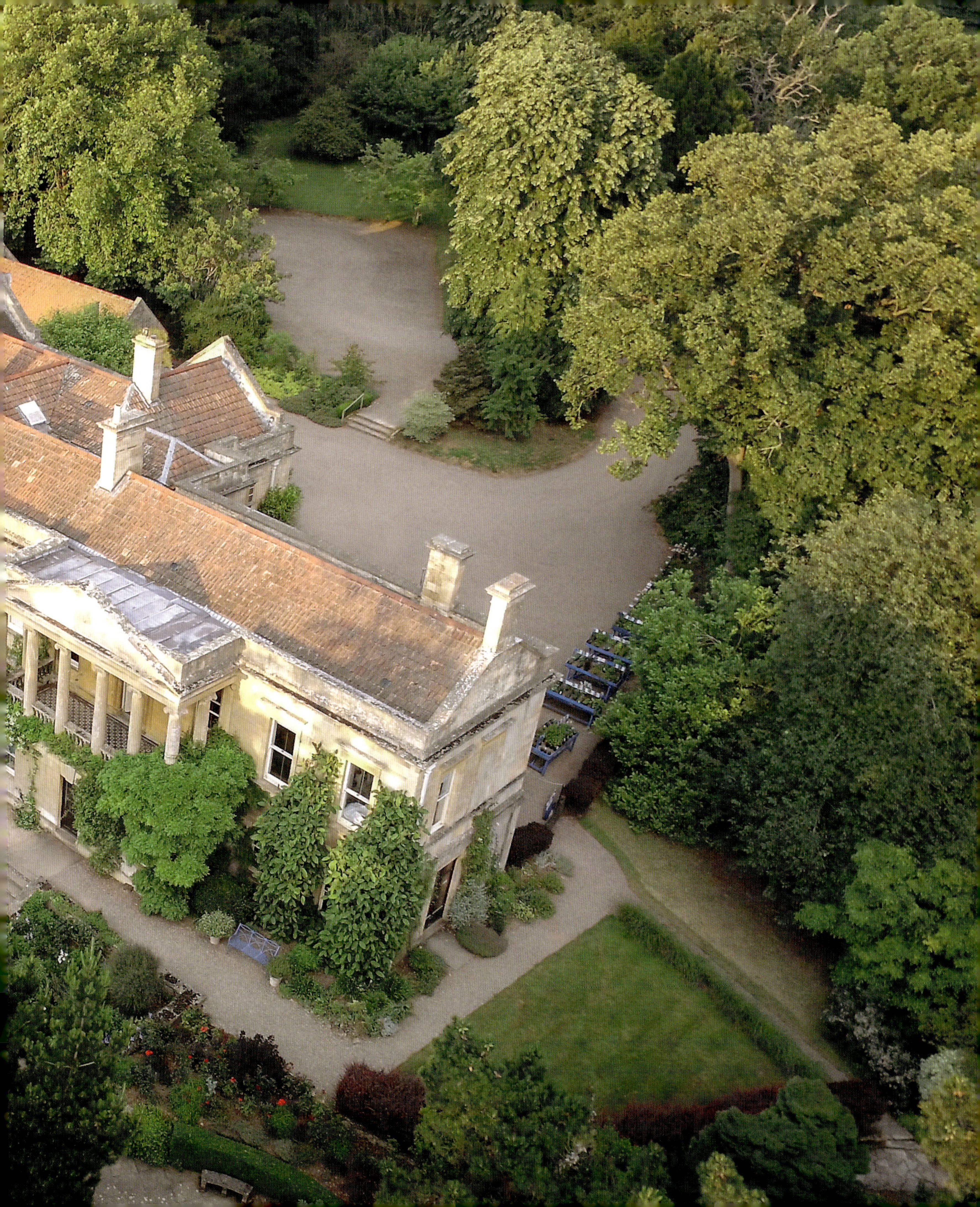

Arrival at Kiftsgate

Baker's Hill winds its way up from Mickleton to Kiftsgate. The road is impassable in snow, but, on a clear winter's day, the Grecian portico and Sidney Graves Hamilton's row of Monterey pines are visible above the valley. This view, full of promise, was probably the first sight that Jack and Heather Muir had of their future home.

The top lane runs along the edge of the Kiftsgate estate, past fields and a row of hollies planted in the 1970s by Diany Binny to continue the line of trees from the gardens. Hidcote and Kiftsgate are divided by just this lane, for Heaven's Gate at Hidcote can be seen up to the right, making apparent the close proximity of two of England's most important gardens.

Kiftsgate Court Gardens are entered through wrought-iron gates, supported by tall stone piers. These were once flanked by enormous Victorian laurels, which were cleared in 1932 by the Muirs, leaving only a beech seedling to grow into a large tree by the kitchen-garden wall.

By the gates is Front Lodge, to which first Jack and Heather Muir and then Diany Binny moved after leaving the main house. Heather spent more of her retirement in London, but Front Lodge was Diany's home for over thirty years, until her death in 2006. She filled its garden with her favourite plants, juxtaposing *Viburnum* × *burkwoodii* and *Osmanthus delavayi* as she had by the front door of the main house, and planting potentillas, peonies, deutzias, philadelphus, geraniums and *Acer campestre*. The lodge is now let, but the Chambers maintain the garden, for it is the visitor's introduction to Kiftsgate. In April a lavish cherry-red chaenomeles (*Chaenomeles japonica*) sprawls over the low wall; it is pruned two or three times a year to keep it in shape.

When the Muirs first came here in 1919, the avenue was still lined by William Shenstone's limes, but now only three of his great trees remain. Over the years, they have been replaced with weeping silver limes (*Tilia tomentosa* 'Petiolaris'), which scent the air in summer and are irresistible to bees. There are many other mature trees besides the limes, creating a splendid parkland approach. These include yews, holm oaks, sophora (*Styphnolobium japonicum*), *Metasequoia glyptostroboides*, *Fagus sylvatica* 'Pendula', *Robinia pseudoacacia*, the Caucasian *Quercus pontica*, *Fraxinus mariesii* and stands of *Rhododendron ponticum*. Between them, they provide a variety of tree shape and foliage colour, with dark junipers, *Juniperus horizontalis* 'Glauca' and *J. procumbens*, added by Diany for winter contrast.

But this is not just a classic tree-lined avenue, for there are tiers of interest, like a rich piece of embroidery into which each generation of the family has woven colourful threads. Amid the stately trees are smaller trees and shrubs, perennials and bulbs, an earnest of the mixed planting so evident at Kiftsgate.

Beyond Front Lodge are two rough-barked *Eucryphia glutinosa*, the only survivors of a line that Diany planted in the 1970s along the south-facing wall of what was once the kitchen garden (now the nursery). Also from Diany's time are pink, red and blue climbing roses, including 'Debutante', 'Crimson Shower', 'Veilchenblau' and 'Bleu Magenta'. Anne Chambers prunes the roses hard every autumn, fanning them out against the wall. Below the roses is a line of irises, inspired by a garden in the South of France. Because irises have such a short season, Anne chose to make the border here rather than in the main garden, and in a position where

Opposite: A pair of stone piers makes an emphatic entrance to Kiftsgate Court Gardens. To the left of the entrance is Front Lodge, to which both Heather Muir and Diany Binny retired when they handed over the garden to their daughters.

Below: The cherry-red flowers of a *Chaenomeles japonica* hedge outside Front Lodge are a cheerful welcome for spring visitors to Kiftsgate.

ARRIVAL AT KIFTSGATE

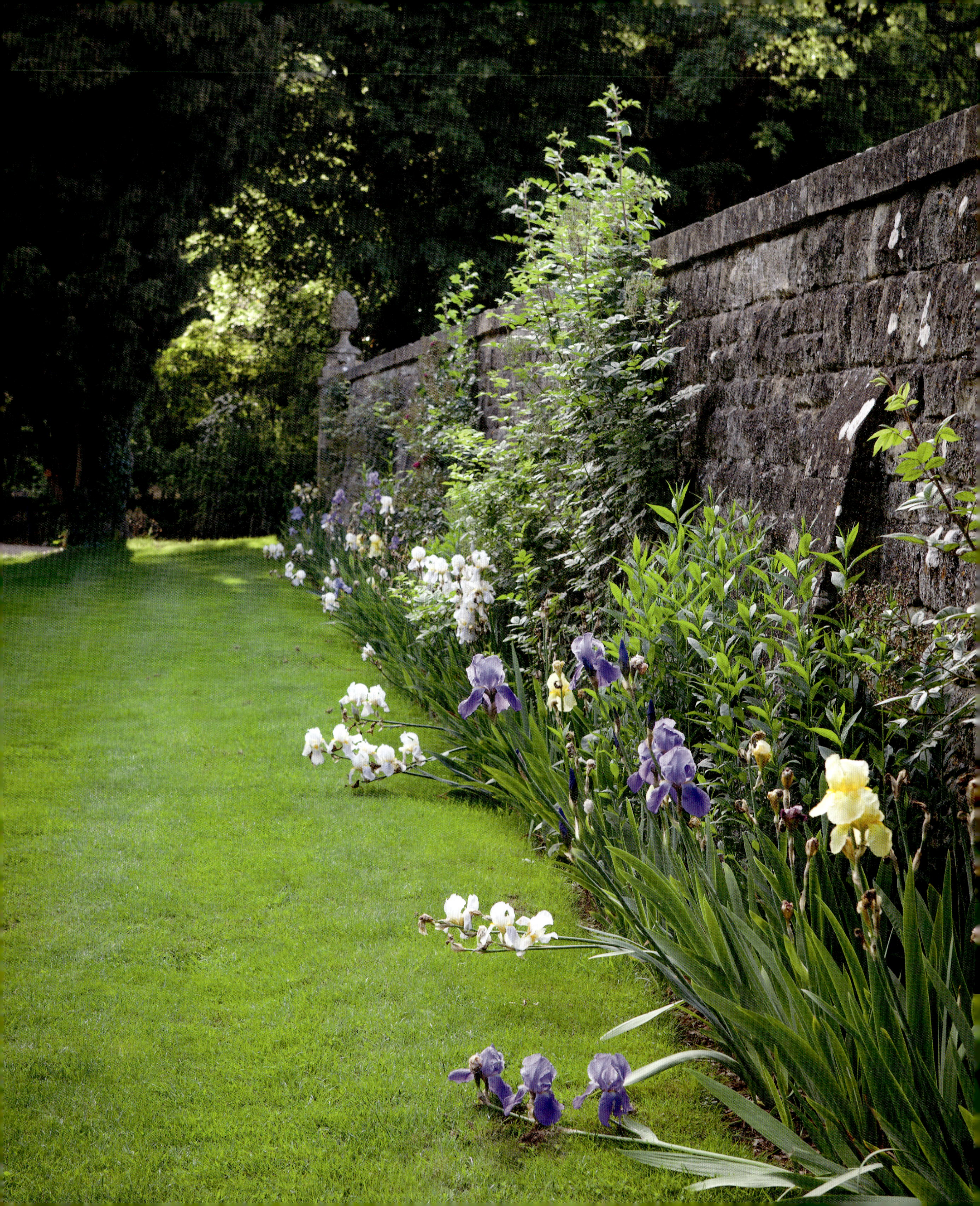

their rhizomes can bake in the sun after the flowers have finished.

Beyond the nursery wall, the drive dips and bends round to the left, with head-high banks rising on the right-hand side, before flattening out again towards the house. At this first bend is Berberis Corner, planted with several varieties, including *Berberis × stenophylla* 'Pink Pearl' and *B. thunbergii* 'Tricolor'. Their different-shaped leaves give good autumn colour, aided in September by the white flowers of *Heptacodium miconioides*.

Adjacent is a small grove of specimen acers, planted by the Chambers' elder son, Robert, his first contribution to the garden. Near the acers is a Bhutan pine, grown from a cutting taken from a historic tree at Isola Madre on Lake Maggiore in northern Italy. It was given to Anne by the Isola Madre head gardener, who had visited and admired Kiftsgate.

From here, the drive is lined by white daffodils, some dating from Heather's time. Many of them are 'Mount Hood', supplemented annually by Anne. A collection of specimen

Opposite: Against the wall of the nursery, Anne Chambers has created an iris border that peaks in May, allowing the rhizomes to bask in the sun throughout the summer.

Top: In April, white *Osmanthus delavayi* flowers in front of the house as the garden opens for business. Old-fashioned white daffodils fill the grass beneath a *Ginkgo biloba*.

Above: Originally planted by Heather, the daffodils flood the verges and banks alongside the drive beneath weeping silver limes planted by Diany.

ARRIVAL AT KIFTSGATE

KIFTSGATE COURT GARDENS

trees, planted by Diany in the 1960s and 1970s, features another eucryphia (*Eucryphia* × *nymansensis*); *Davidia involucrata*, with flowers like white pocket handkerchiefs; the Judas tree, *Cercis siliquastrum*, which has heart-shaped leaves and, in spring, rose-pink flowers; *Malus* × *floribunda*; a weeping beech, *Fagus sylvatica* 'Pendula'; and *Callicarpa bodinieri*, covered with livid purple berries in autumn. The leaves of a katsura (*Cercidiphyllum japonicum*) turn orange, yellow and pink in autumn and smell of burnt sugar. Also here is a walnut, *Juglans regia*, planted in the spring of 1998 to mark sixty years of the garden's opening for the National Garden Scheme.

Individual magnolias have been chosen for interest from spring through to late summer. *Magnolia campbellii* subsp. *mollicomata* has cerise-pink flowers in March and April, followed in June and July by the white flowers of M. *macrophylla* subsp. *ashei* × *virginiana*. On a corner of the house is M. *grandiflora* 'Exmouth', which has lemon-scented, butter-yellow flowers in August.

The drooping spindle flowers of *Pterostyrax hispida*, a native of Japan and China, grown from seed by Diany against the odds, provide a pretty white flash in summer between the car park and the picnic lawn. Also around the car park are a tree heather, *Erica arborea*; a pine dating from 1900; *Amelanchier* × *grandiflora* 'Ballerina'; and a line of youthful *Syringa* × *josiflexa* 'Bellicent', the last replacing trees and bushes damaged in the severe winter of 2017–18. *Cornus* 'Kenwyn Clapp' and C. *alternifolia* 'Argentea' (repeated elsewhere in the garden) are sentinels on either side of the steps leading from the car park to the house forecourt. Across this low bank spread *Alchemilla mollis*, a foam of lime green in June; prostrate *Baccharis patagonica*; and *Cistus* × *argenteus* 'Silver Pink'.

A bluey-grey *Abies koreana*, *Ginkgo biloba* and a weeping silver lime stand together on an apron of grass jutting out in the forecourt of the house. This area is especially lovely in April, when the daffodils are out and the planting by the front door is entirely white. The nutmeg-scented *Viburnum* × *burkwoodii*, an equally fragrant, white-flowered *Osmanthus delavayi* and a spreading *Magnolia denudata*, with large white, lily-shaped flowers, were all planted by Diany. Other planting against the house includes *Philadelphus* 'Sybille', the narrow-leaved *Actinidia pilosula*, *Camellia cuspidata* (the only camellia in the garden) and various hybrid hellebores that flower through winter into spring, to be superseded by *Paeonia* × *lemoinei* 'Souvenir de Maxime Cornu'. The white theme of the viburnum and osmanthus is picked up in summer by the deciduous *Schizophragma integrifolium*, which scrambles up the wall on its aerial roots. With large flowers resembling those of a lace-cap hydrangea, it is something of a rarity. In 1987 Diany provided Hillier Nursery with seeds of the plant, receiving a fulsome letter of thanks: 'We shall endeavour to germinate them and see how we progress … Perhaps with luck we can return a few young plants to you sometime in the future.'

A schizophragma is also planted against the house by the gate into the garden, along with the early May-flowering *Ceanothus* 'Puget Blue' and the white rambler *Rosa* 'Dentelle de Bruges'.

In the 1960s and 1970s, Diany planted a small arboretum beside the drive. In May the handkerchief tree, *Davidia involucrata*, is covered with glorious creamy-white flowers (seen in detail above).

ARRIVAL AT KIFTSGATE

Bluebell Wood

Below: Naturalized *Crocus tommasinianus* grow happily amid beech tree litter.

Right: For a month from early February, the woods are carpeted with snowdrops.

Specimen acers, dotted through the taller parkland trees along the drive, peak in spring and autumn. Planted by Anne and Johnny, they include *Acer palmatum* 'Aoyagi'; *A. griseum*, which has attractive peeling bark; and *A. sieboldianum*.

Specimen acers are also planted through the Bluebell Wood, which falls away sharply to the left. The slopes follow the line of the drive, and are covered with snowdrops in early February. On the slopes facing south rather than south-west, the snowdrops flower two weeks earlier. In late April and through May, the woods are a haze of the deep blue of English bluebells, shafts of light reaching them through the foliage of the trees.

KIFTSGATE COURT GARDENS

BLUEBELL WOOD

Bluebells thrive in the dappled shade cast by the mostly deciduous trees on the slopes below the drive.

BLUEBELL WOOD

Below and right: Anne and Johnny Chambers have planted many specimen acers throughout the Bluebell Wood, including *Acer palmatum* 'Bloodgood', seen in detail below.

Opposite: The banks of the Bluebell Wood were more densely wooded when the Muirs moved to Kiftsgate in 1919. The leaves of the trees, rotted down over the centuries, provided a rich mulch for Heather's rhododendrons, which otherwise do not grow in the alkaline soil of the Cotswolds.

Densely wooded before the Muirs' arrival, these banks were thinned out by Heather in the 1930s to give room and light for such acers as *Acer davidii*, *A. japonicum* and *A. platanoides* 'Drummondii'. Several varieties of *A. palmatum* and *A. pseudoplatanus* 'Brilliantissimum' have since been added. Although the Cotswolds are generally too alkaline for rhododendrons, woodland leaves rotting down over the centuries provided Heather with the right environment here.

Some large trees remain, such as a fine *Populus lasiocarpa*, *Chamaecyparis lawsoniana*, *Nothofagus antarctica* and *Quercus rubra*. Many, however, have fallen in recent years, breaking the canopy and letting in too much light for the bluebells. To fill the gaps, the Chambers have planted several cherries, including *Prunus* 'Shōgetsu' and *P. sargentii*, blackthorn (*Prunus spinosa* 'Purpurea') and a *Malus × zumi* 'Golden Hornet' for spring and autumn colour.

This is not one of the most intensively gardened areas, although some pruning and an annual onslaught on the brambles are required. Anne and Johnny also have a fight on their hands since foxgloves have started seeding themselves competitively among the bluebells.

KIFTSGATE COURT GARDENS
66

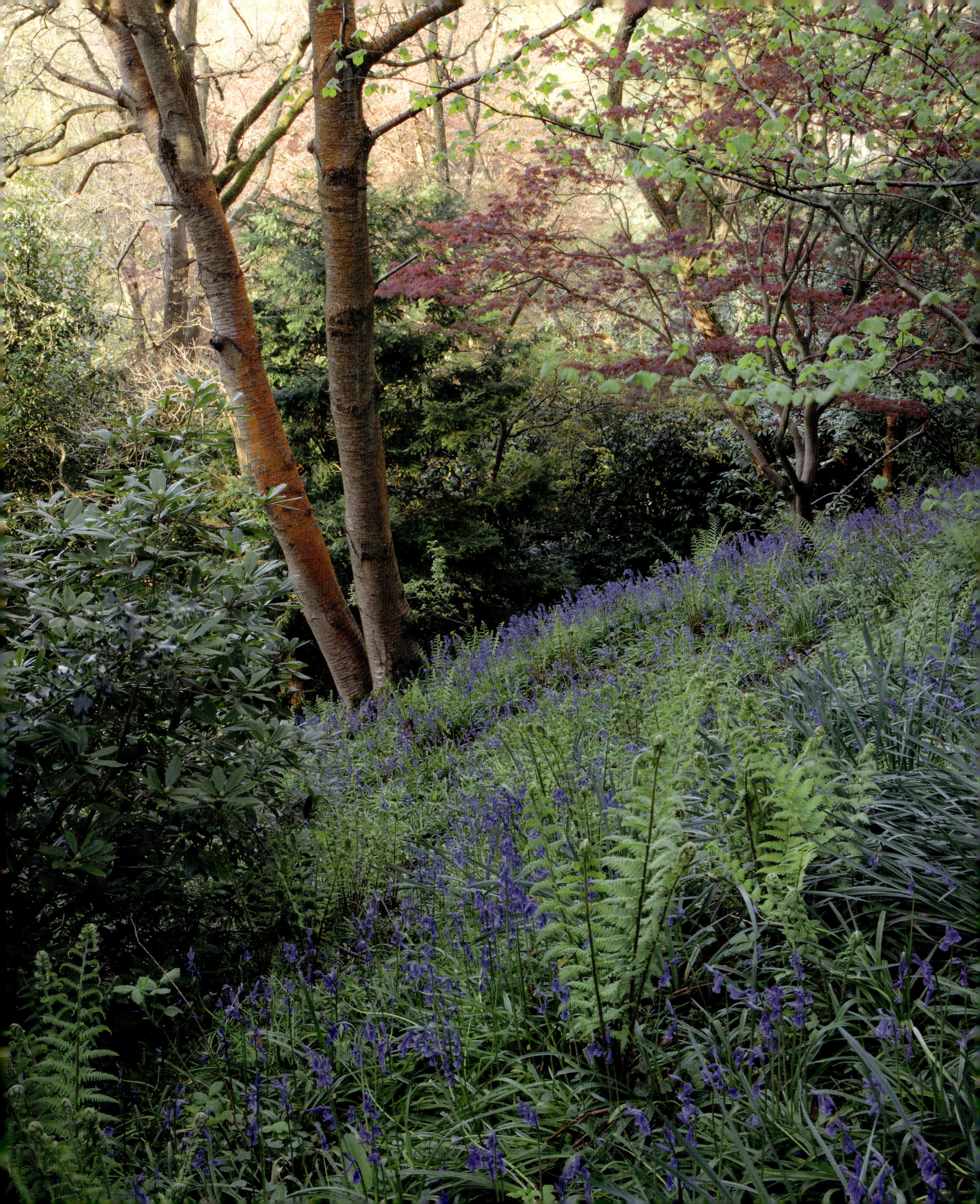

Above: The path into the garden is lined by a low hedge of *Pennisetum thunbergii* 'Red Buttons', which glows red in high summer and rustles attractively in the wind.

Opposite: The view across the rose-packed Four Squares to the portico designed by James Lees-Milne for the Muirs in the 1930s.

House and Side Lawn

Nothing stands still at Kiftsgate, despite the tranquil feeling of continuity. Nor is anything ever wasted. An early decision of Anne's in the 1980s was to create an entrance of more éclat for visitors. To do this, she reused a redundant ironwork gate from the White Sunk Garden, setting it next to the house, where it opens on to a glimpse of Bredon Hill and the Malverns through the Monterey pines. She and Johnny also planted a prunus hedge by the gate, which they then replaced in the winter of 2017–18 with a hedge of *Escallonia* 'Apple Blossom', to be tougher and neater. These may seem small points, but this willingness to adapt and rethink gives Kiftsgate its freshness.

Beneath the boughs of a *Prunus padus* 'Watereri' is a blanket of flowers for late winter and spring, with snowdrops and *Eranthis hyemalis* followed by scillas, snake's head fritillaries, *Anemone blanda* and *A. nemorosa*. The grass here is mown once the fritillaries have set seed.

The long view is foregrounded by a semicircular hedge of *Berberis thunbergii* f. *atropurpurea* 'Rose Glow'. Planted by Diany, this frames a rare area of lawn. Running beside the lawn is another new Chambers introduction: an edging strip of *Pennisetum thunbergii* 'Red Buttons', which replaced lavender planted by Diany. In summer and autumn, when the grasses are longer, they rustle in the breeze and catch the light, their reddish tinge echoing the colour of the berberis.

Heather Muir clothed her house in climbers. Pegs on the side wall show that roses once reached up to the parapet of the roof. These included 'Albertine', a fragrant double pink rambling rose planted in 1921. Although Heather's 'Albertine' has long since died, her granddaughter has recently planted a replacement, which may yet scale the height of Heather's top pegs.

Heather's magnificent, almost century-old *Magnolia delavayi* frames the windows of what is now the tearoom, once the drawing room. Splendid though it is, the magnolia is a work-creator, as its large, leathery leaves do not rot

Below: Euphorbia characias subsp. wulfenii 'Joyce's Giant' with purple honesty.

Right: On the corner of the house above the Four Squares is a magnificent *Magnolia delavayi* planted by Heather in the 1920s.

Opposite: The side lawn is encircled by a hedge of *Berberis thunbergii* f. *atropurpurea* 'Rose Glow', planted by Diany. A forty-year-old Scots pine seedling and one of Sidney Graves Hamilton's Monterey pines soar up beyond the hedge. In the foreground is *Rosa* 'Albertine'.

down, and need picking up by hand. It is also pruned every other year, and does not flower in the year of pruning.

Beside the magnolia grows a *Wisteria floribunda*, which has scaled the Grecian portico since Heather's time. In the beds beneath the magnolia are large blue *Scilla hyacinthoides* for early spring and an architectural *Phillyrea angustifolia*, a present from Diany's younger gardening friend Timothy Leese. Spotting *Xanthoceras sorbifolium* at Sissinghurst inspired the Chambers to plant this upright, deciduous shrub with star-shaped white flowers in late spring. On the other side of the portico grow *Hydrangea serratifolia*, *Actinidia kolomikta* and *Rosa* 'François Juranville'. In the recess to the left of the portico stands a blacksmith-made bench, one of many seats commissioned by Diany in the 1960s. Elsewhere are sprung metal chairs dating from the 1930s. Painted bottle green by Heather, they are all now the azure blue favoured by Diany, a striking contrast against dark foliage.

One of the charms of Kiftsgate is its virtual indifference to gardening trends. While many garden designers have now adopted the fashion for block planting of particular species, Anne has stuck to her last. Her planting in any area is just as abundant as that of the block-planters, but it comprises plants used individually and then repeated either nearby or in other parts of the garden. Sometimes similar, yet different, varieties are used for a subtle shift in emphasis. The honey-scented *Euphorbia mellifera* on one side of the portico, for example, is echoed by *E.* × *pasteurii*, comparable in size and shape, and also with a honey fragrance, but having yellower flowers in mid-summer and red-tinted leaves in autumn. Lily-of-the-valley-scented smilacina (*Maianthemum racemosum*), a favourite of Anne's,

HOUSE AND SIDE LAWN

runs through these beds around the house, and reappears throughout the garden.

A yellow *Rosa banksiae* 'Lutea' was originally planted by Heather on the wall at a right angle to the Grecian portico. It is not long-lasting, so Anne has already replaced it two or three times, again maintaining the link with her grandmother's choices. She has also replanted Diany's beloved *Rosa* × *odorata* 'Mutabilis', a classic China rose that opens buff yellow and fades to cerise pink. It flowers on and off for about six months and, unusually, is grown at Kiftsgate as a climber; it is more often seen as a border shrub rose.

Anne and Johnny also experiment against this warm, west-facing wall. A new rose to them is *Rosa* 'Cooperi', a tender, glossy-leaved rambling rose more often seen in the South of France and in Italy, but here already reaching the first-floor windows. Early in the season, it has single white flowers with noticeable yellow stamens. This grows above the slightly tender

Geranium palmatum, also a May flowerer, as is *Ceanothus* 'Puget Blue', which came from Betsy Muir's garden at Hidcote Boyce. In August, *Anemone* × *hybrida* 'Montrose' flowers against the wall behind large terracotta pots of *Hydrangea paniculata* 'Phantom', olives and oleander.

A nearby step leads to the 1930s portico, which matches the Graves Hamilton façade and encloses a terrace with tables and chairs. Scented pelargoniums are arrayed along the portico wall: lunching there on a sunny day, and looking out across the Four Squares at the Monterey pines, you could well be in the South of France. This newer portico was designed by a youthful James Lees-Milne. Lees-Milne – whose mother, Helen, was a friend of Heather Muir – was instrumental in Lawrence Johnston's handing Hidcote to the National Trust in 1948.

Below the newer portico stands a row of terracotta pots, bought cheaply in Italy by Diany in the 1960s and then transported to Kiftsgate at vast expense. They are not frost-proof, so need wrapping in winter. These terracotta pots are interspersed with small stone troughs, which once belonged to Betsy. All are planted each year with different tulip varieties and, in one year, 'Blood Red' wallflowers from Sarah Raven. The pots are then replanted in May for the late season, with blues and greys, including *Malva sylvestris* (a gift from the Irish gardener Helen Dillon), *Cerinthe major* 'Purpurascens', argyranthemum, melianthus and artemisia.

More of Diany's Italian pots on the semicircular terrace below the Four Squares are planted with the same foliage plants. But there the colour theme is red, with bright pelargoniums, *Salvia confertiflora* and *S.* 'Hot Lips'.

Spilling on to the terrace is an old rose, 'William Lobb', a dark crimson purple, with violet reverses. This is trained along the top of the wall, growing up from the Wide Border below. At the corner of the terrace is an *Itea ilicifolia*, an evergreen shrub with tassels of white flowers in high summer. Self-seeded bronze foxgloves, *Digitalis ferruginea*, peep out from cracks in the walls.

Opposite: Naturalized snake's head fritillaries (*Fritillaria meleagris*), wood anemones (*Anemone nemorosa*) and *A. blanda* grow near the house under the spreading boughs of a *Prunus padus* 'Watereri'.

Right: In spring, the first sight that visitors encounter on entering the garden are the large pink flowers of *Magnolia* × *soulangeana* 'Picture'.

HOUSE AND SIDE LAWN

KIFTSGATE COURT GARDENS

Four Squares

Kiftsgate is a garden of many moods and aspects. The trapezoid shape of the top garden permits no long avenues or grand central spaces. Instead, the various borders and gardens are connected by a more informal network of stone and grass paths, with glimpses from one to another offered through a framework mostly of yew. But, if there is a major statement, it is the Four Squares. Backed by the Georgian portico – covered in May with purple wisteria and in June with yellow *Rosa banksiae* 'Lutea' and coral-pink *R.* 'François Juranville' – this is the most familiar image of the garden.

Heather Muir began with the Four Squares, first of all planting yew hedges to face the two wings of the house and form a dark backdrop to her tiers of planting. Pre-Muir photographs show that Heather did not start entirely afresh here, but worked instead with the existing retaining walls, steps and cruciform layout. She preserved the Yorkstone paths and central sundial, converting the four square lawns into flower beds edged with small-leaved box (*Buxus microphylla*). Heather's original yew and box still frame the planting today, and are kept razor-sharp by annual pruning. Box cuttings from the ankle-high hedges are used for propagation: never having had to buy in box, the Chambers have been spared the box blight that has ravaged so many other gardens.

In the Four Squares, Heather put down her benchmark. Here, and throughout the garden, she shunned the conventional herbaceous border popularized by Gertrude Jekyll, instead mixing shrubs with roses, peonies and hardy perennials. Although she planted mainly for spring and summer, her bold use of shrubs, both deciduous and evergreen, and of box and yew, gives structure year-round, with the box providing crisp, frosty edging in winter.

Heather's fondness for foliage shape and texture as much as for flower colour was also first demonstrated here: peonies, for instance, have a short flowering season, but the gradual transformation of their dark-green leaves into reddish bronze maintains interest as summer progresses. For the roses in the Four Squares,

Opposite: The façade of Kiftsgate Court, covered with wisteria and roses, is framed by two yew pillars, planted in the 1920s by Heather Muir.

Top: The colour scheme of pale pink and lilac in the box-edged beds of the Four Squares has been maintained ever since it was established by Heather.

Above: Pale *Rosa* Eyes for You and darker *R.* 'Magenta' are mixed with perennials such as the pink-flowered *Rodgersia pinnata* 'Superba'.

FOUR SQUARES

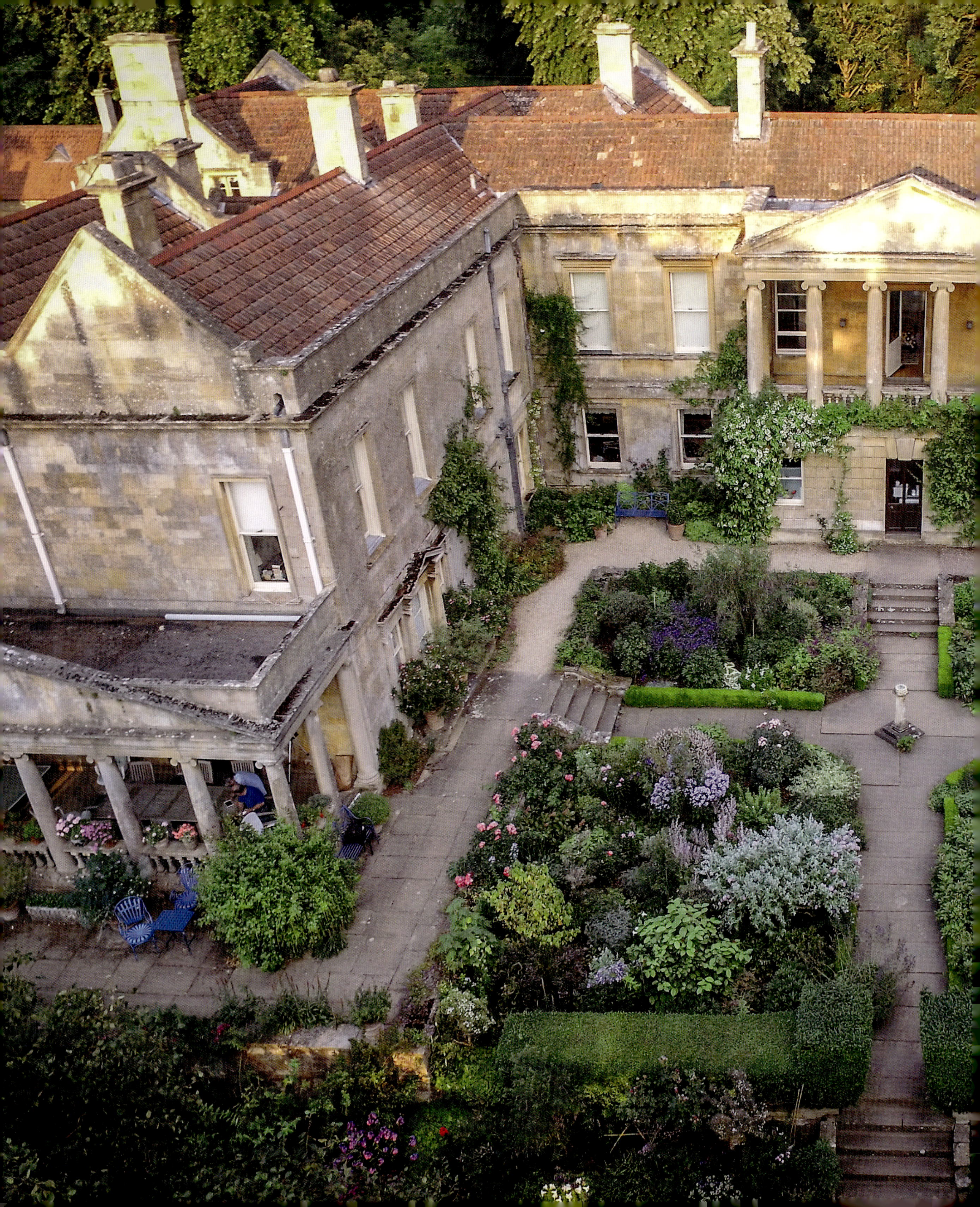

An aerial view shows the strong structure and shapes of the planting in the Four Squares. Encircling the lawn to one side of the house is the brilliant hedge of *Berberis thunbergii* f. *atropurpurea* 'Rose Glow'.

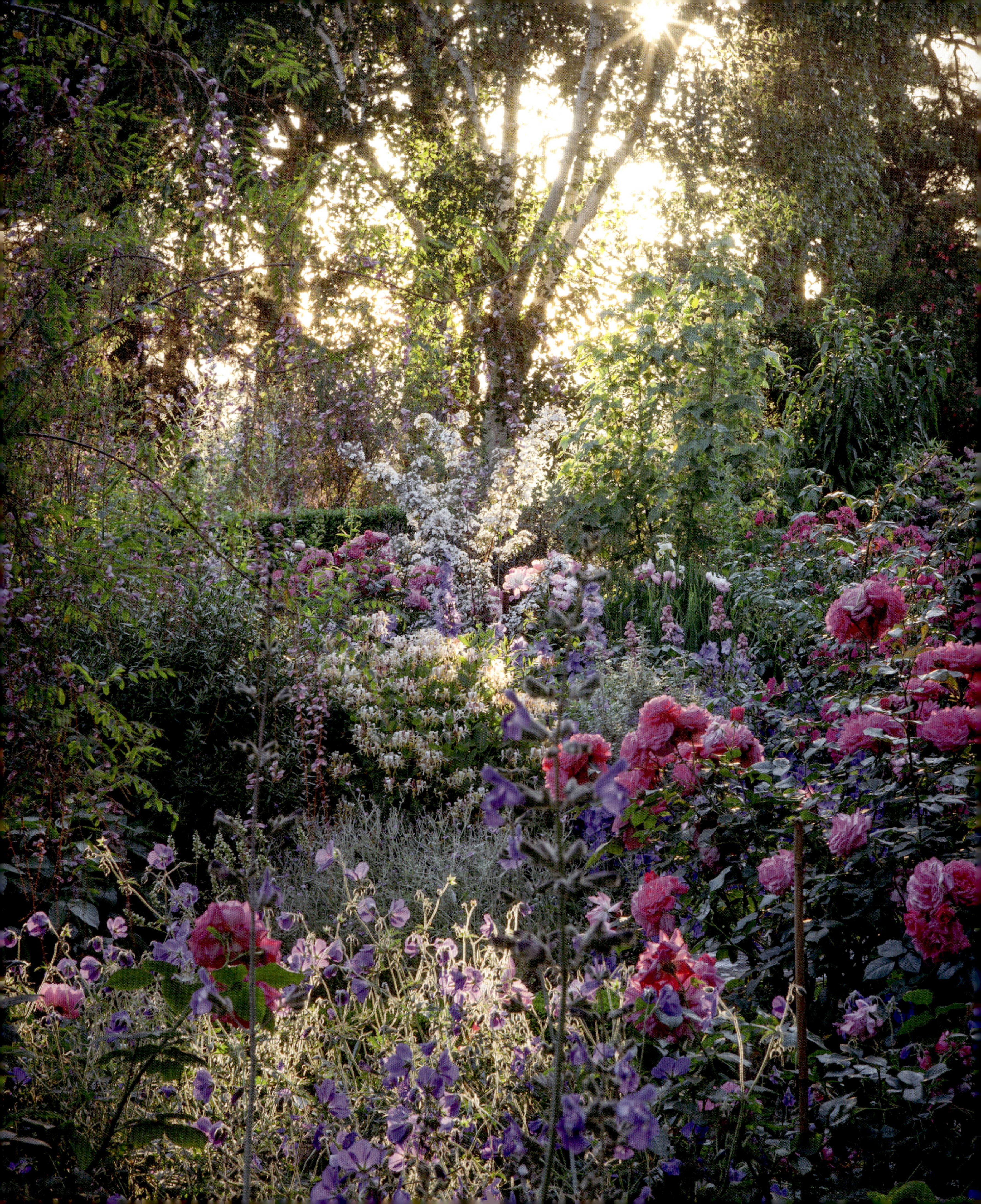

Heather chose delicate shades of mauvy pink, described by the Chambers as 'the colour of grannies' knickers'. This soft palette is echoed throughout the garden, where, on the whole, bright colours are shunned. Reds tend to be crimson or purply pink rather than scarlet, yellows lemony rather than egg yolk, and orange virtually absent.

The deep-pink climber 'American Pillar' (a rose bred in 1862) may well have been in the Four Squares since Heather's time. This rose is pruned hard each year by Anne, who then trains it in a fan shape through a network of wires. These run up and over the retaining wall behind, so the rose flowers at the foot level of visitors on the house terrace. This unfamiliar method of training climbers was devised by Heather, and is also used for clematis. Each clematis is seen individually, rather than climbing through roses as in so many other gardens. Anne and her mother both favoured small-flowered clematis, such as *Clematis alpina* for spring and then, for summer and autumn, *C.* 'Étoile Rose' and 'Perle d'Azur'.

Many of the roses are post-Second World War introductions planted by Diany, such as the American floribunda 'Lavender Pinocchio', 'Lilac Charm' and 'Magenta'. A perfect new rose for this colour scheme is the lilac Eyes for You. Another rose in the Four Squares is a rarity: 'Rita', a deep-pink floribunda, was bred and given to Diany by Hilda Murrell.

The flowering season begins with the appearance of mauve drumstick *Primula denticulata*, swiftly followed by different tulip varieties each year, the bulbs an innovation of Anne's of which Diany disapproved. These are accompanied by purple honesty and the mottled foliage and dainty blue flowers of *Brunnera macrophylla* 'Variegata'. In late May the tree peonies come into their own: *Paeonia rockii* 'Double White' and *P.r.* 'Baron Thyssen Bornemisza', both introductions from the Swiss-based champion peony-grower Sir Peter Smithers. *Lactiflora* peonies include the double pink *P. lactiflora* 'Bowl of Beauty' and an unknown white peony, a gift to Diany from Victoria Wakefield, the owner of Bramdean House garden in Hampshire.

Flowering shrubs include rosy-pink *Deutzia* × *elegantissima* 'Rosealind', introduced by Diany; flowering from spring into early summer, it remains a favourite. The silvery foliage of three *Olearia* × *scilloniensis* throws the mauves and pinks of the roses into relief in June and July when their own spring flowers are over; this half-hardy shrub survives in the microclimate enjoyed by this Cotswold escarpment garden. *Calycanthus* × *raulstonii* 'Hartlage Wine', a large shrub with bold claret-coloured flowers, is a recent planting. Further contrast is provided by the acid-green foliage of *Heuchera cylindrica* 'Greenfinch' and

Opposite: Exuberant summer planting in the beds of the Four Squares: dazzling pink *Rosa* 'Rita' is mixed with *Deutzia setchuenensis* var. *corymbiflora, Salvia candelabrum*, a bush honeysuckle, *Geranium robustum* and *Indigofera pendula*.

Above: The view from the balcony of the Georgian portico shows that Heather largely retained the layout of the original garden when she created the Four Squares in the 1920s.

FOUR SQUARES

Shape is important. Dotted through the beds are shrubs pruned into neat domes, witness to the influence of Diany's sister, Betsy, who was a fiercely tidy gardener. Domed shrubs include *Syringa meyeri* 'Palibin' and the bush-form honeysuckle *Lonicera periclymenum*. These were a present from Peggy Munster, another gardening friend of Diany and aunt of Sir Simon Hornby, president of the Royal Horticultural Society in the 1990s. They contrast with tall uprights, such as *Indigofera pendula*, which appears in three of the four beds, and has long tassels of purple wisteria-like flowers throughout the summer. Louisa Arbuthnott's Stone House Cottage Nursery was their source.

As summer advances, the spires of *Salvia candelabrum* spill out from the bed over the box hedging and on to the Yorkstone paths. For late summer and autumn, there are asters ('Twilight', for example), *Kirengeshoma palmata*, *Lobelia* × *speciosa* 'Hadspen Purple', *L.* × *s.* 'Russian Princess' and dark *Penstemon* 'Burgundy'.

Steps through the yew hedge to the south open on to a semicircular terrace like an amphitheatre, with a view past a *Trachycarpus fortunei* to the Mediterranean Banks below. Above retaining banks of box are two semicircular rose borders. In one are silvery-pink, gnarled 'Felicia' roses, the only example of mass planting by Heather; she planted them in the late 1920s. Anne prunes them hard in the autumn and deadheads them in late June for a second flowering in September. When her daughter, Clare, was married in October 2014, 'Felicia' flowers were used as buttonholes for the men in the wedding party.

The border on the other side is a rare exception to the soft colours prevailing in the garden. This bed is planted with brilliant-red repeat-flowering floribunda roses, including 'Frensham', Lilli Marlene, 'Europeana' and 'Wilhelm'. Appearing almost like an extension of the berberis hedge around the side lawn, this bed was made by Diany, who laughingly described it as her answer to the Red Borders at Hidcote. Other Hidcote-style plants here include red lilies, cannas, salvias and penstemons.

As one leaves the Four Squares towards the west, a pair of yew pillars opposite the Grecian portico frame the view to the shelter belt of Monterey pines on the other side of the majestic Wide Border. Steps lead down to this border, where planting themes in the Four Squares are reiterated and new themes taken up.

Clockwise from top left: Lilium regale; Buddleja crispa; Geranium palmatum; Calycanthus × raulstonii 'Hartlage Wine'.

by the copper-coloured, deeply veined *Rodgersia pinnata* 'Superba'. Tumbling among the roses and shrubs are ground-covering hardy geraniums, planted by the Chambers. The cerise, black-eyed *Geranium psilostemon*, striated *G. renardii*, *G. clarkei* 'Kashmir Purple' and *G. wallichianum* 'Buxton's Variety' all help to make the pink roses sing.

KIFTSGATE COURT GARDENS

Left and below: In summer, *Rosa* Rosy Cushion makes a bright display in the Four Squares, but the emphasis on shape lends interest year-round. Neatly domed shrubs contrast with the verticals of the pines and a white-stemmed birch, *Betula utilis* var. *jacquemontii*, which stands out in winter in the Wide Border beyond the yew hedging.

Overleaf: Diany described the raised bed on the terrace beside the Four Squares as 'Kiftsgate's very modest answer to Hidcote's red border'. This late-summer border is planted with *Penstemon* 'Chester Scarlet', *Dahlia* 'Bishop of Llandaff', *Rosa* Lilli Marlene and *Cotinus coggygria* 'Royal Purple'. It is fringed by a hedge of *Berberis thunbergii* f. *atropurpurea* 'Rose Glow'.

FOUR SQUARES

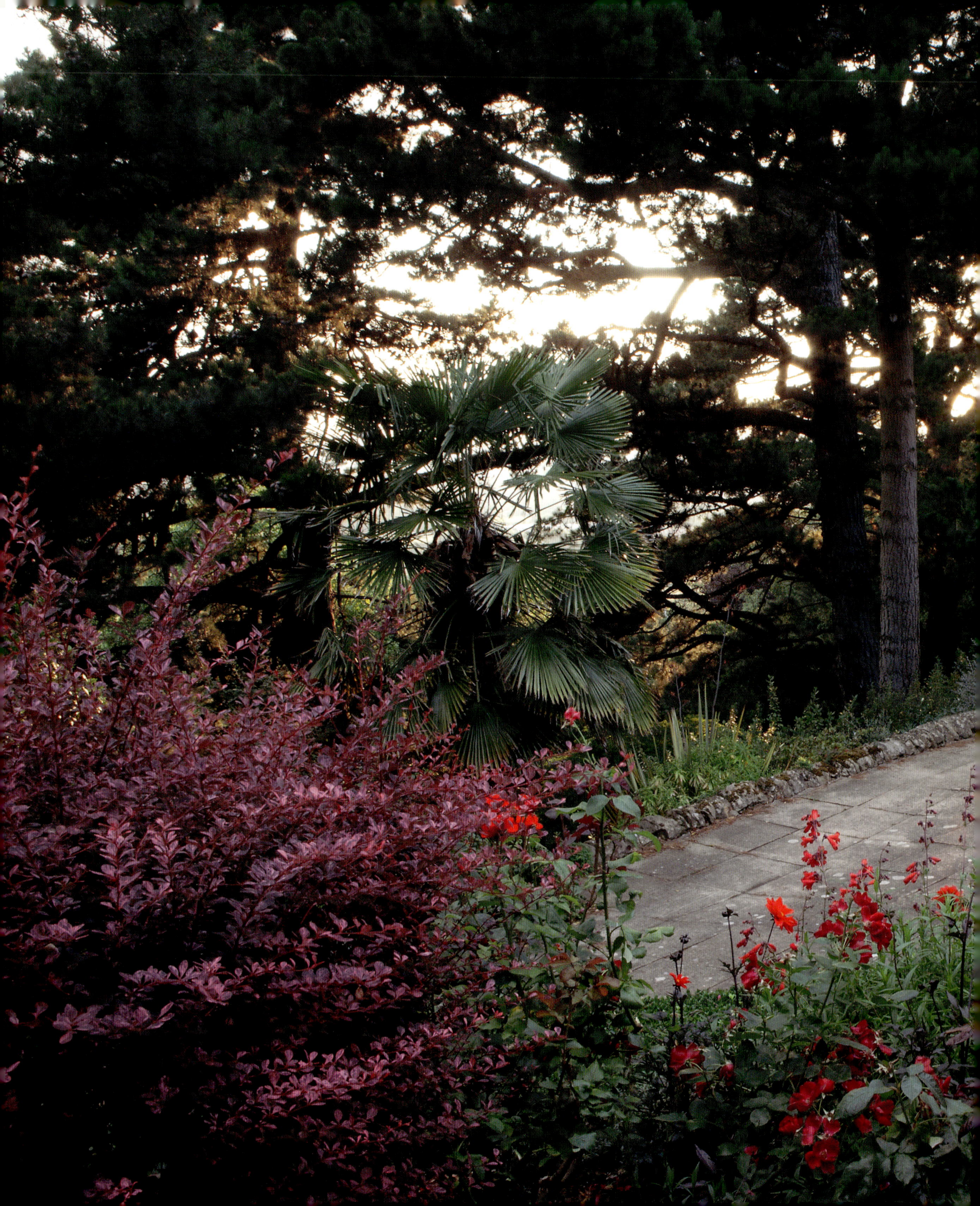

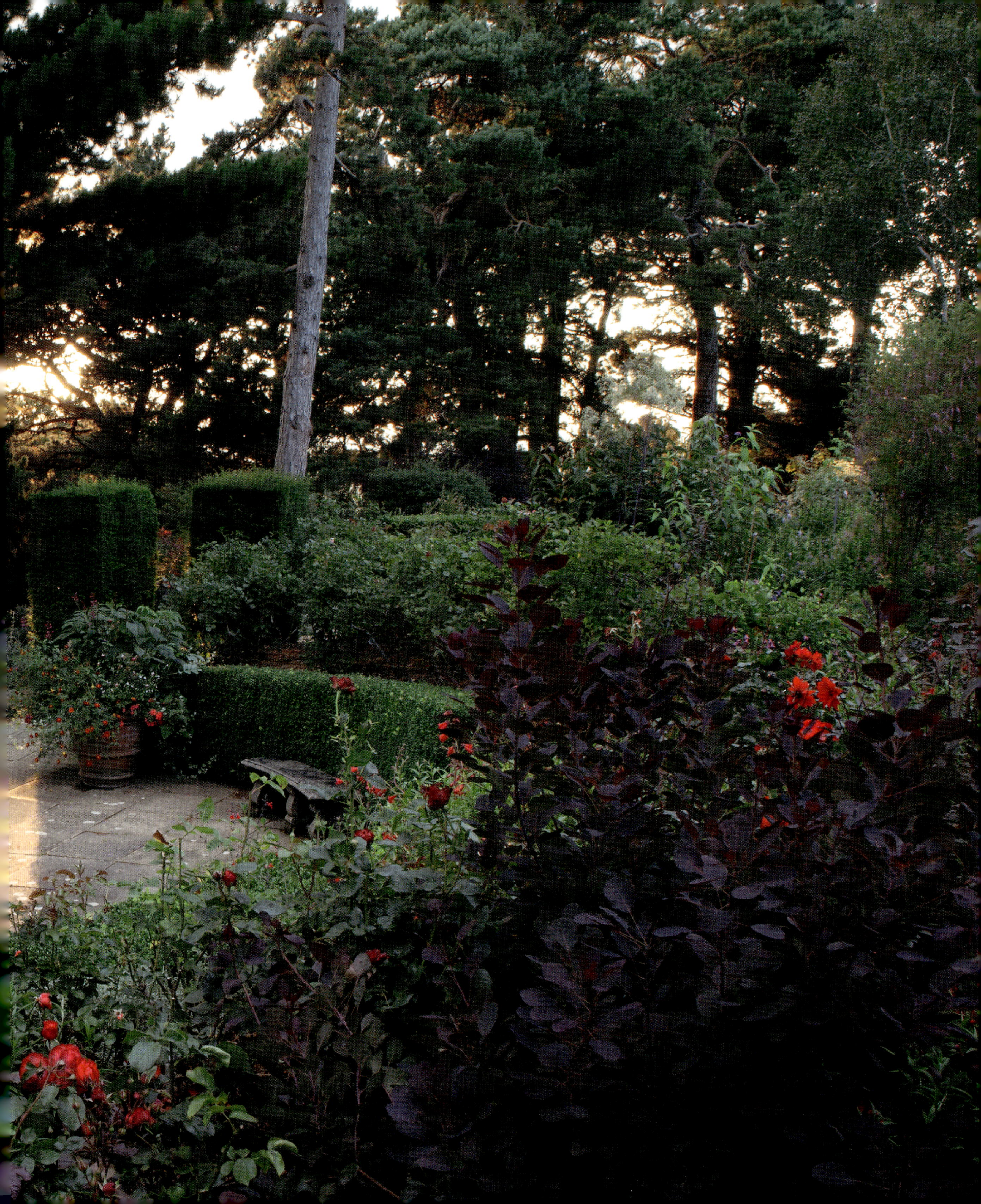

The Wide Border is a wonderful swirling mass of shapes, textures and colours in summer (below), including *Geranium* 'Brookside', *Carpenteria californica* 'Ladhams' Variety', *Gladiolus communis* subsp. *byzantinus*, *Rosa* 'Highdownensis', *R.* 'Vanity', *Dictamnus albus* var. *purpureus*, *Crambe cordifolia*, *Stachys byzantina* and a tall *Paulownia kawakamii*. In spring (opposite), the outlines of the shrubs are more clearly defined.

Wide Border

The Wide Border consists of two semi-parallel borders running in front of the 1930s portico commissioned by Heather Muir from James Lees-Milne. The border immediately below the house terrace is narrower and straighter, probably no more than 10 feet (3 m) deep. But on the other side of the grass path the border is actually an enormous wedge-shaped bed that sprawls across 30 feet (9 m) at its widest, tapering to a point against the holly-and-yew hedge that divides it from the North Border. The path between these borders links the Banks and the Four Squares with the White Sunk Garden, the Bridge Border and the Yellow Border.

Heather laid the Wide Border with a standard straight edge. Over the years, however, it has become increasingly serpentine, particularly on the wider side, as first Diany and then Anne allowed the plants and shrubs to grow out and spread across the grass, in a style inimical to Betsy's taste for greater control. Colour-themed in shades of pink and mauve, with the occasional splash of very pale yellow, the border has the characteristic Kiftsgate mix of shrubs, roses, perennials, some annuals and even trees.

Structure is given by shrubs, such as deutzias, hebes, bay and the dwarf lilac *Syringa meyeri* 'Palibin', with its upright panicles of lilac-pink flowers. Like bold full-stops, they are pruned as domes, reminiscent of shrubs in the Four Squares. These roundels ripple irregularly along the edge of the border and through its width like boulders in an ocean of blue and green, with *Crambe cordifolia*, which was listed in the border forty years ago, rising like sea spray among them. Also here is *Deutzia setchuenensis* var. *corymbiflora*, a compact deciduous shrub with small white flowers, one of Kiftsgate's signature plants (see p. 175).

Roses are trained in a variety of ways above other planting. Some have their branches worked down over an umbrella shape, with radiating wires, like the brolly's spokes, pinned down to the ground. Always on the lookout for ways of fine-tuning, Anne had these frames made after spotting the method in a garden designed by Xa Tollemache at the Chelsea Flower Show.

Other roses, such as the blush-pink 'Fantin-Latour', are trained fan-shape on frames, while a cerise 'Vanity' scrambles through a Magnolia × loebneri 'Leonard Messel'. The mostly pink and white roses also include Alden Biesen (a gift to Anne from a Dutch breeder), 'Prince Charles' and the stripy 'Ferdinand Pichard'. At the bed's centre is the large rose 'Highdownensis', a moyesii hybrid with wonderful hips in autumn and early winter. At the back of the narrow border, a purple 'William Lobb' rose is fanned out across wires along the parapet of the terrace, in the characteristic Kiftsgate method, like 'American Pillar' in the Four Squares.

These borders are perhaps the most high-maintenance, with staking and tying-up required in high summer, and intensive pruning and training in autumn and winter. Hoops, circles and meshes of wire, many of them from Diany's day, are kept in the apple store behind the Hydrangea Border (see White Sunk Garden). All have to be erected in the Wide Border for support through the spring and summer.

The seasons unfold in the Wide Border like a four-act drama. Winter reveals the basic structure and the care taken to feed and manure the soil. There are tiers of interest, even in January and February. Evergreen shrubs, such as Olearia nummularifolia, Osmanthus yunnanensis and the shiny red foliage of Photinia × fraseri 'Red Robin', create a backdrop for the skeletal outlines of the deciduous shrubs, including Syringa meyeri 'Palibin', ceanothus and buddleja.

Having trees in such a border lends stature and variety, but it is a balancing act, as they compete voraciously for water, light and nutrients. The silver-white trunk of Betula utilis var. jacquemontii looks lovely in winter, but is virtually invisible in summer. Planted by Diany, the tree is almost fifty years old and is under threat, for it steals moisture from the surrounding area, water pouring out of its roots when they are cut into. A large purple acer was another Heather Muir legacy until it died in about 2014; its demise opened up the bed and let in more light. It has now been replaced by a Paulownia kawakamii, chosen for its architectural leaves and to retain height above the lower planting.

In spring the perennials and bulbs emerge, starting with the ribbed leaves of Veratrum nigrum; the pixie-cap flowers of various erythroniums; Brunnera macrophylla 'Variegata'; shy violas; purply-blue, pea-like Lathyrus vernus; and Fritillaria pyrenaica. Above them bloom smilacina and Exochorda ×

Above, clockwise from top left: Clematis × diversifolia 'Hendersonii'; Lobelia bridgesii; Dahlia merckii; the bush honeysuckle Lonicera periclymenum.

Opposite: In July, Lilium 'Scheherazade' is arresting against the gentler colour scheme of pinks and mauves in the Wide Border.

KIFTSGATE COURT GARDENS

WIDE BORDER

Below: Anne, unlike her predecessors, enjoys planting tulips. 'White Triumphator' tulips spring up in May amid the emerging perennials at the Banks end of the Wide Border.

Right: Welsh poppies, *Allium hollandicum* 'Purple Sensation', *Euphorbia characias* subsp. *wulfenii*, *Rosa sericea* and blue, self-sown aquilegia.

macrantha 'The Bride', its spray of white flowers recalled in high summer by *Crambe cordifolia*.

Many different varieties of hardy geranium run between the other perennials throughout the season. Comparing today's plant lists with Diany's from the 1970s, we can see that *Geranium* 'Ballerina' has remained here for more than forty years. Newer varieties include the early, almost black *G. phaeum* var. *phaeum* 'Samobor', with rust-splashed leaves, while later in the summer the violet-blue 'Brookside' and the cerise, black-eyed *G. psilostemon* make a strong showing.

A good companion for geraniums is a Mediterranean perennial, *Amsonia orientalis*, bought originally from the hellebore expert Elizabeth Strangman. With its small blue, star-shaped flowers and grey-green foliage, it also complements *Artemisia* 'Powis Castle' and a pale-azure veronica. Picking up the blue further down the border is the low-growing herbaceous *Clematis* × *diversifolia* 'Hendersonii'.

When summer really gets going, lacy *Thalictrum aquilegiifolium* and *T.* 'Elin', and crimson button-heads of grey-leaved *Knautia macedonica*, are juxtaposed with the glossy foliage of roses and peonies. Dotted along the front of the border are self-sown, purply-red *Gladiolus communis* subsp. *byzantinus*, with, behind them, tree peonies and *lactiflora* peonies. The tree peonies were planted by Diany because of Tony's affection for them: the only horticultural legacy of a man who was much less involved in the garden than Johnny Chambers has been. 'Guardian of the Monastery', a tree peony, is the perfect colour here, with its mauvy-pink petals and dark-magenta centre.

Diany also introduced her favourite *Carpenteria californica* (here the white-flowering 'Ladhams'

KIFTSGATE COURT GARDENS

WIDE BORDER

Above: Planting here includes *Staphylea colchica*, *Photinia × fraseri* 'Red Robin', *Elaeagnus angustifolia* and variegated weigela.

Left: Autumn reveals the roundels of clipped shrubs that give structure to the Wide Border, while deep-pink sedums continue to flower as the leaves begin to fall.

Opposite: Winter sun filters through the Mediterranean pines at the far end of the Wide Border, which tapers to a point beside a hedge of yew and holly. The two holly mopheads are known as 'Roy's Balls' after Sir Roy Strong, who suggested this topiary.

Variety'), buddlejas, campanulas and several indigoferas, to which Anne has added purply-pink *Indigofera hancockii* from Pan-Global Plants at Frampton-on-Severn. The Chambers have also planted black-stemmed *Philadelphus delavayi* f. *melanocalyx* 'Nyman's Variety', the white flowers of which have a dark calyx.

As elsewhere, heritage and adaptation work together. Dark-red martagon lilies, introduced by Heather, have naturalized through the border (as well as through the Banks), while Diany began planting one or two penstemons and astrantias. *Achillea millefolium* 'Cerise Queen' was there in the 1970s; it remains in the border today. Arrestingly, Anne has planted 4-foot-high (1.2 m), deep-red *Lilium* 'Scheherazade': different in style, shape and hue from anything else in the border, it is a wonderful starburst of colour in July. Penstemons, planted cautiously by Diany, who believed them to be tender, thrive here in abundance, with Anne's introductions including 'Garnet', 'Hidcote Pink' and 'Sour Grapes'. The only astrantias grown in the Wide Border by Diany were the species *major* and *maxima*; now featured are such astrantia cultivars as the deep-red 'Ruby Wedding' and the pale-pink-flecked 'Buckland'.

For late summer and autumn, there are sedums (*Hylotelephium* 'Herbstfreude' and 'Red Cauli') and asters. Anne's more recent introductions have been dahlias and half-hardy and tender salvias. Dahlias are left in the ground to fight for their survival in winter: *Dahlia merckii* has proved itself completely hardy. An eye-catcher, planted the length of the wider border, is *Dictamnus albus* var. *purpureus*, another survivor from Diany's days. The borders fade gracefully in the autumn, yet remain a feast of textural contrasts, with late-flowering blue asters maintaining the colour. Diany's notebook for 1985 listed, among many others, this instruction to herself: 'Take out or move aster Corymbiflorus from centre of wide border.' The item is ticked, but the aster remains on the plant list today. The first frost serves only to enhance these borders, outlining the seed heads of phlomis and the umbelliferous flower heads of the sedums, and turning the grass path white.

Sir Roy Strong, on a visit to Kiftsgate, complained that the holly-and-yew hedge dividing the Wide and North borders was 'rather boring'. Anne was piqued but, at his suggestion, allowed two holly leaders to grow above the hedge at the point of the border. These, she clipped and trained into mopheads, now known satirically as 'Roy's Balls'.

Opposite Roy's Balls is a line of hellebores, planted for spring effect by Heather against a dark yew hedge. Steps lead up through the yew into the White Sunk Garden and another world.

White Sunk Garden

There are no photographs of pre-Muir days at Kiftsgate to indicate what previously existed where Heather created her White Sunk Garden. What does seem likely, however, is that she carried out more extensive landscaping here than she did when designing the Four Squares on the other side of the house. Heather dug out a central area for a sunken lawn, above which she made shallow, stone-edged beds, and planted yew hedging on two sides to mirror that around the Four Squares. On the other two sides are the house and the high courtyard wall, against which is a salmon-pink rose, 'Follette', often seen in the South of France, and replacing a vanished *Rosa brunonii* 'La Mortola' planted by Heather. Planting began in the 1920s, thereby anticipating Vita Sackville-West's legendary White Garden at Sissinghurst by more than twenty years. Actually larger than the Four Squares, the White Sunk Garden nevertheless feels more intimate, its effects created by alpines and rock plants studding the low walls and narrow beds.

An early planting was *Rosa* 'Pax', a hybrid musk rose bred by the Reverend Joseph Pemberton in 1918 to mark the end of the First World War. Its papery white flowers and very yellow stamens are a beautiful introduction in high summer to this enclosed garden. Nearby is a rose named for Heather herself: *Rosa sericea* 'Heather Muir', a long-flowering shrub rose with pure-white, simple flowers. Other roses include 'White Wings'.

For height above the lower planting, Heather chose the serrated-leaved *Osmanthus armatus*, *Hoheria lyallii*, a belichened *Hamamelis mollis* (a joy in mid-winter) and possibly the mossy *Viburnum carlesii* 'Aurora'. The garden is still framed by such white-flowering shrubs as *Staphylea colchica*, abutilons, two *Deutzia monbeigii*, *D. setchuenensis* var. *corymbiflora*, *Philadelphus microphyllus* and eucryphia.

Heather kept mostly to a simple colour palette, adding to the whites with grey-leaved plants in soft shades of blue, such as *Allium cristophii*, the seed heads of which are visible in a photograph taken in the early 1950s (see p. 40). Heather and Diany sit on the lawn, while Betsy prunes a rose on the terrace above. It is a vision of three accomplished plantswomen.

Although Diany adapted and extended Heather's planting throughout the garden, the White Sunk Garden was one of only two places where she added to the infrastructure laid down by her mother. Diany altered the layout completely in the 1970s by further lowering the garden floor and laying paving instead of lawn, with 'Skyrocket' junipers (since replaced with box roundels) to mark each set of steps. At the centre, she installed a raised pool with a fountain, in the style of a medieval cloister, which in itself takes its inspiration from ancient Persian gardens. The well-head fountain came from the Pyrenees and was bought from an exhibitor at the Chelsea Flower Show, which Diany attended most years. The plash of water on a hot summer's day, together with the silvery foliage, grey stone and Heather's sprung chairs, painted azure blue by Diany, make this garden feel like a corner of the Mediterranean.

The White Sunk Garden became Diany's own, a place where she enjoyed gardening when she could no longer attempt the Banks.

Opposite: Rosa sericea 'Heather Muir'.

Below: The White Sunk Garden is the only area that Diany substantially altered. In early summer it is structured by white-flowering shrubs.

WHITE SUNK GARDEN

Right: A key plant in early spring is Trillium *chloropetalum* var. *giganteum*, seen in the foreground.

Opposite, top: The White Sunk Garden is full of spring jewels, including an unknown pink anemone, planted by Heather or Diany, and the grey-leaved *Tanacetum haradjanii*.

Opposite, bottom: Subtle spring shades are provided by muscari, *Primula* 'Tie Dye' and self-sown wild primroses. Anne tends this part of the garden herself.

KIFTSGATE COURT GARDENS

Her mother's affection for it is the reason why Anne personally continues to tend the host of little treasures that could easily be dug out by anyone unfamiliar with Diany's meticulous planting. She prunes the roses here in February.

The terraces are dry and well drained, so the planting is mostly drought-tolerant. In spring an unknown pink anemone pops up, along with white and blue *Anemone nemorosa*, trilliums and several types of erythronium, including *Erythronium californicum* 'White Beauty'. Anne and Johnny keep the self-seeding primroses under control, as they do not want too much yellow, however pale. Towering near the garden is a copper beech, its rosy-pink emerging leaves heart-stoppingly lovely at this time of year.

In May the pace quickens with the cup-shaped brilliant-white flowers of Diany's *Sanguinaria canadensis* f. *multiplex* 'Plena', the daisy blooms of *Olearia* × *scilloniensis* above the soft-grey edging of *Stachys byzantina*, tiny white *Anemone leveillei* (an early version of *A. rivularis*)

WHITE SUNK GARDEN

Above: Heather's Hydrangea Border runs along the top of the White Sunk Garden and carries the season through high summer into autumn. Planting here features *Cornus kousa*, *Hydrangea paniculata* 'Praecox', *H. cinerea*, *H. serrata* 'Grayswood' and various hostas along the front of the border.

Right, anticlockwise from bottom right: *Hydrangea involucrata* 'Hortensis', *H.i.* 'Viridescens', *Hosta* 'Halcyon', *Salvia sclarea* var. *turkestaniana* and self-sown Japanese anemones.

Opposite: The pink shot-silk tree peony 'Madame Louis Henry' (also seen in detail) provides a splash of colour in the White Sunk Garden, with *Rosa* 'White Wings' behind and the rock plants *Stachys byzantina*, *Veronica austriaca* 'Ionian Skies' and *Erodium macradenum* in front.

KIFTSGATE COURT GARDENS

and sprays of aquilegia. Heather's big-headed *Allium cristophii* also feature in late spring, and are followed in mid-summer by mauve *A. cernuum* along the front of the encircling borders and later by the purple drumsticks of *A. sphaerocephalon*, for continuity across the seasons.

The White Sunk Garden at Kiftsgate is less of a purist's garden than Sissinghurst's White Garden, for, in high summer, the colour palette has widened since Heather's time. Various shades of pink and mauve enter the arena, including a shocking-pink alstroemeria brought back by Diany from a nursery at Slieve Donard in Northern Ireland; a lilac-flowered harebell, *Campanula patula*, from Scotland; and a rich-pink, shot-silk tree peony, *Paeonia* × *lemoinei* 'Madame Louis Henry'. For contrast, Anne bought a white peony from Piet Oudolf in The Netherlands. *Paeonia lactiflora* 'Jan van Leeuwen' took a while to flower, but it is now one of Anne's favourites, as is a tiny, star-shaped smilacina.

Other summer perennials and shrubs planted here include phlox, hardy geraniums, erodiums, pulmonaria, *Astrantia maxima*, sisyrinchiums, parahebes and helianthemums, with navy-blue agapanthus for July and August. Iris 'White Swan' edges a stepped bed, an idea inspired by Emma Keswick's garden at Rockcliffe House in Upper Slaughter. The silver-leaved *Eryngium* × *oliverianum* makes a sole appearance at Kiftsgate, chosen as much

WHITE SUNK GARDEN

for its foliage as for its flowers, like the hostas that thrive in a moist border by the house, fortunately unassailed by slugs. On the walls of the house are a creamy-pink rambling rose, 'Phyllis Bide'; *Schizophragma corylifolium*; escallonia (grown from a cutting stolen guiltily by Diany from Crathes in Aberdeenshire); and *Actinidia kolomikta*, which looks as though it has had its leaves dipped in pink paint.

Summer is really the climax, although interest carries on into late summer/early autumn, when *Hydrangea involucrata* 'Hortensis' flowers and delicate wands of pink dierama, introduced by Johnny, are matched by the grasses *Miscanthus yakushimensis* and *Pennisetum orientale*. The garden's strong underlying structure creates pleasing shapes and outlines, even in winter.

The Hydrangea Border was another of Heather's creations, running from an ideal damp and shady corner by the house along the courtyard wall. Before the hydrangeas come into their own, the season starts slowly with *Anemone rivularis* along the front of the border and the flowering of the various cornus planted by Diany and added to by the Chambers: *Cornus alternifolia* 'Argentea' (another favourite Kiftsgate shrub), *C. alba* 'Sibirica' and *C. kousa* var. *chinensis* 'China Girl'.

Then, in late summer and autumn, the star feature is more than twenty varieties of

KIFTSGATE COURT GARDENS
98

Opposite, left: Japanese anemones in the White Sunk Garden.

Opposite, right: Gladiolus communis subsp. *byzantinus* and alliums grow around the box roundels by the steps in the White Sunk Garden. James Lees-Milne's portico behind gives this sheltered garden a distinctly Mediterranean feel.

Left: Heather's Hydrangea Border at its floriferous best, with white *Hydrangea paniculata* 'Praecox', *H. aspera* subsp. *sargentiana*, *H.* 'Preziosa' and white *Phlox paniculata* 'Fujiyama'.

Below: Agapanthus 'Midnight Star' stands out against paler *Dierama pulcherrimum*, *Allium cristophii*, white cosmos and *Pennisetum orientale*. Both the grasses and the dierama are introductions by Anne and Johnny.

WHITE SUNK GARDEN

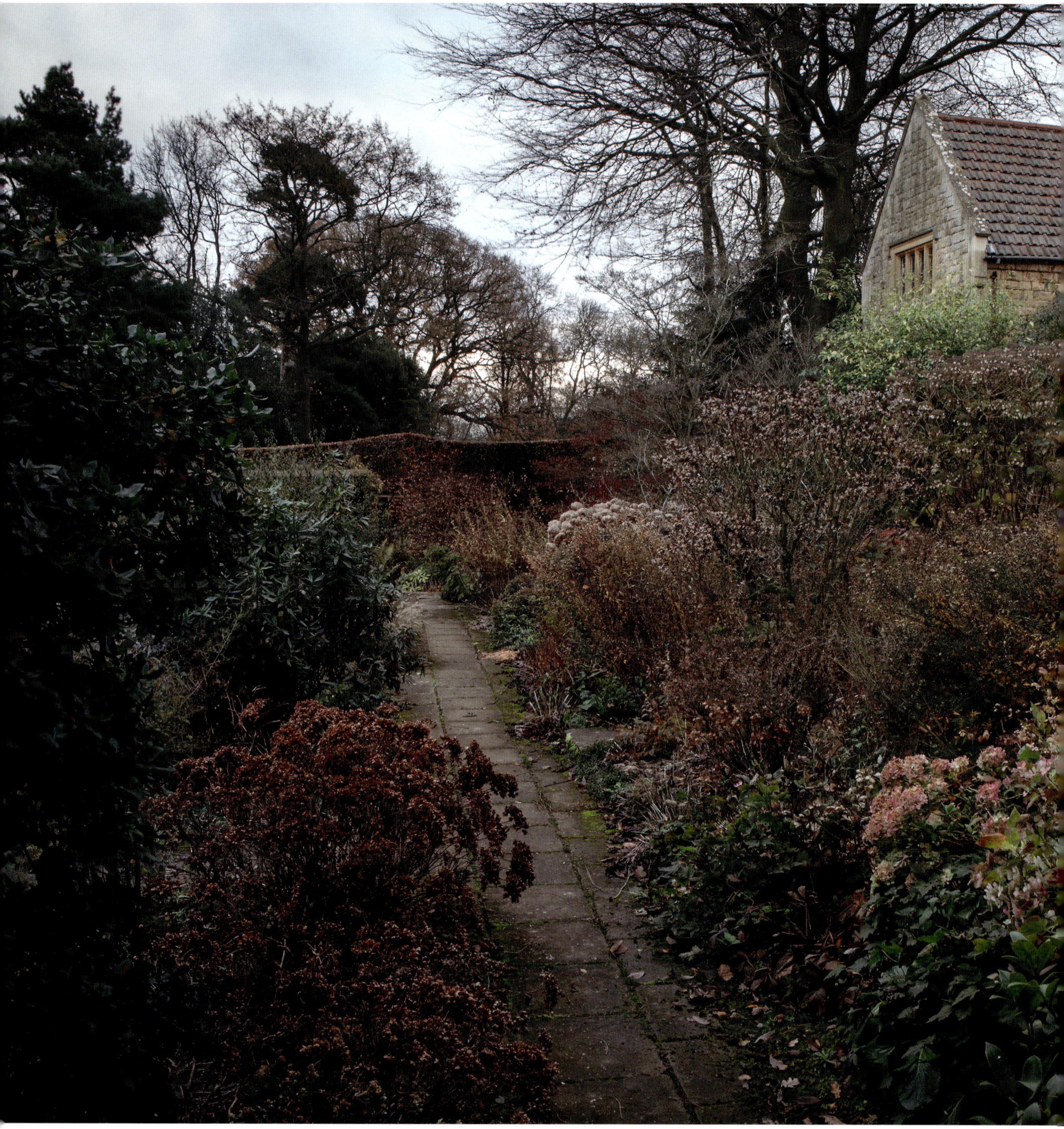

hydrangea, offering different textures, colours and leaf shapes. These include *Hydrangea aspera* Villosa Group (which dates from Heather's time), *H.a.* subsp. *sargentiana*, *H. paniculata* 'Praecox', *H. quercifolia* and *H. arborescens* 'Grandiflora'. All are cut hard back by Anne in spring.

The hydrangeas are underplanted with hostas, rodgersias, asters, phlox, Japanese anemones (deadheaded furiously to stop them from spreading) and – favourites of Johnny's – the toad lilies *Tricyrtis formosana*, *T. lasiocarpa*, *T. latifolia* and *T.* 'Shimone'. Hostas edge the far end of the Hydrangea Border. The idea came from Betsy Muir's garden at Hidcote Boyce, where she grew a hosta border in which she mixed different shapes, colours, sizes and variegations. Every corner of Kiftsgate bears the stamp of a family member, giving it resonance and intriguing layers of interest.

Left: Colour lingers on the hydrangeas in this border until long after the first autumn frosts. The bright-pink flowers of *Hydrangea* 'Preziosa' darken at the end of the season.

Below: The stone framework and box roundels give winter definition to the White Sunk Garden.

WHITE SUNK GARDEN

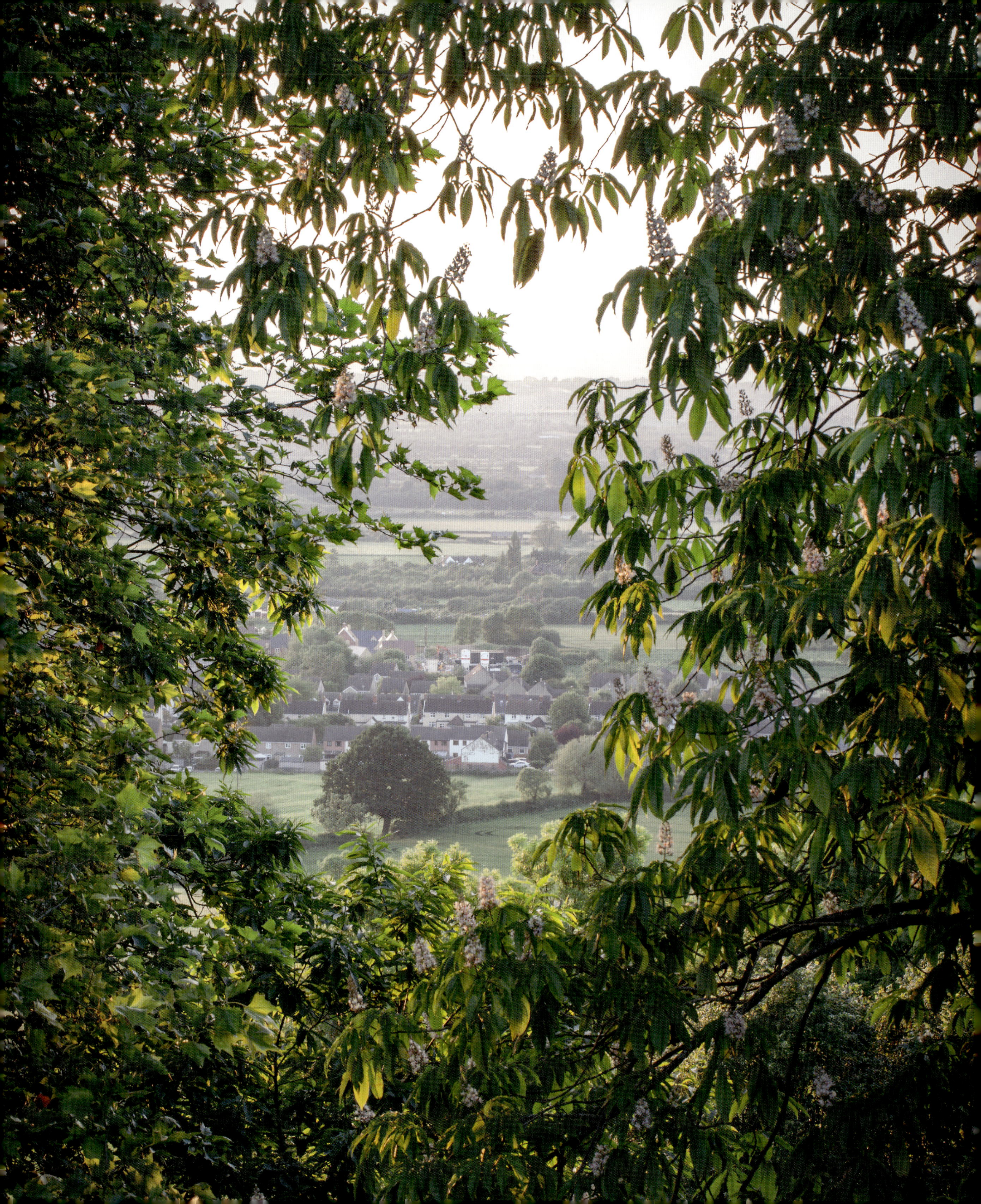

Bridge Border

Beyond the Hydrangea Border, the Bridge Border marks another change of register. You seem to step out from the Cotswold escarpment and into a Cornish valley, for this border is very different, being the only place with a low pH (acidic soil). Anne Chambers believes that her grandmother dug in peat here in the 1920s and 1930s to enable her to plant a rhododendron and azalea border, at its best in April and May.

The Bridge Border is so called because it is planted above a tunnel that once led down to the laundry cottage where the family's washing was taken in the pre-war years. The border feels almost like a tunnel itself, framed as it is with parallel high hedging. On one side is a wide bed, against the yew hedge of the White Sunk Garden, with perennial and other planting beneath hydrangeas, azaleas and rhododendrons, and a colour scheme broadly of blue and yellow. Hellebores are succeeded by white tulips, then foxgloves, smilacina, *Astrantia* 'Roma', martagon lilies and, in late summer, *Anemone* × *hybrida* 'Honorine Jobert' and the double white *A.* × *h.* 'Whirlwind'; flowering in sequence, they maintain a band of interest through the seasons. Above them grow *Ceanothus* × *pallidus* 'Marie Simon'; the snowdrop tree, *Halesia carolina*; and such lace-cap hydrangeas as *Hydrangea aspera* 'Macrophylla'.

Facing this border, in full sunshine most of the day, is a waist-high hedge of *Viburnum davidii*, with which Diany replaced Heather's earlier skimmia hedge. Behind the planting in this border is Heather's only major borrowing from Lawrence Johnston's Hidcote: her Tapestry Hedge of green and copper beech, plain and variegated holly, and yew. Now dominated by copper beech, the near-purple hedge is still the perfect backdrop for

Opposite: At the end of the Bridge Border, a gap in the trees offers a glimpse down to Mickleton and to the Vale of Evesham beyond.

Right: 'White Triumphator' tulips and a self-sown red acer in early May, beneath the white flowers of *Halesia carolina*.

Above: Mauve Hydrangea aspera subsp. *sargentiana*, white H. *heteromalla* f. *xanthoneura* 'Wilsonii' and H. *aspera* 'Macrophylla' at one end of the Bridge Border.

Right: The Belvedere was constructed between the Wide, Bridge and North borders after a massive chestnut tree fell down. Over it flowers *Cornus kousa* 'Miss Satomi', with *Elaeagnus angustifolia* below Roy's Balls.

Opposite: Tender *Magnolia laevifolia* 'Gail's Favourite', first spotted by the Chambers in a Cornish garden, grows surprisingly well on the Cotswold escarpment.

KIFTSGATE COURT GARDENS

BRIDGE BORDER

bright-blue rhododendrons, such as 'Blue Haze' and 'Blue Tit'. After admiring it in Cornwall, the Chambers have planted a Magnolia laevifolia 'Gail's Favourite', which has brown buds and white flowers. Another of their introductions is the scarlet-flowered Chilean fire-bush tree *Embothrium coccineum* 'Inca Flame', a daring contrast to the rest of the bed. Anne and Johnny saw the embothrium in a garden on the west coast of Scotland, and half-feared the landlocked Cotswolds might prove too cold for it. But it has flourished and indeed needs firm pruning.

The purple flowers of a borage family member, *Moltkia doerfleri*, run through the gravel by the Tapestry Hedge from May to July. An archway through the hedge leads into the Rose Border. Diany's elder sister, Judy, was photographed in this archway at the age of twelve or thirteen, showing that the Tapestry Hedge was an early planting of Heather's and already well established by the mid-1920s (see p. 27).

Seedlings of *Helleborus × hybridus* (seen in detail above) have spread themselves around under the *Halesia carolina* tree where the Wide and Bridge borders meet.

KIFTSGATE COURT GARDENS

Right: Rhododendron 'Blue Tit'.

Far right: Rhododendron 'Princess Anne'.

Below: A waist-high hedge of *Viburnum davidii* was planted by Diany to replace an earlier hedge of skimmia. Spring is the peak time in the Bridge Border, when the bright-red Chilean *Embothrium coccineum* 'Inca Flame' also flowers.

BRIDGE BORDER

Rose Border

The Rose Border is, in fact, a rose garden with other perennial planting, enclosed by hedging on four sides. Entering from late June through the Tapestry Hedge, you cannot but be impressed by the sheer volume of the 'Kiftsgate' rose as it flows along and through the right-hand bed and climbs remorselessly to top a 60-foot-high (18 m) copper beech. Filling the air with its strong musk fragrance, it is, along with the Grecian portico and the wisteria, a symbol of this alluring and complex garden. It is the first thing that many visitors head for.

The 'Kiftsgate' rose, however spectacular and dominant, is just one of more than forty different roses established here. Running through the centre are thigh-high hedges of *Rosa gallica* 'Versicolor'. Many of the stripy roses that Heather planted have now reverted to their crimson parent, *Rosa gallica* var. *officinalis* (or the Apothecary's rose). The rose hedges flank a blue-brick path, laid by the Chambers in the 1990s as the grass path was being eroded by a greater number of visitors.

Most of the roses are old-fashioned single flowerers in white, pink and shades of red, with just a hint of blue from the climber 'Veilchenblau'. The pretty single *Rosa* 'Una' has attracted the attention of Henry Robinson, holder of the National Collection of Rambler Roses at Moor Wood in Gloucestershire; he has taken cuttings of this rare white rose. Other white roses are 'Pax', also in the White Sunk Garden, and 'Blanche Double de Coubert', one of two rugosa roses on the Mound. Colours shade from pale-pink R. Bonica and 'Fantin-Latour', deeper-pink Gertrude Jekyll and 'Charles de Mills' to crimson-purple 'Prince Charles' and 'Tuscany Superb'. In high summer, the garden is a deeply perfumed and radiant mix of colour and form.

The roses themselves are trained on frames arranged through the Rose Border almost like theatrical flats, with the roses pulled down to the horizontal to spur flowering. Many of these rusty iron frames were bent from metal that Diany found in a scrapyard at the bottom of the hill. Blithely unconcerned about her safety, she would scramble across the heaps of reclaimed materials, searching for what she wanted.

KIFTSGATE COURT GARDENS

Framing the Rose Border is the Tapestry Hedge, inspired by neighbouring Hidcote. The path is edged by thigh-high hedges of *Rosa gallica* 'Versicolor'. Above it, the 'Kiftsgate' rose flowers for a few weeks from late June.

ROSE BORDER

Top, left: Diany laid the curving path through the back of the Rose Border to make gardening easier here.

Top, right: 'Angélique' tulips begin the season in the Rose Border.

Above, left and right: The roses are trained over elaborate frames, many of them made by Diany from scrap metal picked up in reclamation yards.

Opposite, top: The view through the arch of *Sorbus aria* 'Lutescens' in winter across the Rose Border towards the Tapestry Hedge.

Opposite, bottom: In late spring, the silvery leaves of the Sorbus Arch stand out beautifully against dark yew on either side. To the left is *Deutzia × rosea*, complemented by 'Angélique' tulips.

KIFTSGATE COURT GARDENS

ROSE BORDER

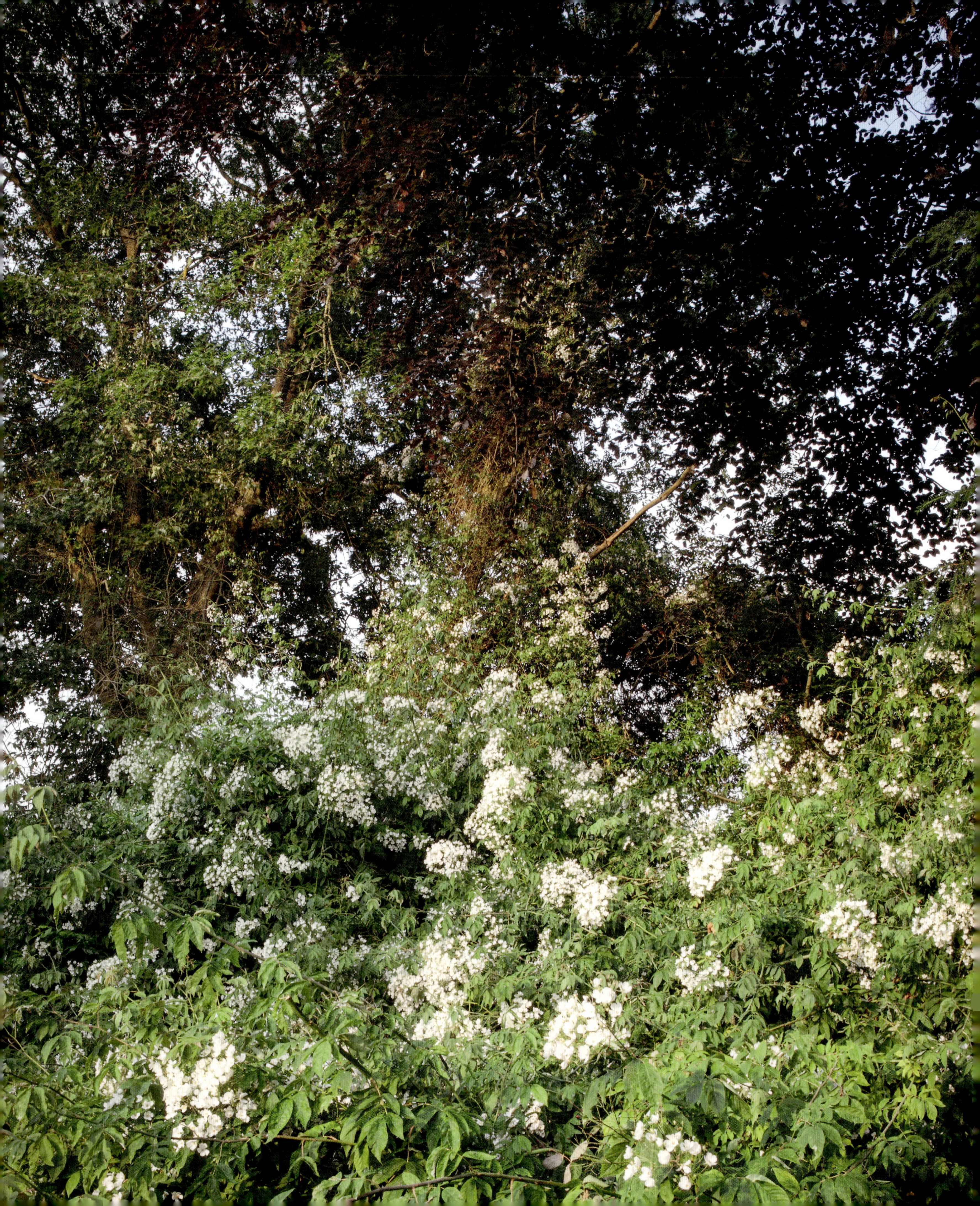

The roses peak from June into early July, but Diany and the Chambers have put their mark on Heather Muir's original 1920s conception so that the Rose Border is attractive throughout the year. Diany laid a paved, curving walkway around the damp side of one border, to make gardening easier. Edged with *Astilbe* 'Sprite', this walk is particularly effective in high summer, with other astilbes coming on later. Planting has been introduced by Anne and Johnny to start the season earlier and to maintain interest for themselves when visitors leave at the end of summer. Pink 'Angélique' tulips open for the first visitors, followed by pink *Deutzia* × *rosea*, which Diany trained over metal supports to flower like a parallel hedge before the rows of *Rosa gallica* var. *officinalis* get under way. Also here are French tree peonies, such as 'Guardian of the Monastery', picking up the theme from the Wide Border and the Four Squares.

Other companion planting includes *Geranium pratense*; *Thalictrum delavayi* 'Hewitt's Double'; *Astrantia major* 'Sunningdale Variegated'; the multi-stemmed, fragrant wine-red shrub *Calycanthus* × *raulstonii* 'Hartlage Wine'; and, for later, the white sprays of *Francoa ramosa* and many different asters, in shades of deep blue and purple.

The border culminates in the Sorbus Arch, set in a semicircle of yew hedging, both of which Diany planted in the late 1970s. In her

Opposite and below, left: Rosa filipes 'Kiftsgate', bought by Heather Muir in 1938 in mistake for a less rampant moschata rose, soars up into tall trees beside the Rose Border.

Right: Philadelphus delavayi f. melanocalyx 'Nyman's Variety'.

Below, right: Deutzia × rosea.

ROSE BORDER

notebook for 1976, she had jotted down the name and contact details of the sculptor Simon Verity, whose work she had appreciated at Rosemary Verey's garden at Barnsley House in Gloucestershire. In 1978 she commissioned Verity to sculpt the figure of a seated woman from two tombstones that she had found lying abandoned in a country churchyard. Two whitebeams, *Sorbus aria* 'Lutescens', form a frame for the statue from the rose garden, their silvery spring leaves and the statue beautifully placed against the dark green of a yew hedge behind. The whitebeams are trained across an arch of scrap metal, but, eager to grow straight, they require pruning two or three times a year in order to keep them in shape.

Above: Pink *Ceanothus* × *pallidus* 'Marie Simon', *Geranium pratense* 'Mrs Kendall Clark' and *Aconitum napellus* 'Carneum' are planted with pale *Rosa* 'Penelope' and darker R. 'Tuscany Superb'.

Right: Rosa William Shakespeare.

Far right: Rosa gallica 'Versicolor'.

KIFTSGATE COURT GARDENS

114

Left: In the foreground, the *Rosa gallica* 'Versicolor' hedge has reverted in places to the plain pink Apothecary's rose, next to which grows the pale *R*. 'Fritz Nobis'. On the other side of the path, beneath the 'Kiftsgate' rose, are *Geranium psilostemon*, the double white *Philadelphus* 'Manteau d'Hermine' and *Rosa* 'Tuscany Superb'.

Overleaf: The path laid by Diany behind the Rose Border is edged with pale *Astilbe* 'Sprite', behind which grow the darker *A*. 'Fanal' (× *arendsii*) and *Astrantia major* 'Sunningdale Variegated'.

ROSE BORDER

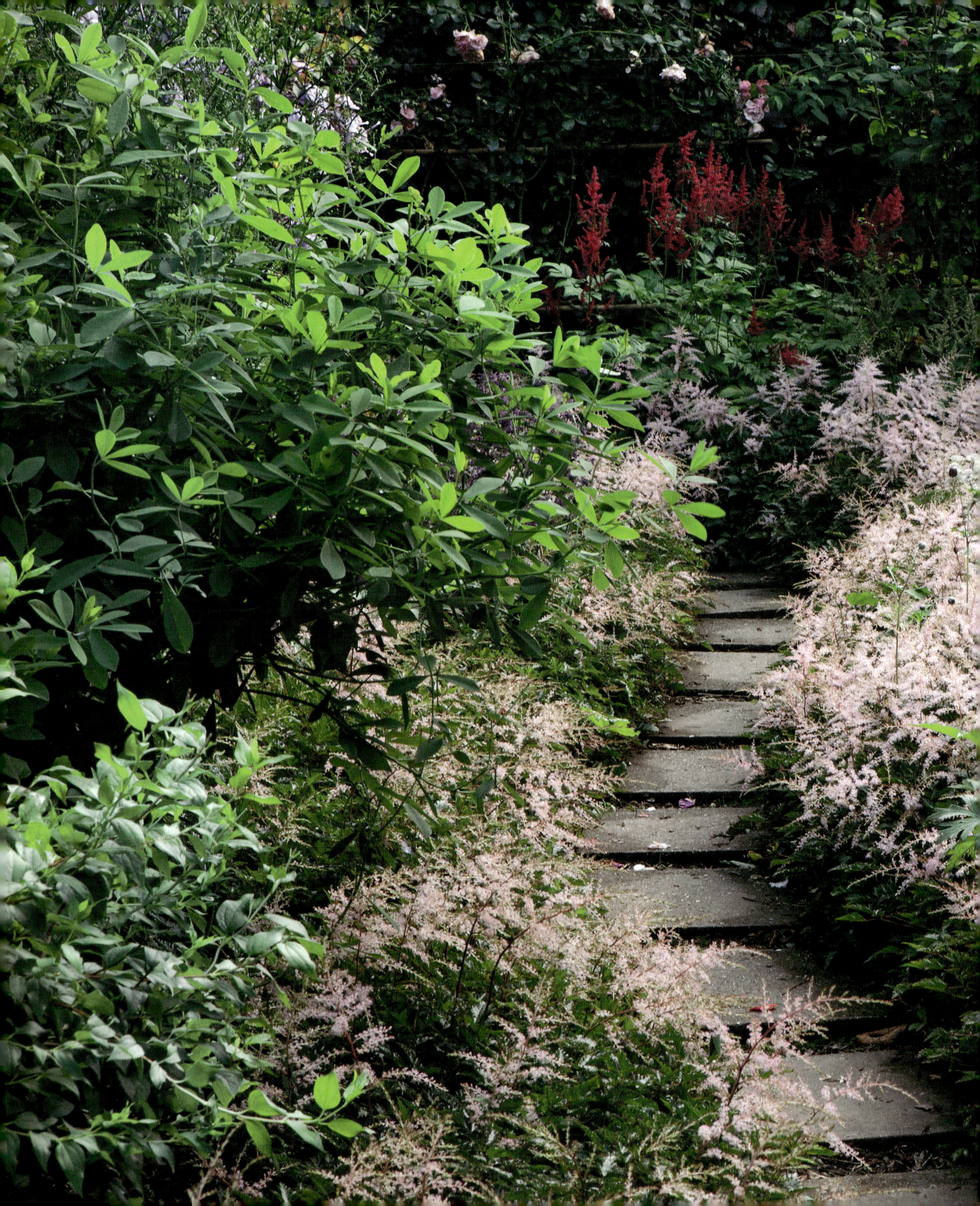

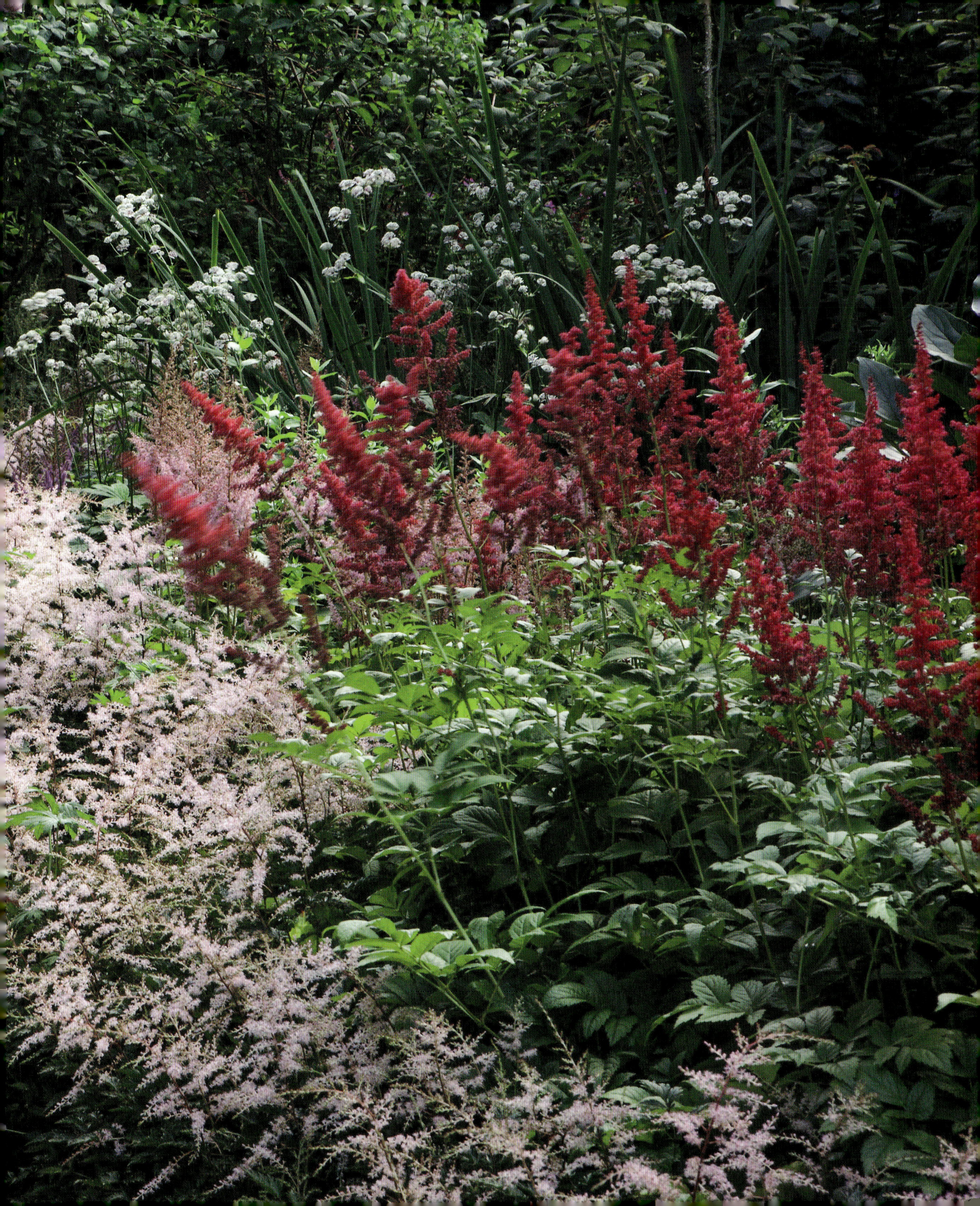

Fern Border and Wild Flower Corner

The planting of the Sorbus Arch and flanking yew hedges created a shady corner around Simon Verity's statue. Diany turned this into the Fern Border, another of the variations of pace at which the creators of this garden have all been so skilled. The pure-green border, planted with ferns and grasses, is unexpectedly cool and viridescent after the intensity of the Rose Border.

Among the ferns are the five-fingered, black-stemmed maidenhair fern, *Adiantum aleuticum*; the Japanese painted lady fern, *Athyrium niponicum* var. *pictum*, with grey lance-like, red-spined fronds; the evergreen hart's tongue fern *Asplenium scolopendrium* Crispum Group; and the deciduous royal fern, *Osmunda regalis*, which has strong autumn colouring. Juxtaposed with the shapely ferns are both tall and short grasses, including the transparent, almost blue *Molinia caerulea* subsp. *arundinacea* 'Transparent'; *Calamagrostis brachytricha*; *Miscanthus sinensis* 'Silberspinne'; and the stripy *M.s.* 'Zebrinus'. The black strappy leaves of ground-hugging *Ophiopogon planiscapus* 'Nigrescens' and foaming *Alchemilla mollis* edge the beds. The only hint of colour is the scarlet climbing nasturtium *Tropaeolum speciosum*, threaded through the yew hedging.

A gate leads into the Wild Flower Corner, a small wedge contained within a beech hedge, and marking a transition from the formal garden to the Orchard and Mound beyond. This has been the work of Anne and Johnny, who have struggled to seed a successful meadow in their fertile soil. They removed 18 inches (50 cm) of top soil, but the ground remained too rich for an annual wild flower seed mix. In 2017, therefore, they started sowing perennial seeds instead, along with bulbs and such half-hardy annuals

Left: The pure-green Fern Border changes the pace of a stroll after the pinks and reds of the Rose Border. In spring, the unfurling leaves of the Sorbus Arch catch the early-morning sunlight.

Opposite: Set against a yew hedge and surrounded by *Alchemilla mollis*, the statue of a seated woman was carved from gravestones by Simon Verity in the 1970s.

KIFTSGATE COURT GARDENS

FERN BORDER AND WILD FLOWER CORNER

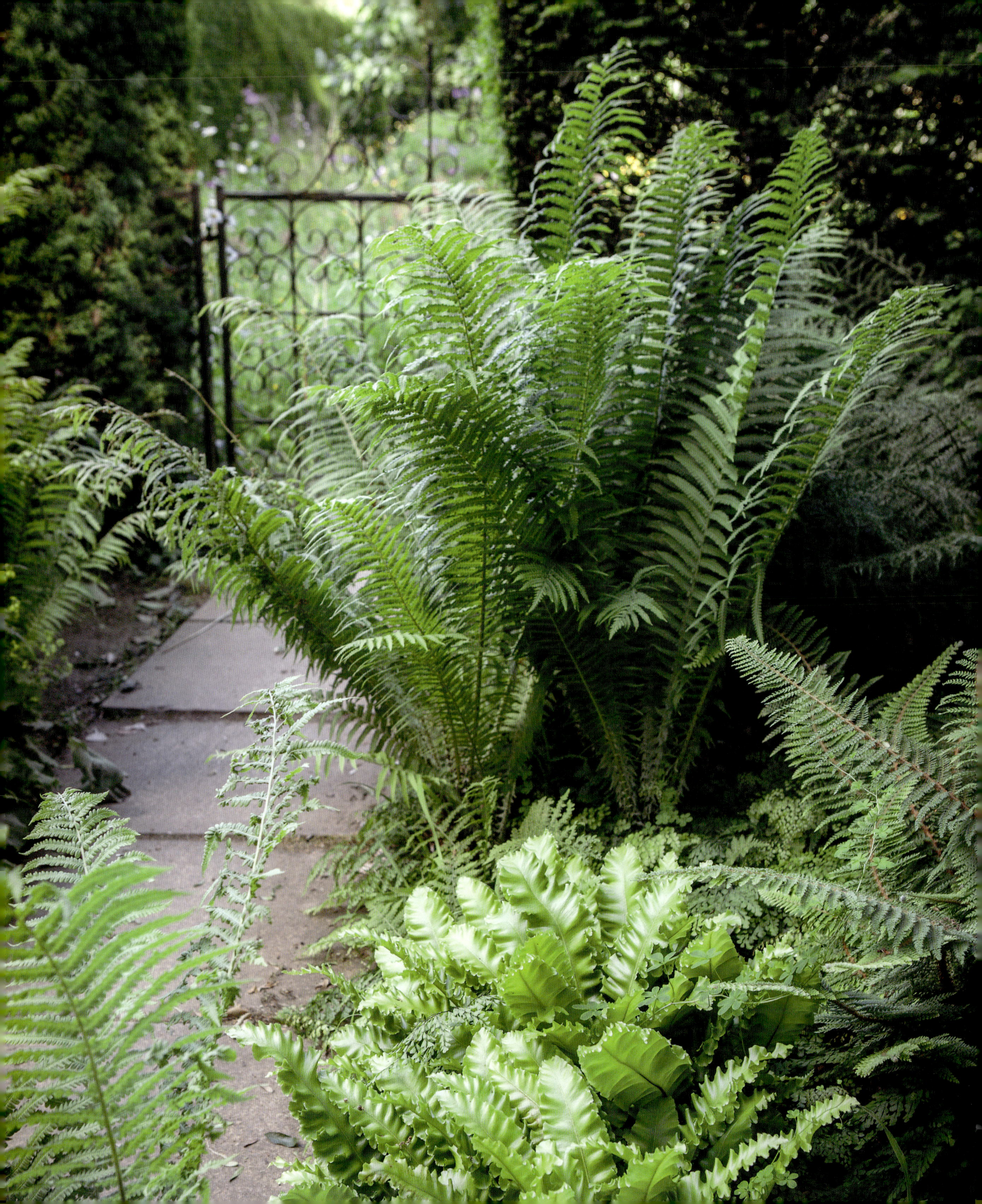

Opposite: The cool damp of this enclosed area is ideal for shuttlecock ferns (*Matteuccia struthiopteris*) and *Asplenium scolopendrium* Crispum Group.

Right: One of the charms of the garden at Kiftsgate is the way in which each area beckons the visitor on to another; here, the Wild Flower Corner is glimpsed through the foliage of *Aruncus dioicus* 'Kneiffii'.

Above and right: Allium hollandicum 'Purple Sensation' and yellow buttercups are interplanted in the Wild Flower Corner beneath *Cornus controversa* 'Pagoda', which is like a layered wedding cake in May.

as ammi and cerinthe. Other planting here includes *Allium hollandicum* 'Purple Sensation', fennel, umbellifers and the odd wild flower, such as buttercups and *Dianthus carthusianorum*. Despite the Chambers' difficulties, this area has the look, if not of a wild flower meadow, at least of a cottage garden. To one side of the path is a layered white *Cornus controversa* 'Pagoda', like a glorious wedding cake.

The Worshipful Company of Fruiterers presents a tree each year to the winner of the Historic Houses Association/Christie's Garden of the Year Award. When Kiftsgate won the award in 2003, the Chambers' gift was a 'Burbank's Tangerine' plum tree, planted across the path from the cornus. The tree was bred in the 1930s by E.A. Bunyard, the nurseryman from whom Heather Muir bought her 'Kiftsgate' rose, and was chosen on account of Bunyard's important association with the garden.

Left: To the left of the path through the Wild Flower Corner is a 'Burbank's Tangerine' plum tree, presented to Anne and Johnny by the Fruiterers' Company when Kiftsgate won the Historic Houses Association/Christie's Garden of the Year Award in 2003.

Below: Although the Wild Flower Corner is primarily a spring and summer garden, the autumnal colours of the cornus reignite this area of the garden.

FERN BORDER AND WILD FLOWER CORNER

Orchard, Mound and Tulip Tree Avenue

A small wrought-iron gate leads from the Wild Flower Corner to the Orchard, a triangle of long grass and spring bulbs, bordered on two sides by yew and beech hedging. There is a feeling of timelessness, but, in fact, Anne and Johnny have worked hard on what had once been a rather neglected space. No 'Things that need doing' are listed in Diany's notebooks for areas beyond the confines of the formal garden.

Gnarled old apple trees are now overrun with *Rosa* 'Leverkusen' and *R. multiflora* 'Grevillei', the latter a present from a gardening friend of the Chambers. To these ancient apples, Anne and Johnny have added pears, medlars, quinces and Gloucestershire varieties of apple, 'Gilliflower of Gloucester' and 'Lady Sudeley'. 'Lady Sudeley' has resonance for the family, for Sudeley Castle is at Winchcombe, just across the fields from Postlip Hall, where Heather's sister Clara lived. Judy, Diany and Betsy spent time at Postlip Hall as children with their cousins Gill and Kim, and would have known the Dent-Brocklehursts, who owned Sudeley Castle. Also planted here is 'Barnack Beauty' (Johnny's godfather lived at Barnack). So many of Kiftsgate's plants hint at the family's strong local traditions.

The ground is spotted with celandines in April, followed by white narcissi, fritillaries, primroses, camassias and daisies. Dark-crimson 'Jan Reus' tulips have naturalized in the grass and are added to every year. A shorter, mown path meanders through the longer grass, which has been sown with yellow rattle to reduce its vigour. The route of this path is changed every year on the advice of Ursula Cholmeley, who in 2001 began the much acclaimed restoration of Easton Walled Gardens at the family estate near Grantham in Lincolnshire. This allows the grass to grow evenly across the Orchard.

Work on the Orchard began as a foreground to Anne and Johnny's most daring project. When they created the Water Garden in 1999–2000, thousands of tons of soil were excavated and then dumped in what had been

Opposite: Camassias and late *Narcissus poeticus* var. *recurvus* (pheasant's eye) flower in May in the Orchard, just by the gate leading to the Wild Flower Corner.

Above: Heritage and local varieties of fruit tree have been planted among ancient trees in the long grass of the Orchard.

Left: Ox-eye daisies and yellow rattle flow through the Orchard in high summer.

ORCHARD, MOUND AND TULIP TREE AVENUE

Above: To allow wild flowers to flourish and not be swamped, the grass through the Orchard must be mown at various times during the season.

Right: Wooden steps lead enticingly up from the abundant white daisies in the Orchard to the Mound.

KIFTSGATE COURT GARDENS

Right and below: The smooth banks of the Mound were created from the spoil when the Water Garden was dug. The banks are surmounted by a semicircle of purply-red and white rugosa roses 'Roseraie de l'Haÿ' and 'Blanche Double de Coubert', the loose habit of which suits this area's informality.

the pony paddock. This huge embankment, initially an unsightly embarrassment, eventually presented itself as an opportunity. The Chambers turned the mound into a modern-style belvedere, and threw out an avenue of trees up the hill towards the north-east, parallel to the line of venerable chestnut trees along the top perimeter of the paddock.

The effect is startling. Wooden steps lead up from the Orchard through cotoneaster-covered slopes to the top of the Mound. The middle has been scooped out and laid with black and white stones and crushed green glass, set in grey stones in a chevron pattern, decorated solely by small olive trees in square faux-lead tubs. Along the rim runs a hedge of rugosa roses, white 'Blanche Double de Coubert' and purply-red 'Roseraie de l'Haÿ', chosen because their loose habit suits the informal aspect of the Mound. They also have lovely hips in autumn and early winter.

ORCHARD, MOUND AND TULIP TREE AVENUE

Above: The Mound is kept deliberately minimalist, with olive trees in small faux-lead pots the only ornament.

Right: A chevron pattern has been created using crushed green glass and black and white stones set amid grey.

The grass banks are difficult to mow, but otherwise this area has been designed more or less to look after itself, a necessity when the formal garden requires so much attention. To one side of the Mound is a grove of silver birches that decorated the marquee for the wedding of Clare Chambers at Kiftsgate in October 2014.

Beyond the Mound, the avenue of tulip trees (*Liriodendron tulipifera*), planted in 2007, leads up to a 20-foot-high (6 m) stainless-steel leaf sculpture. The work of Pete Moorhouse, it is outlined against the sky and, in early summer, fields of yellow rape beyond. The Mound and the sculpture hint at the Middle East, both partly inspired by Johnny's visits to Persian gardens during business trips to Iran in the early 1980s. The intricate filigree pattern of the three-sided sculpture reflects the light, and was based on an Islamic pattern taken from the Hunat Hatun Mosque in Kayseri, Turkey.

KIFTSGATE COURT GARDENS

Like the black pool of the Water Garden, the Mound and Avenue are a moment's calm away from the palpating succession of bravura planting in the flower garden and on the Banks. If you stand by the leaf sculpture and look back, you will understand the intricate structure of Kiftsgate Court Gardens. Visible are the outlines of yew hedging, the towering pines – which could be on the French Riviera – and the English parkland trees. From here, it is impossible not to appreciate the mighty backdrop against which three remarkable plantswomen have created and maintained an even more impressive garden.

The avenue of tulip trees (*Liriodendron tulipifera*), planted in 2007, looks even more spectacular after a heavy fall of snow.

ORCHARD, MOUND AND TULIP TREE AVENUE

KIFTSGATE COURT GARDENS

A stainless-steel leaf sculpture by Pete Moorhouse is a fitting climax. Looking back from this vantage point, you glimpse the yew hedging, parkland trees and Scots pines that form the backbone of this extraordinary garden.

ORCHARD, MOUND AND TULIP TREE AVENUE

Water Garden

The Water Garden is the still heart of Kiftsgate. It was a courageous move by Anne and Johnny Chambers to dig up Heather Muir's 1930s clay tennis court and replace it with a black pool distinct from the ethos of almost every other area of this plantswomen's garden. But the surface of the court was breaking up, making every set of tennis a lottery, and the Chambers had the opportunity to do something radical: the only other place where water plays at Kiftsgate is through the Pyrenean fountain in the plant-packed White Sunk Garden. The Water Garden could hardly be more different. This beautiful, understated haven showed that Kiftsgate's gardens could be extended to reach out towards the twenty-first century from their planterly, 1920s beginnings. The apparent straightforwardness of the design belies its complex, abstract origins.

The main inspiration for the Water Garden was the work of the landscape architect Sir Geoffrey Jellicoe (1900–1996) at Sutton Place, near Guildford in Surrey. Trained as an architect, Jellicoe had studied Italian Renaissance gardens in his youth before coming under the influence of the Constructivist Movement, and such sculptors as Henry Moore, Ben Nicholson and Barbara Hepworth. Jellicoe and these sculptors were all interested in spatial relations and the way in which an abstract idea is realized in stone, paint, wood – or, in Jellicoe's case, in the garden. The hallmark of his work was unadorned simplicity, as exemplified by the Long Canal at RHS Garden Wisley and the Kennedy Memorial at Runnymede, both in Surrey, and the elegant rill garden at Shute House in Dorset. At Sutton Place in the early 1980s, Jellicoe created within yew hedging a black lily pond in which to reflect a huge abstract relief in white marble by Nicholson.

Left: From the Yellow Border, the pool can be glimpsed past the pavilion, which is covered by a prolific *Rhodochiton atrosanguineus*.

Opposite: The sound of water dripping from gilded bronze philodendron leaves in the Water Garden is refreshing on a hot summer's afternoon.

KIFTSGATE COURT GARDENS

WATER GARDEN

Windows cut into the surrounding yew hedge offer views into the Water Garden from the Fern Border.

Both Jellicoe's Garden at Sutton Place and the Water Garden at Kiftsgate have something of the atmosphere of Hidcote's Theatre Lawn, a green interval between dramas being enacted elsewhere. The courtside hut, which the Chambers retained, was copied from Hidcote. Once thatched and used as a tennis pavilion, it is now roofed with cedar shingles, the entrance covered with *Rhodochiton atrosanguineus*.

As ever, innovations at Kiftsgate build on the work of previous generations. The starting point for the Chambers' new garden was Heather's existing yew hedges, and the rectangular pond, when completed, covered the area of the doubles court. The project proved a major challenge, as two of the yews within the hedging had to be taken out to allow access for machinery. These yew trees were potted up to await replanting; rather to the Chambers' surprise, they survived their manhandling and grew back seamlessly to reunite with the rest of the hedge. A lower yew hedge, like a bench seat around the garden, was planted against the existing high yew. The ground slopes, and so the whole design of the garden, with its simple lines, would otherwise have looked askew.

The pool itself was dug down to 5 feet (1.5 m) over the winter of 1999–2000 by the Chambers' handyman, Bernard Gardner, his son, Stuart, and a friend. (The soil removed would subsequently form the Mound beyond the Orchard.) Anne had wanted grass right up to the edge of the pool, but Johnny convinced her that a border of stone was required. Haddonstone Portland cast stone was used for this border and for the steps that lead across the pool to a central platform of lawn. The stone is power-washed twice a year. Black dye in the pool water cuts out the light to slow the growth of weed. Nevertheless, the pool must be emptied every February so that blanket weed and leaves from the surrounding trees can be removed.

These parkland trees, so much a feature of the garden at Kiftsgate, are also an important aspect of the Water Garden, their leaves and branches reflected, along with a bronze-and-steel sculpture, in the black water of the pool.

This water sculpture, at one end of the pool, was commissioned from a New Zealander, the sculptor Simon Allison, who lives near Banbury, not far from Kiftsgate. Allison was chosen because he appreciated

KIFTSGATE COURT GARDENS

that the sculpture needed to give height and movement, as well as to be a delicate and airy contrast against the dark yew and water. The gilded bronze leaves were moulded from a philodendron leaf that Allison found in the Oxford Botanic Garden. The twenty-four leaves are supported by graceful stainless-steel stems, which sway in the breeze. Many a visitor enjoys sitting for a while in the former tennis pavilion, watching the water drawn up the philodendron stems and listening to the sound of it dripping from the gilded leaves.

Below: The bare branches of parkland trees are a spectacular backdrop to the Water Garden. The sculpture is by Simon Allison, who moulded the leaves from a philodendron leaf that he found in the Oxford Botanic Garden.

Right: Magnolia sieboldii subsp. *sinensis* grows by the yew hedge surrounding the Water Garden.

WATER GARDEN

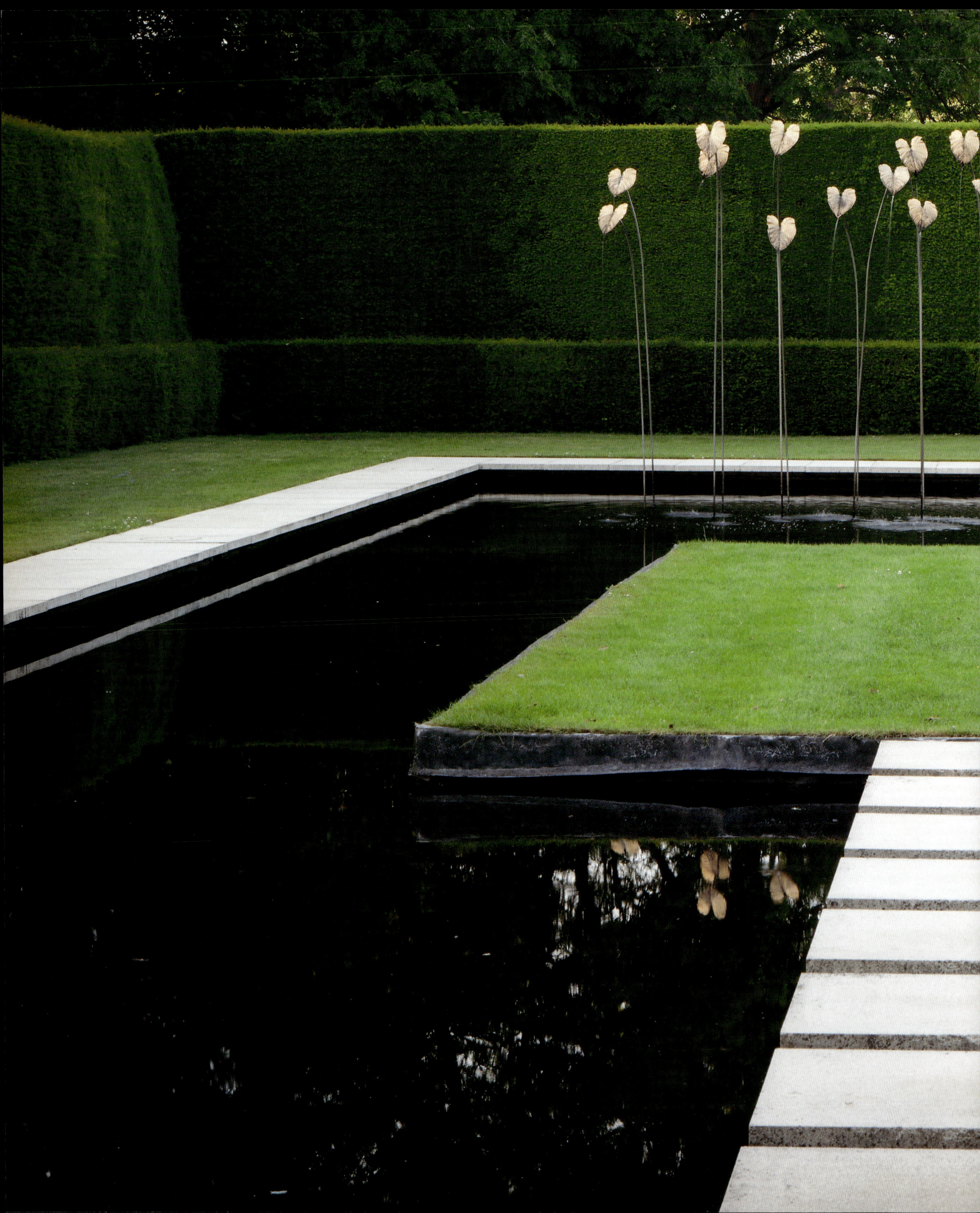

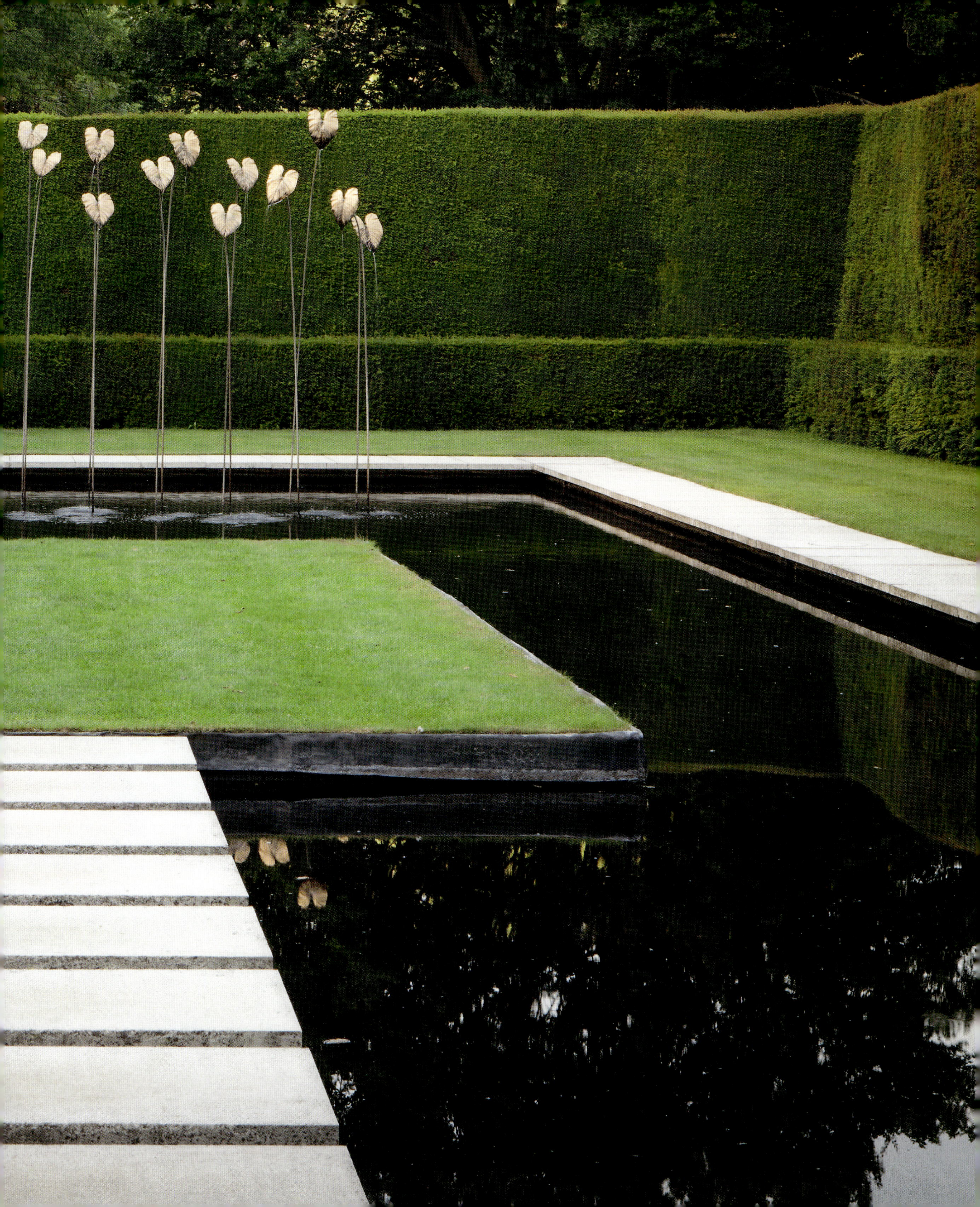

KIFTSGATE COURT GARDENS

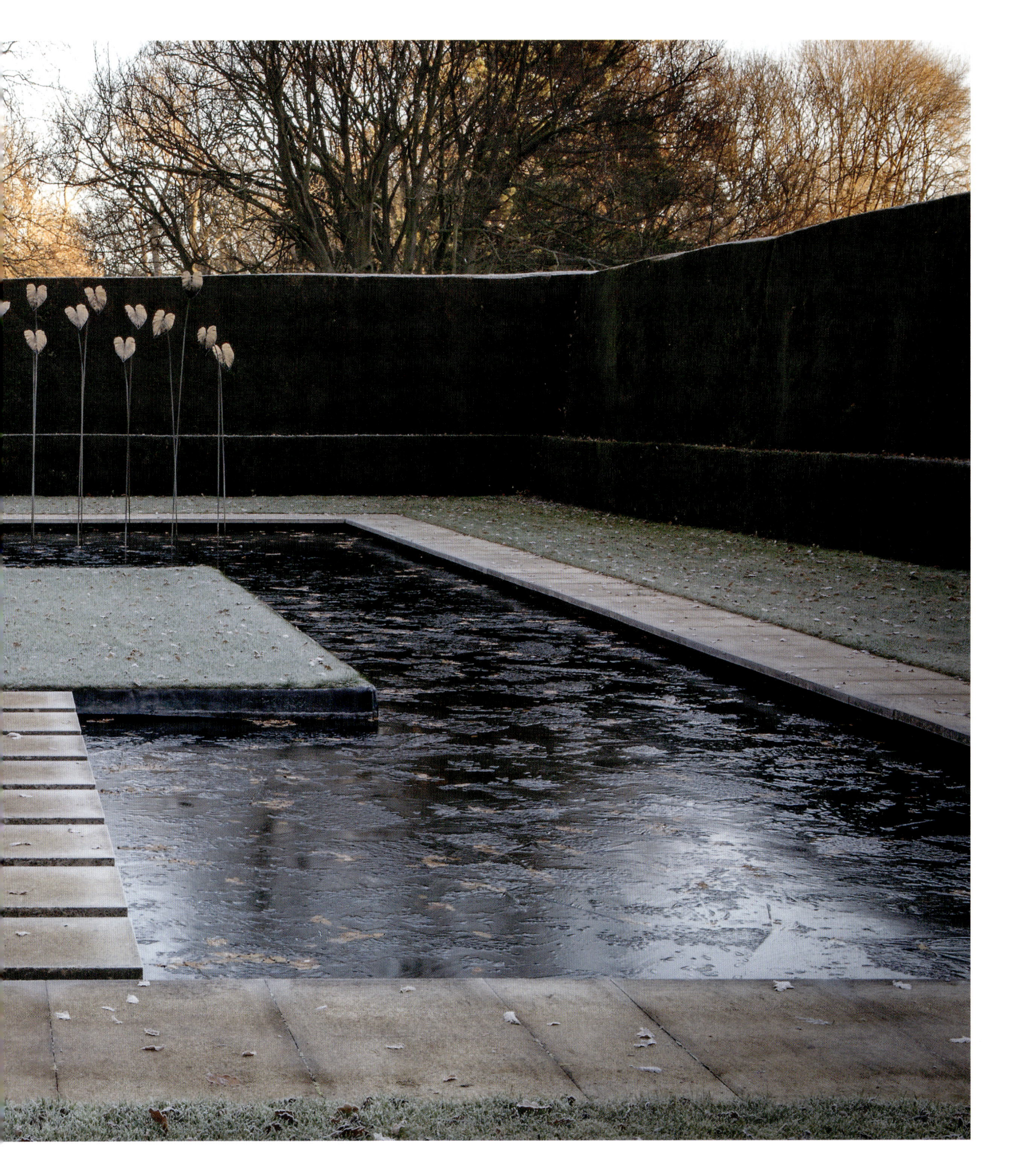

WATER GARDEN

KIFTSGATE COURT GARDENS

Yellow Border

The yew-backed Yellow Border stretches from the Water Garden to the Bridge Border. By the Water Garden hedge stands a spreading sorbus and in the grass nearby is what looks like a dolmen. It is, however, a gatepost from Kiftsgate Farm, installed by Diany as a piece of sculpture near a hedge of *Escallonia virgata*.

Facing the border is chest-high box hedging, planted by Heather, over which can be glimpsed through the parkland trees views across the Vale of Evesham towards Wales. *Rosa* 'Paul's Himalayan Musk' rambles up into trees near the Water Garden, while further along, outside the box hedge, is *Rosa* 'Diany Binny'. This cross between *R. soulieana* and *R. filipes* 'Kiftsgate', registered by the Royal National Rose Society in 1975, is almost as rumbustious as its latter parent.

When the Yellow Border was first laid out in the 1920s, it was cutting edge because its effects were created as much by contrasts in foliage as by flower colour. In a period when reds and pinks were mostly in favour, Heather selected here dazzling shades of bronze mixed with sulphurous to pale-lemon yellow, and occasional splashes of azure blue. She chose two acers for height, one with gold foliage (*Acer shirasawanum* 'Aureum') and one mahogany (*A. palmatum* 'Dissectum Atropurpureum'); both remain in the border today. *Cotinus coggygria* 'Royal Purple' and Golden Spirit continue the thematic contrast of purply bronze and yellow, along with gold-tipped *Berberis thunbergii* 'Aurea' and a deep-purple B.t. f. *atropurpurea* 'Helmond Pillar', the latter picking up the copper of the beech in the Tapestry Hedge at the Bridge end of the border. Golden hop (*Humulus lupulus* 'Aureus') runs through the bronze leaves of dark hazel (*Corylus maxima* 'Purpurea'). *Cornus alternifolia* 'Argentea', a much-repeated shrub, appears here, a clashing silver waterfall in spring.

Diany honoured her mother's memory by keeping the same colours in the border and by her choice of rose. Her task lists indicate that in 1985 she planted a yellow Graham Thomas rose to replace a spirea, representing the importance of Thomas's friendship to Heather, as well as to Betsy and herself. Diany described the Kiftsgate garden in one interview as 'mixed beds with roses predominating', but this is less true of the Yellow Border: the only other rose here is *Rosa xanthina* 'Canary Bird'. Could that be the one referred to in her notes for autumn 1970? 'Order new yellow rose middle yellow border.'

The Yellow Border, perhaps because of its tricky, north-facing position, preoccupied Diany. In her lists of 'Things that need doing', she comes back year after year to this border. In 1970, for example, she listed 'replant end of yellow border', but did not tick it, although she ticked 'Robinia pseudoacacia Frisia yellow border' (the false acacia is no longer there). In 1979 she took out a phlomis in the middle of the border, but failed to 'replace small delphiniums, grey poppy & grasses'. In the following year, she removed a *Potentilla fruticosa* 'Tangerine' from the border, replacing it with '3 or 4 hemerocallis corky and new tangerine'. *Hemerocallis* 'Corky' is still there; 'Tangerine' has disappeared.

Like Heather, Diany disliked the formality of traditional herbaceous borders, which tended to run from low at the front to high at the back. In the Yellow Border, having set the colour scheme, Heather and Diany mixed the levels, creating the

Pages 140–41: The spring colours in the Yellow Border are dazzling: the fresh new foliage of *Acer palmatum* 'Dissectum Atropurpureum' is teamed with orange 'Ballerina' tulips and lemon Molly-the-Witch peonies (*Paeonia mlokosewitschii*; also seen in detail).

Above, clockwise from top left: Euphorbia palustris 'Walenburg's Glorie'; Astrantia major; Lilium lancifolium; Epimedium × warleyense 'Orangekönigin'.

KIFTSGATE COURT GARDENS

The Yellow Border is backed by a yew hedge, beyond which lies the Rose Border. It is bookended by two trees planted by Heather Muir: *Acer palmatum* 'Dissectum Atropurpureum' and *A. shirasawanum* 'Aureum'.

Nectaroscordum siculum self-seeds vigorously through one end of the border.

YELLOW BORDER

Spires of delphiniums, including dark-blue 'Faust', give the Yellow Border height and also contrast with *Rosa* Graham Thomas, *Gentiana lutea* and *Astrantia major*.

KIFTSGATE COURT GARDENS

YELLOW BORDER

Above, left and right: Rosa 'Paul's Himalayan Musk' scrambles along the fence and through trees opposite the Yellow Border, marking the boundary of the formal garden.

Opposite: Tall delphiniums wind themselves upwards into the branches of the dark-red acer.

same rippling effect as in the Wide Border. In both, there is an understorey of clump-forming and herbaceous shrubs and perennials, here hypericums, potentillas, astrantias, euphorbias and rodgersias. Comparing Diany's plant lists from the 1970s with today's list indicates that the species and cultivars may have changed, but these genera are the enduring backbone. Diany amused herself by planting among lower, structural plants red-hot pokers when they were beyond the fashion pale, using such lemon-yellow varieties as *Kniphofia* 'Bees' Lemon' and *K. caulescens*. These and other varieties still feature in the border.

Spring begins gently with the shy, roseate-leaved and yellow-flowering *Hacquetia epipactis*, similar to an eranthis. Anne has mostly stayed with her predecessors' colour scheme, although she has added flashes of orange: 'Ballerina' tulips for late April and May. The Molly-the-Witch peony, the pale-yellow, spring-flowering *Paeonia mlokosewitschii*, is the perfect colour for this bed, and is followed by *Geum* 'Marmalade' and 'Totally Tangerine' in summer.

A silvery bank of *Nectaroscordum siculum* flowers in May, along with aquilegias such as the eagle-headed *Aquilegia chrysantha* 'Yellow Queen' and red-and-orange *A. skinneri*, and tall yellow *Gentiana lutea*, which grows wild in Switzerland, where it is used to make a drink. Next up are both orange and yellow tiger lilies, fiery *Euphorbia griffithii*, hemerocallis, *Cephalaria gigantea*

and the daisy heads of *Anthemis tinctoria* 'Sauce Hollandaise'. Tall blue delphiniums ('Faust' and 'Nicky Woodfield') spear through the mid-summer planting. These were bought from the Clifford Chambers nursery of the Woodfield brothers, once cattlemen whose interest in plants led to their becoming multiple Chelsea gold medallists. In autumn, the deep-blue *Salvia patens* runs along the front of the border. Large-leaved hostas (*sieboldiana*, 'Sum and Substance' and 'Frances Williams') and the smaller *Hosta* 'June' give a fleshy, muscular dimension, picked up by the leaves of *Ligularia* 'Britt Marie Crawford', which remain dark purple into autumn. *Crocosmia* × *crocosmiiflora* 'Citronella' and *C.* 'Emberglow' are vibrant in late summer.

As well as introducing splashes of orange, and turning up the heat on some of the yellows with, for instance, the bright South African iris-like *Moraea spathulata*, Anne has also threaded grasses through the border. Grasses do not appear in Diany's notebooks, and are a rare nod by Anne towards contemporary garden fashion. They work well here, with golden *Hakonechloa macra* 'Aureola' at ground level. The stems of carex, miscanthus and *Panicum virgatum* 'Warrior' catch the light of the setting sun, providing winter interest before they are cut down in February or March. Yellow *Phlomis russeliana* earns its place, too; its frosted seed heads are attractive when little else is to be seen.

KIFTSGATE COURT GARDENS

YELLOW BORDER

North Border

A small belvedere at the end of the Wide Border, just below Anne's mocking mophead hollies known as Roy's Balls, replaced an enormous chestnut tree that fell in the early 2000s. Just beside it grow Cornus kousa 'Miss Satomi', with flat, star-shaped, dark-centred flowers in a gorgeous shade of pinky apricot, and a silver-leaved, scented Elaeagnus angustifolia. Step down from there to your left, and you will be greeted in spring by the lily-of-the-valley scent of a small hedge of white-flowered Osmanthus delavayi, marking the start of the North Border. Diany Binny wrote a striking account of the border's creation in 1972. She chose, in her own words, 'the unpromising situation of a dirty grass slope facing north'. She went on:

> Along it, a low containing wall was built by my Italian gardener of that moment, but when we started to cultivate it, my heart sank. The soil turned out to be solid yellow clay, so obviously the house foundations had been dumped there. However, by this time, I was determined to succeed, so contrary to all the rules, it was lightly forked over with a lot of very coarse peat spread on top. Planting was exciting, as it was the first time I had made a border from scratch. I decided to have entirely silver and grey foliage with some white flowering plants ... This grey border was a Godsend during the appalling drought of 1976. It was one part of the garden that continued to look reasonably healthy.

Diany's initial planting plan was quickly adapted as two Elaeagnus × submacrophylla outgrew their situation and Eucalyptus gunnii became a tree. All were removed within a few years. The border may have held its own in the drought of 1976, but a north-facing, clay slope was not ideal for the grey-leaved Mediterranean sun-lovers that Diany had in mind. As a result, Anne

Left: The long-flowering Cornus kousa 'Miss Satomi' foams over the Belvedere at the junction of the Wide, Bridge and North borders.

Opposite: The Cornus alternifolia 'Argentea', which once arched over the path, was felled by snow in the winter of 2017–18 and has now been replaced by a Magnolia wilsonii.

KIFTSGATE COURT GARDENS

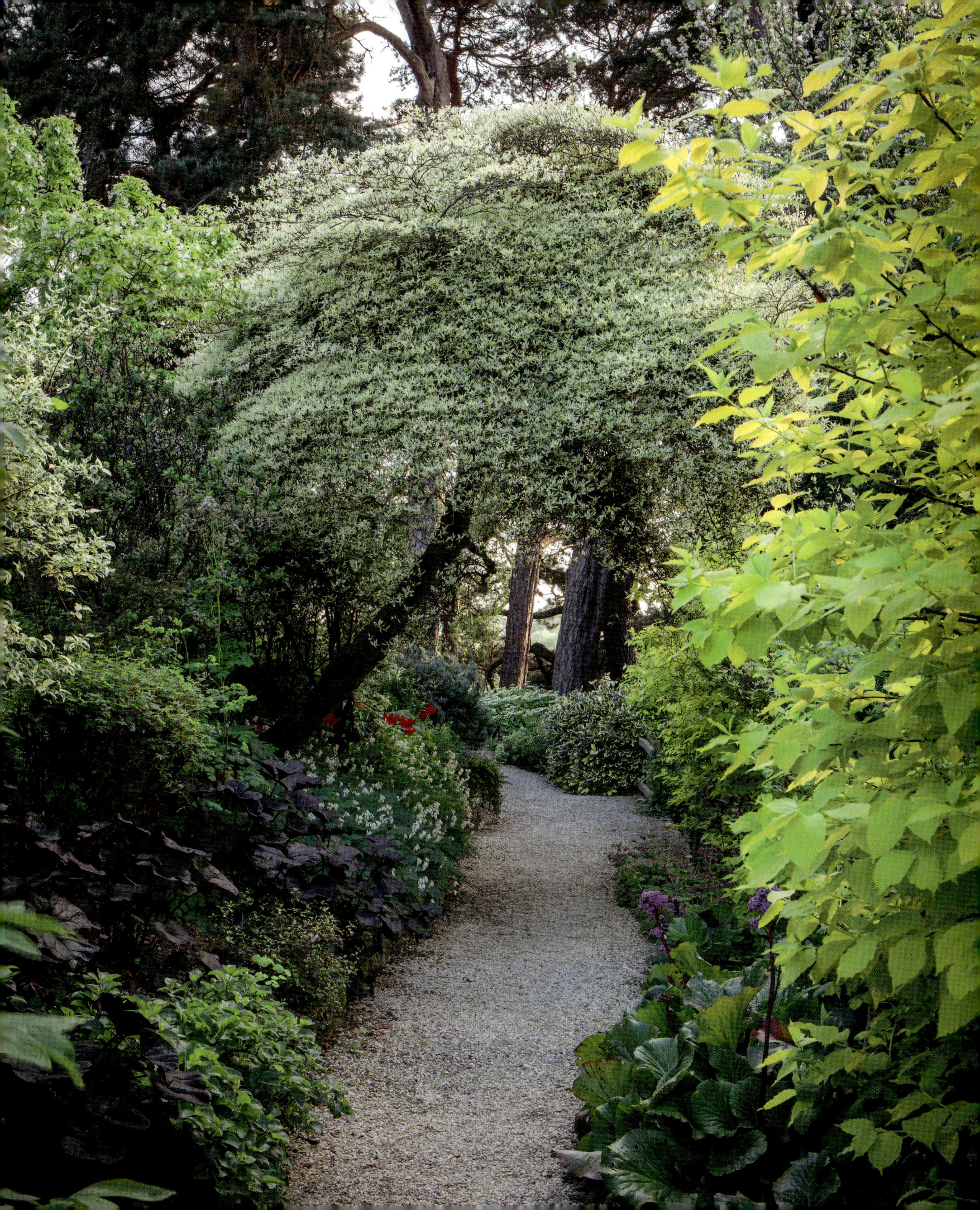

Right: Anne has introduced bright-red *Rosa* Trumpeter into her mother's originally grey North Border.

Below: Dicentra formosa f. *alba* is punctuated by 'Red Shine' tulips. Towards the back is an unknown white tree peony and a signature dark-leaved plant of both the Yellow and North borders, *Ligularia* 'Britt Marie Crawford'.

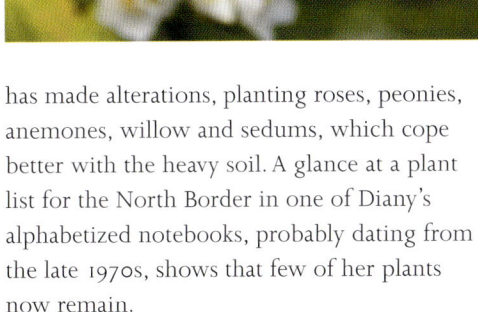

has made alterations, planting roses, peonies, anemones, willow and sedums, which cope better with the heavy soil. A glance at a plant list for the North Border in one of Diany's alphabetized notebooks, probably dating from the late 1970s, shows that few of her plants now remain.

Over the opposite fence are planted the yellow-leaved *Philadelphus coronarius* 'Aureus' and the creamy-white *Rosa* 'Nevada', developed in Spain in 1927, while a 'Paul's Himalayan Musk' rose rockets up into a tree. Between them, they fill the air with fragrance in June. A *Cornus alternifolia* 'Argentea', which once arched over the path, was felled by snow in the winter of 2017–18 and has been replaced by a *Magnolia wilsonii*, presented to Anne and Johnny in 2018 on the eightieth anniversary of the garden's opening for the National Garden Scheme.

The border is now essentially red and white, beginning in spring with 'Red Shine' tulips and then *Dicentra formosa* f. *alba* along the front and Anne's signature plant, creamy smilacina, through the other planting. In early summer, red *Papaver orientale* 'Beauty of Livermere' appears along with *P.o.* 'Snow Goose' and the single white *Paeonia* 'Chalice', set against salmon-red *Phygelius* × *rectus* 'African Queen'. The roses have all been chosen for their intense colour, such as the reddest of red, La Sévillana, as well as Hommage à Barbara, the repeat-flowering Trumpeter and, for contrast, Iceberg. A favourite of Diany's remains in the border, *Deutzia setchuenensis* var. *corymbiflora*, its white summer flowers arresting beside the red roses. Otherwise, there are few traces of her original conception, apart from the glaucous foliage of the tall, wispy *Thalictrum flavum* subsp. *glaucum*.

Colour themes from other borders are reprised, like symphonic motifs adding to the subtle, byzantine pattern across the whole garden. Here, the dark-purple foliage of *Ligularia* 'Britt Marie Crawford' is repeated from the Yellow Border, as are cheerful hemerocallis and different cultivars of crocosmia. Red *Crocosmia* 'Spitfire' and 'Lucifer' are accompanied in later summer by the deep pinky-red *Hydrangea macrophylla* 'Merveille Sanguine'.

The border curls around the yew hedge at the Banks end to merge with the widest section of the Wide Border. Planting here unites the colour schemes of both borders, with the reds of the North Border transitioning to purply pink before turning purply blue as they join the main drag of the Wide Border. There are fuchsias, penstemons and knautias, with the violet blue of *Geranium* × *magnificum* and the blue of the species *G. ibericum*. A pure-white lace-cap hydrangea, philadelphus, viburnums and *Daphne odora* give structure.

The path past the North Border leads to the Top Banks, where William Shenstone's Scots pines frame the view of the village of Mickleton below.

Above, from left to right:
Philadelphus coronarius 'Aureus'; double white P. 'Manteau d'Hermine'; P. *coronarius* 'Variegatus'.

NORTH BORDER

The Banks

Few gardens have a more spectacular setting than Kiftsgate, hundreds of feet up on the north Cotswold escarpment. Its three guardians have always been aware of that backdrop, but have wisely never allowed it to overshadow the garden itself. In the enclosed areas, the eye is seduced by the rich, multilayered planting, and yet the surrounding trees – Scots pines, Monterey pines, oaks and beech – also draw the eye up to the garden's skyline framework. And, along the rim of the garden, clever pruning of surrounding shrubs and trees has left windows of opportunity for visitors to enjoy the views as well. Foreground and background work in perfect concord.

Nowhere is this better achieved than on the Banks, where there is the shock of the unexpected. As visitors pick their way gingerly down winding and precipitous paths, they can look past spiky phormiums to the dark half-moon pool framed by the branches of Sidney Graves Hamilton's Monterey pines. The spirit of the Italian and French Riviera is evoked, although a Cotswold hillside grazed by sheep, not the blue waters of the Mediterranean, lies below.

Before making the descent, it is worth wandering along the Top Banks, through guardian pillars of yew and on to the terrace below the Four Squares. Purple berberis, cotinus, santolina and sambucus line the path in the dry shade of William Shenstone's pines, which are underplanted with *Tulipa sprengeri*, alliums and both spring and autumn cyclamen. There are new treasures for the twenty-first century: Johnny Chambers has recently planted *Zanthoxylum piperitum*, the rare Japanese pepper plant, with dark-purple pinnate foliage. Such new planting coexists with reminders of the past, such as the last of three or four early-flowering, tough and weather-resistant *Rosa* 'Frühlingsgold', planted in the 1930s by Heather Muir and once forming a ribbon of gold running along the top edge of the Banks.

KIFTSGATE COURT GARDENS

Opposite: A hedge of Ilex × altaclerensis 'Golden King', planted by Diany Binny, runs like a river of gold alongside the steps leading down the Banks, which are planted with *Geranium macrorrhizum* and *Pittosporum tenuifolium*. Beside the path soars *Magnolia dawsoniana*, planted by Heather Muir in the Lower Garden.

Left: Ceanothus arboreus 'Trewithen Blue' and the sculptural form of a Monterey pine frame the view out towards Bredon Hill and the Malverns.

Overleaf: The statue on the viewing point is of a mother and child, sculpted for Diany in the 1970s by Simon Verity.

THE BANKS

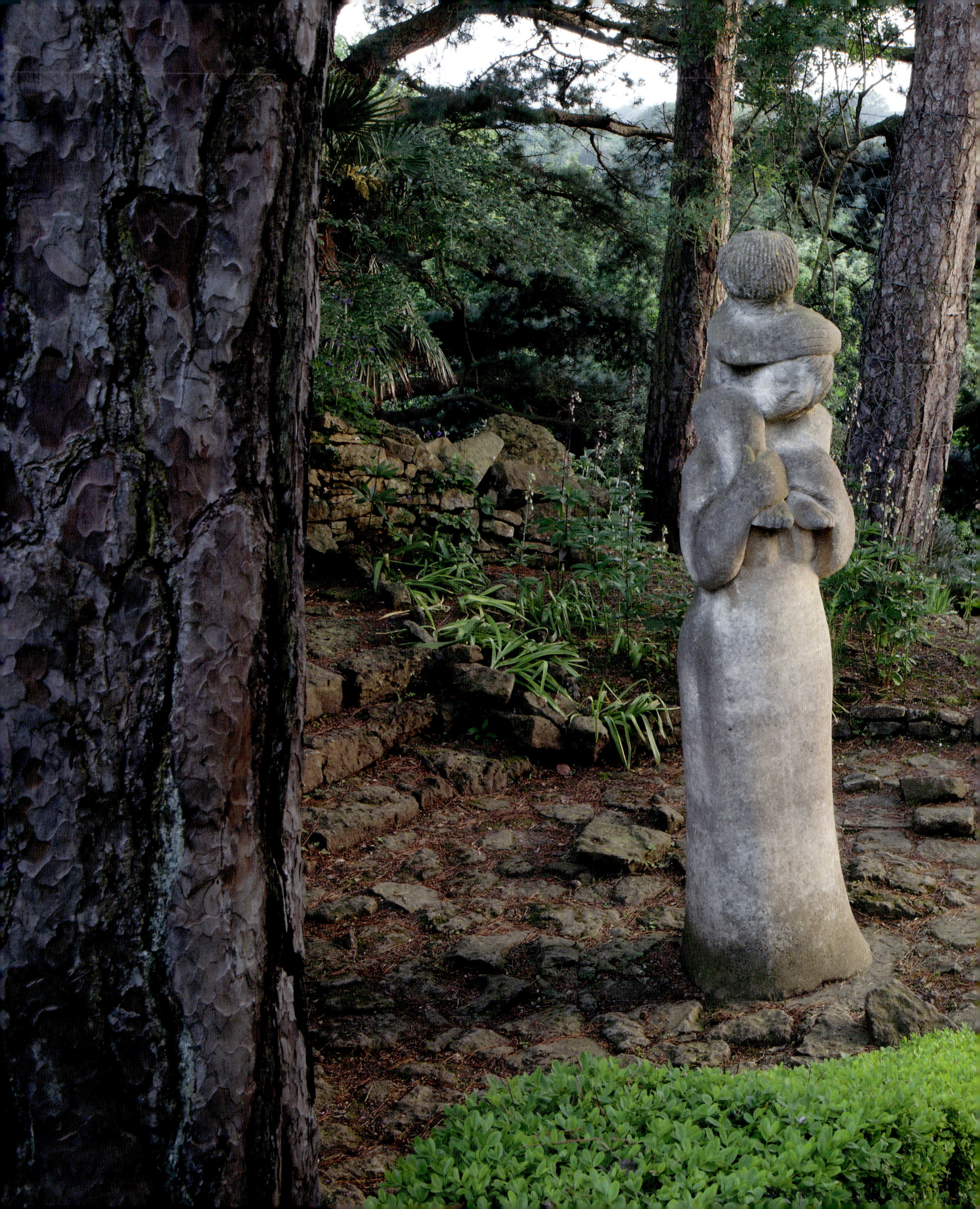

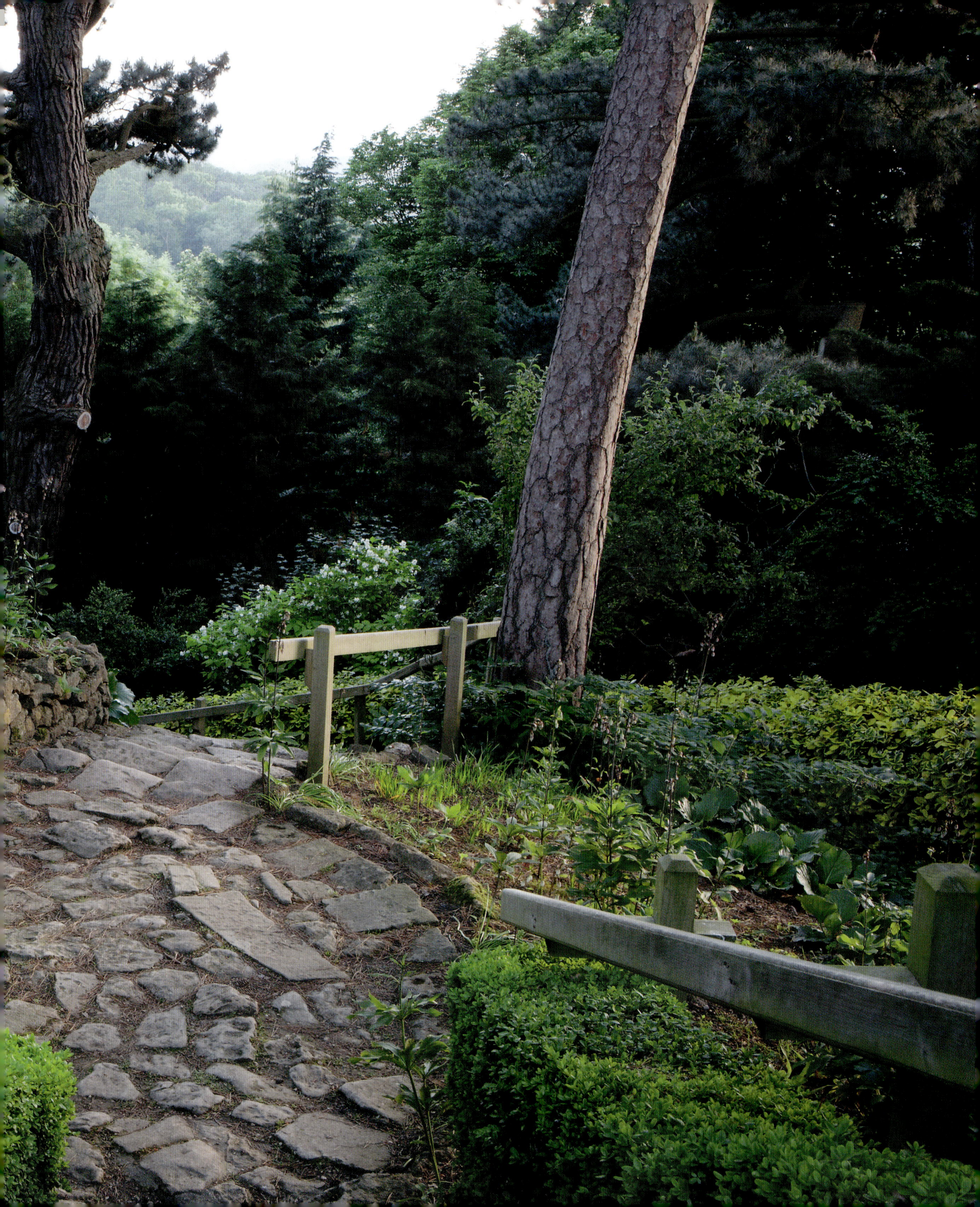

More than eighty years after the Banks were first gardened by Heather, they are still an astounding sight. The inspiration is evident: the Muirs spent their winters in the Mediterranean and would have been familiar with Sir Thomas Hanbury's cliffside garden, La Mortola, and Ellen Willmott's Villa Boccanegra, both near Ventimiglia in Italy, and with Serre de la Madone at Menton in the South of France, created in the 1920s by their Gloucestershire neighbour Lawrence Johnston. A watercolour in the Kiftsgate collection painted by Aubrey Waterfield is an artist's impression of what Heather was trying to achieve here in the 1930s (see p. 28). It shows the towering pines flanking the Banks, and a Grecian-style rotunda, the Ionic columns of which are in line with those on the Georgian portico of the house. The rotunda was not built, rather a wooden, pitched-roof summer house on the cross-paths of the Banks.

Otherwise, Waterfield's watercolour is an evocation of how Heather had the vision to turn a Gloucestershire hillside into a Mediterranean paradise, and the courage to set her team of Italian gardeners to work on a 100-foot (30-m) drop. She must have realized that this bowl-shaped, south-west-facing bank had a microclimate that would allow her to grow plants generally too tender for the harsh Cotswold winters. Frosts roll over the slope, and, when winds howl in from the north and

Above: The descent through the Banks is often precipitous, down steps made from the stalks of staddle stones.

Above, right: The original path through the Banks was laid using staddle-stone caps.

Opposite: Kiftsgate Court on the hill is reflected in the swimming pool, which was created by Diany in the 1960s. Halfway down the Banks is the 1930s summer house built by Heather.

KIFTSGATE COURT GARDENS

THE BANKS

Right: Iris pseudacorus var. *bastardii* grows in the pool below the summer house.

Below: Bright acers were planted by Heather in the 1930s beside the pool on the Banks to give this area the Japanese look then fashionable. The stonework is blanketed with *Clematis armandii*.

Opposite, top: Narrow paths wind along the Banks to the summer house past (on the left) *Ceanothus* 'Puget Blue' and *Viburnum rhytidophyllum*. *Ceanothus arboreus* 'Trewithen Blue' flows freely down the Banks above Heather's summer house, along with grey senecio (*Brachyglottis* 'Sunshine'). From New Zealand, this tough plant copes well with the dry conditions.

Opposite, bottom: Ceanothus 'Puget Blue'.

east, the Middle Bank and the Lower Garden are completely still.

There are now two routes down through the Banks, one path and flight of steps laid in the 1930s using hundreds of staddle stones. (These were the stone supports that lifted old country barns away from marauding rats.) Wooden steps and another path, laid with single paviours, were the work of Diany in the 1960s, with rails added in recent years by the Chambers to secure the path for greater numbers of visitors. The steps from the end of the North Border are lined with *Ilex* × *altaclerensis* 'Golden King', also Diany's work. This golden river runs alongside the path to the Lower Garden, providing light under the dark Scots pines.

A statue of a mother and child, sculpted by Simon Verity and commissioned by Diany, stands just below the path in a stone roundel surrounded by Scots pines with trunks like temple pillars. This belvedere is believed to have been created by Heather to take advantage of

KIFTSGATE COURT GARDENS

views through the trees to the church and manor at Mickleton. Cyclamen and martagon lilies have naturalized in the dry shade of the pines, and the planting throughout this area is protected by Diany's windbreak of cypress.

The path winds down through a dry, windy and exposed bank, where self-seeded mahonias, scillas, irises, geraniums (including *Geranium maderense*, *palmatum* and *macrorrhizum* 'Bevan's Variety') and hellebores grow, along with the unusual *Hebe hulkeana*, which comes from New Zealand and has sprays of pale-mauve flowers in May. Plants such as *Osmanthus delavayi*, *Indigofera heterantha* and cotinus forge a link with the flower garden above. These flourish alongside early-flowering *Ceanothus arboreus* 'Trewithen Blue' and C. 'Puget Blue' (for spring colour), elaeagnus, cistus, *Teucrium fruticans*, and a prickly green berberis as a barrier beside the steep path. A pencil cypress recalls the landscape of Tuscany.

Lower down, in a sunnier spot, are aromatic rosemary and thyme, with cistus, lavender, salvias, euphorbias, *Anthemis punctata* subsp. *cupaniana* (also in the White Sunk Garden) and a pittosporum hedge planted by the Chambers.

Halfway down is Heather's wooden summer house. A golden hop along the wall to one side illumines an otherwise dark corner, while fluorescent-orange, scentless *Lonicera* × *tellmanniana* scrambles over the rail in front. Below, a stone arena, a pool with a mask at its centre, is encircled by flights of steps and a wall covered in *Clematis armandii*. In the pool is variegated *Iris pseudacorus* var. *bastardii*, and beside it are two acers, *Acer palmatum* 'Atropurpureum' and *A.p.* 'Sango-kaku'. These were Heather's limited response to the 1930s taste for all things Japanese.

The garden designer Penelope Hobhouse once visited Kiftsgate. Standing on the summer-house terrace, she pointed out, in her uncompromising fashion, that the pool steps – the steps from the Lower Garden to the swimming-pool lawn and the swimming pool itself – are off-centre. For this master of straight

KIFTSGATE COURT GARDENS
160

lines and verticals, such unalignment may be troubling, but for most visitors the ebullient tumble and asymmetry of these heavily planted slopes are part of their appeal.

Along the path from the summer house is an area of luxuriant vegetation that the Chambers call Tresco. Protected by leylandii, it feels subtropical on a warm summer's day, and the Chambers have filled it with mementos of holidays with their children in the Scilly Isles. They have recently planted red, tenderer echiums to add to others on the slopes. Below the path are bamboo, *Magnolia* 'Vulcan', *Rosa banksiae*, pterocarya, *Davidia involucrata*, *Buddleja agathosma* and *Holboellia coriacea*, the last a rarity from Crûg Farm Plants in North Wales.

On the banks behind are ginger lilies (hedychiums), stachys, dieramas, more anthemis, myrtle, Cornish *Olearia* × *mollis* 'Zennorensis', honey-scented *Euphorbia mellifera*, *Callistemon sieberi* and *Azara serrata*, all evoking the climate of the Scillies rather than of the north Cotswolds. Skimmias, planted by Diany in the 1960s and 1970s, when they were especially fashionable, are also a feature here, while smilacina, *Paeonia ludlowii* and *Osmanthus delavayi* again recall the flower garden above.

Snaking past *Olearia macrodonta* and *Viburnum rhytidophyllum*, the path leads to a gate that opens into the wilder Bluebell Wood.

Left: In eighteenth-century style, the formal garden merges almost seamlessly into the fields below the ha-ha. The surprise is that it is grazing land rather than the Mediterranean Sea that lies beyond. Along the Top Banks are planted *Euphorbia mellifera*, *Ceanothus arboreus* 'Trewithen Blue', the pink-flowered Asian shrub *Rhaphiolepis umbellata* and spiky phormiums.

Below: The view down the Banks from the summer house is slightly asymmetric.

THE BANKS

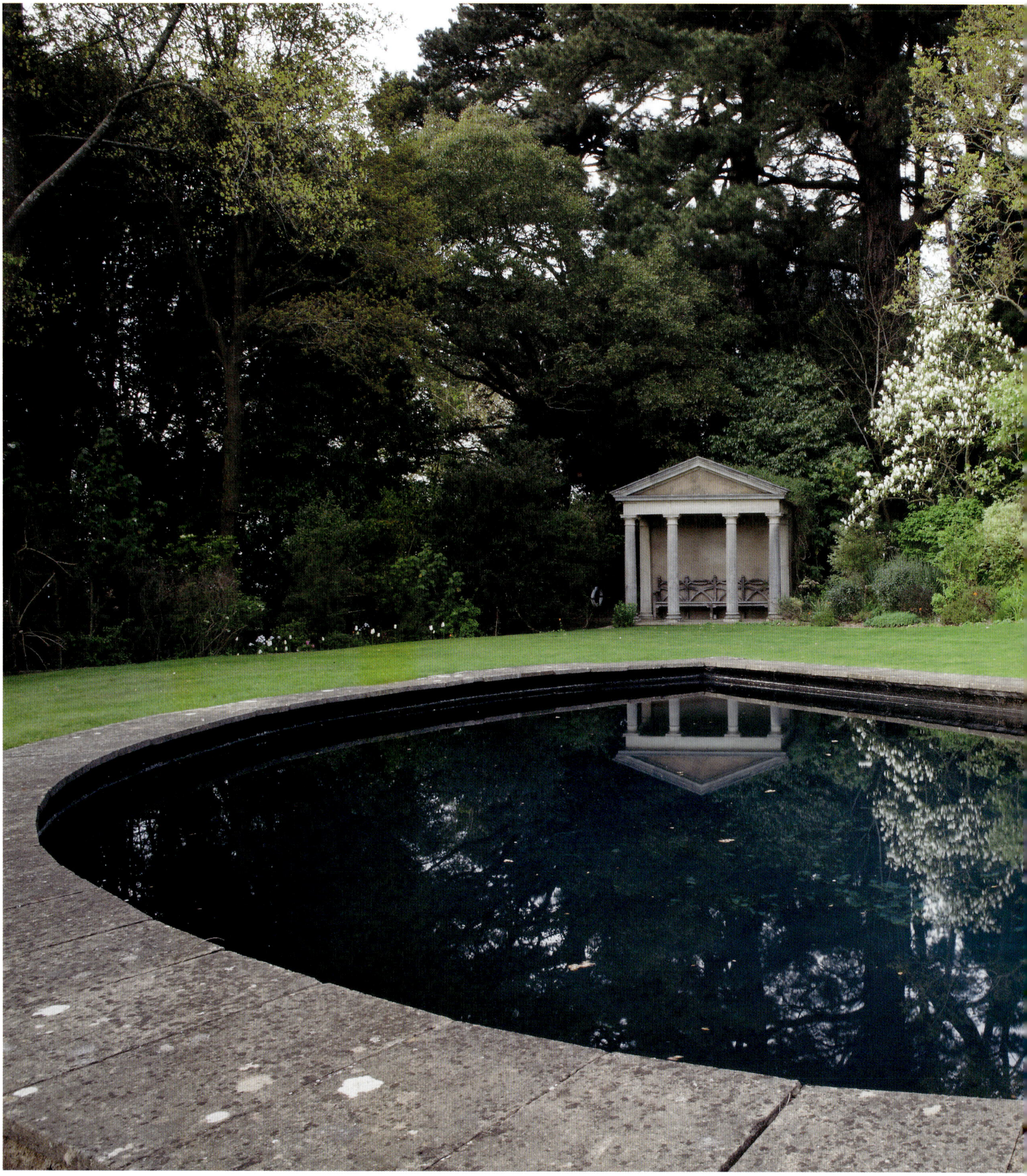

Lower Garden

Stand on the lawn of the Lower Garden looking back up and you will see generations of Muir family history imprinted on the slope. Had you stood here in the 1930s, you would have had an uninterrupted view of the Grecian portico of Kiftsgate Court, Cotswold in colour but pure Mediterranean in style. For many years, the house was obscured from here by a fine old oak-leaved strawberry tree, *Arbutus unedo*, planted as a small sapling when Heather was terracing her Banks. When the heavy snow in early 2018 felled the arbutus, the terracing below had to be replaced, filled with new soil and replanted, but the view to the house from below was reopened. The new terraces are planted with cistus, pittosporum, euphorbia, cornus, lychnis, red echiums and *Olearia* × *scilloniensis*. As so often in gardening, there are swings and roundabouts.

Heather's work is still in evidence around the Lower Garden. To one side is a now immense *Magnolia dawsoniana*, planted by her in the 1930s and then taking more than twenty years to flower. On the other side is her grove of self-seeding *Abutilon vitifolium*, with great mauve saucer-shaped flowers. The abutilons are short-lived, but have perpetuated themselves for eighty years, doing so even more vigorously in the warmer winters of the early 2000s. They are surrounded by purple-leaved lunaria and cerise, black-eyed *Geranium* 'Ann Folkard'.

Curling around the lawn is a semicircular bed of shrubs, including hydrangea, magnolia, *Coprosma* 'Dark Spire', *Cornus kousa* and buddleja with ligularia, hostas, euphorbia, *Thalictrum flavum* subsp. *glaucum*, *Alchemilla mollis* and purple irises. In the fields beyond are parkland trees – walnut, chestnut and oak – dating from Diany's time, and enhancing the landscape beyond the boundaries of the formal garden.

Diany made her mark by framing the lawn with a tulip tree (*Liriodendron tulipifera*) and a walnut (*Juglans nigra*), and planting a leylandii hedge in 1984 to the west of the terrace. She did this partly to provide shelter for tender plants from whipping westerly winds, but also to hide the increasing sprawl of Mickleton. The planning is recorded in shorthand on her list of

'Things that need doing' for 1984: 'Get & plant leylandii on bank below ilex Gold King.' Protected by the hedge, one of Diany's signature plants, *Carpenteria californica*, enjoys the warm conditions on the lawn.

The half-moon swimming pool was made by Diany in the 1960s for her daughters, Anne and Emma, with the intention that it should also be ornamental. As a result, the builders were astonished, both at the shape, which was unusual at the time, and by the fact that no diving board or steps were required. When a falling pine destroyed the wooden pool house in 1984, Diany built a changing room behind the façade of a small Doric temple, a variant on the Ionic portico on the main house above.

Anne and Johnny cut their gardening teeth on the Banks and the Lower Garden, where they formed the kind of gardening partnership that neither Anne's mother nor grandmother had enjoyed. By the time the Chambers moved to Kiftsgate in 1988, Diany could no longer scramble up and down the slopes of the Banks, and was grateful to be able to concentrate on her beloved White Sunk Garden. Anne and Johnny were a couple in their thirties with three young children, and the Lower Garden, with its swimming pool, became a centre of family life. Picnic lunches and teas were brought down to the lawn on sunny days, which the children spent in the pool. The Chambers painted the pool black in the early 1990s, blending it even more into its surroundings.

The Chambers have planted intensively, adding another magnolia, *Magnolia* × *loebneri* 'Leonard Messel' (as they did in the Wide Border), to the magnolia planted by Heather. Diany, having struggled with the bitter winters in the early 1960s, was sceptical of some of Anne and Johnny's planting ideas, and was convinced that the Chilean lantern tree (*Crinodendron hookerianum*), with tassels of red flowers, would never survive. But it has thrived, encouraging the Chambers to become more adventurous. They have planted *Daphniphyllum macropodum*, *Salvia interrupta* and the white-flowered Australian mint tree, *Prostanthera lasianthos*.

But there are also English flower-garden staples: old lavenders, blue *Geranium pratense* (Victor Reiter Group), *G. clarkei* 'Kashmir White' and *Alchemilla mollis*, the last self-seeding through the steps. Welsh poppies also seed themselves, but the Chambers try to stop these vigorous flowers from becoming too prolific.

Pages 162–63: Diany built the little Doric temple with a changing room behind for her swimming pool. In flower beside it is a *Magnolia* × *loebneri*, dwarfed by Heather Muir's *Magnolia dawsoniana* next to the steps.

Above, clockwise from top left: Paeonia lactiflora 'Bowl of Beauty'; *P.* × *lemoinei* 'Argosy'; Rock's seedling tree peony; *P.* × *lemoinei* 'Souvenir de Maxime Cornu'.

Opposite: The multilayered planting through the Banks and the Lower Garden includes acers, *Agapanthus africanus*, *Hebe* 'Watson's Pink' and self-seeded verbascum, with *Nandina domestica* and a tall *Acer palmatum* 'Atropurpureum' behind.

KIFTSGATE COURT GARDENS

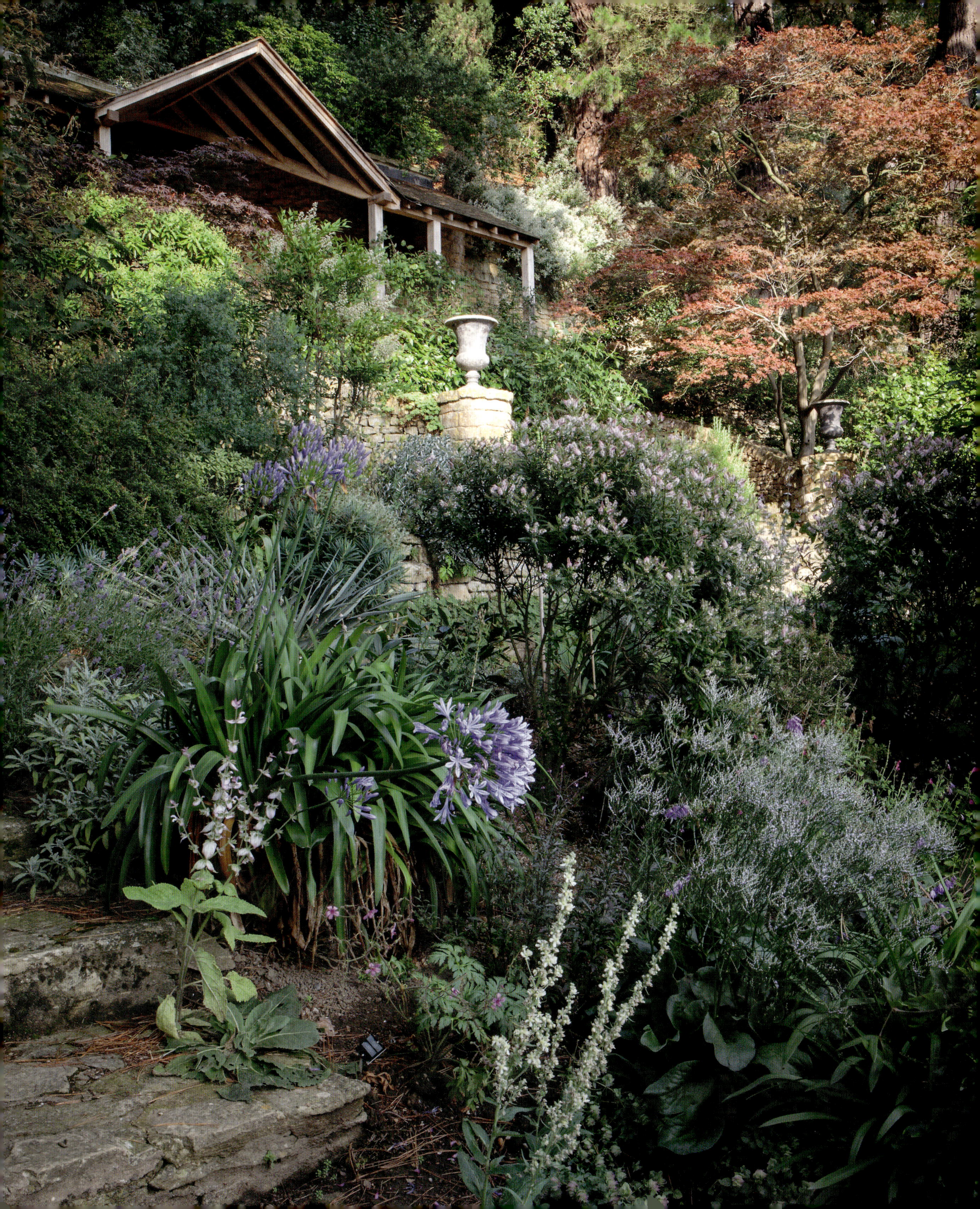

Fragrant Mediterranean plants creep across the stone terrace under the bench beside the swimming pool, with grey *Olearia* × *mollis* and clipped roundels of *Pittosporum tenuifolium* for structure. Behind grow a tree peony, *Paeonia rockii*, and *Rosa* × *odorata* 'Bengal Crimson'.

Planting through the Lower Garden includes an Iceberg rose, *Phlomis grandiflora*, *Euphorbia characias*, *Pittosporum tenuifolium* and *Salvia sclarea* var. *turkestaniana*.

KIFTSGATE COURT GARDENS

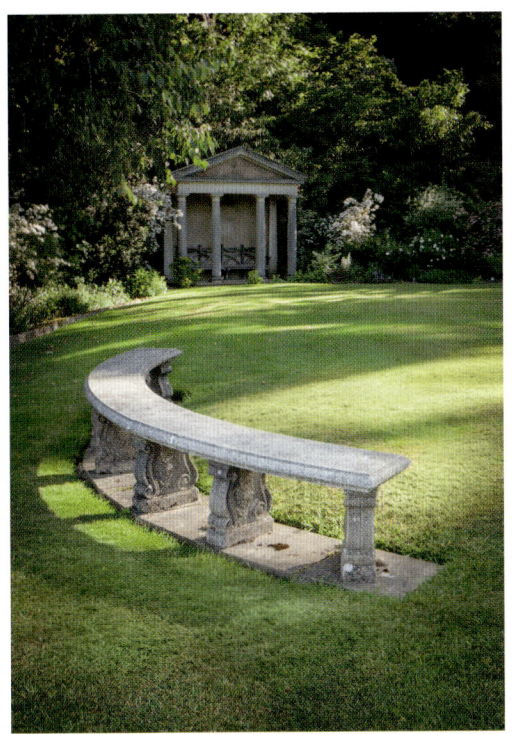

Phlomis grandiflora 'Lloyd's Silver' is planted more for its foliage than for its flowers, although its seed heads put on a good display in winter.

Almost every shrub or tree has a history: the Chilean lantern tree was spotted in the botanic garden at Logan in Scotland; the daphniphyllum was bought at Greenway, Agatha Christie's house at Dittisham, near Dartmouth in Devon; and an old-fashioned blush Rosa × odorata 'Pallida' was planted after Anne had admired the single, long-flowering rose in a friend's garden. A wooden seat on the lawn, along with many others throughout the garden, was made by Nicky Hodges, a friend of Anne's whose parents created a much admired garden at Brook Cottage, Alkerton, near Banbury. Tree peonies here include Paeonia rockii, a historic peony about which Diany corresponded with Graham Stuart Thomas and Anne with Sir Peter Smithers (see p. 176).

Anne has planted a variegated philadelphus to the left of steps leading up from the lawn to cheer an area darkened by Heather's Magnolia dawsoniana when in leaf. A bush-form Lonicera periclymenum 'Red Gables' recalls the domed honeysuckles planted by Diany in the Four Squares, and a startlingly red China rose, Rosa × odorata 'Bengal Crimson', is a link with the roses in the North Border.

Above: Lime-green Alchemilla mollis and lavender flow out on to the stone path below Lonicera periclymenum 'Red Gables' and Olearia × mollis. The little Doric temple is framed by Deutzia setchuenensis var. corymbiflora and Carpenteria californica.

Left: A semicircular bench offers the perfect place to look out from the garden or back up the Banks.

Overleaf: The ground drops sharply away from the swimming-pool lawn, offering a breathtaking view of the countryside beyond.

LOWER GARDEN

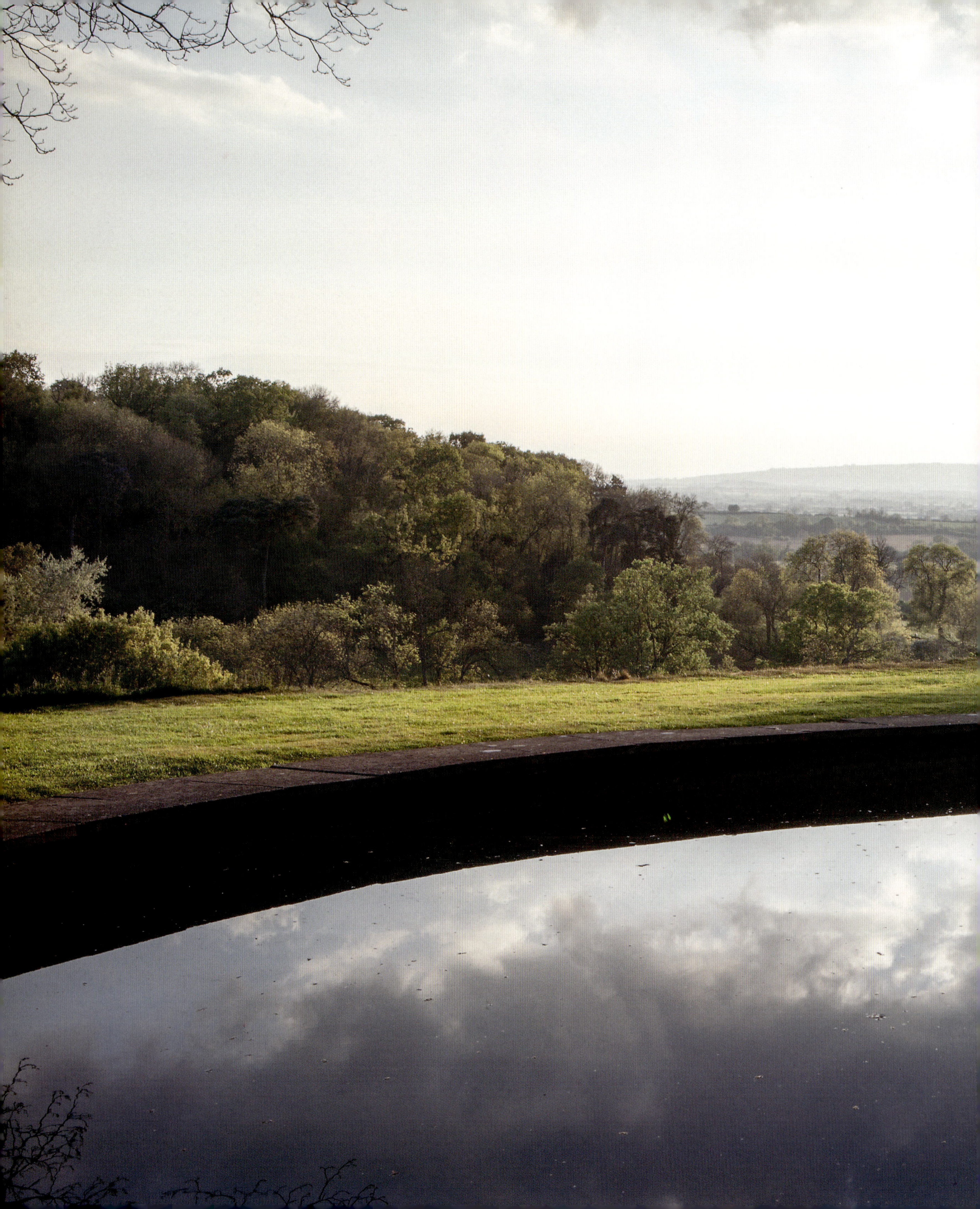

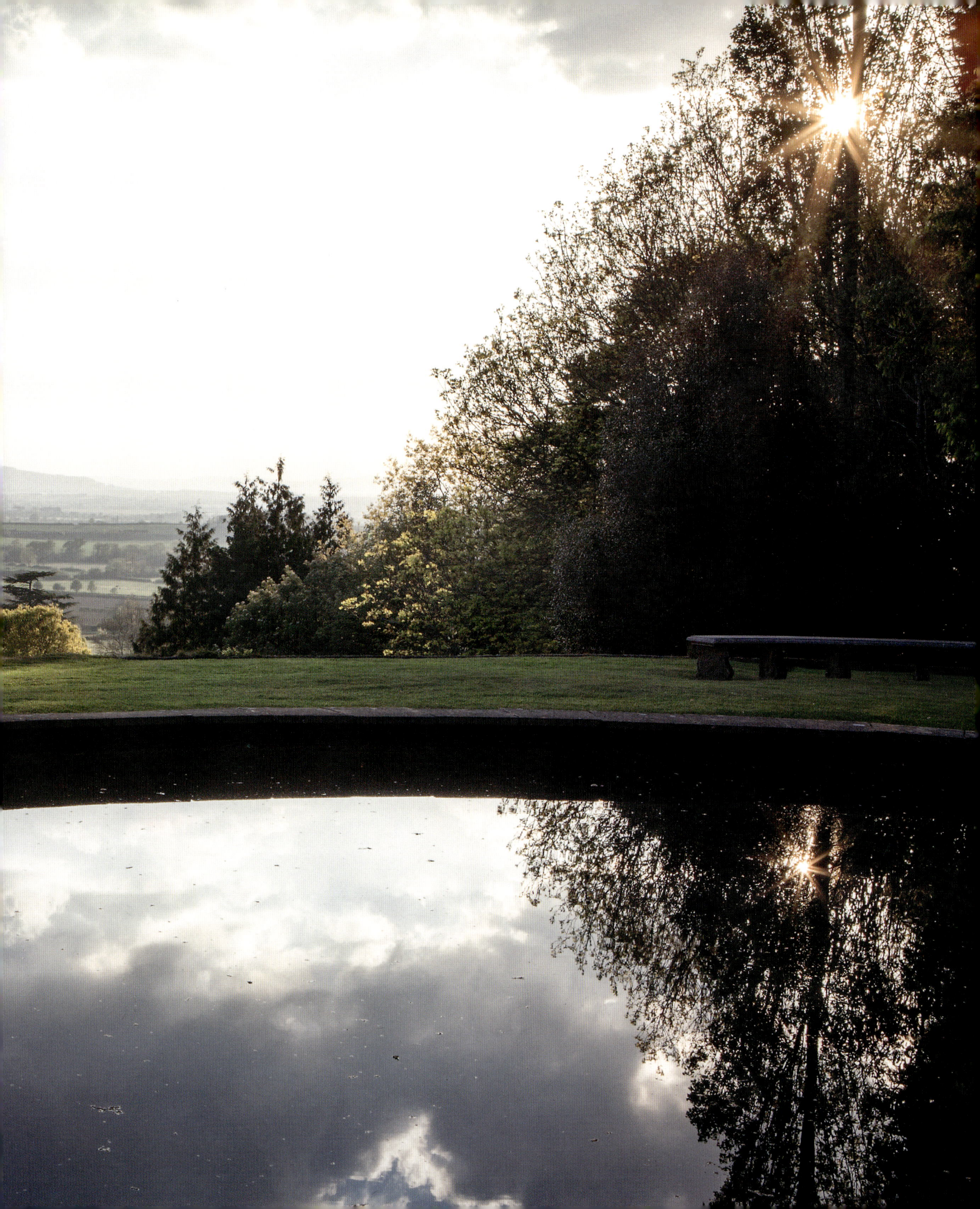

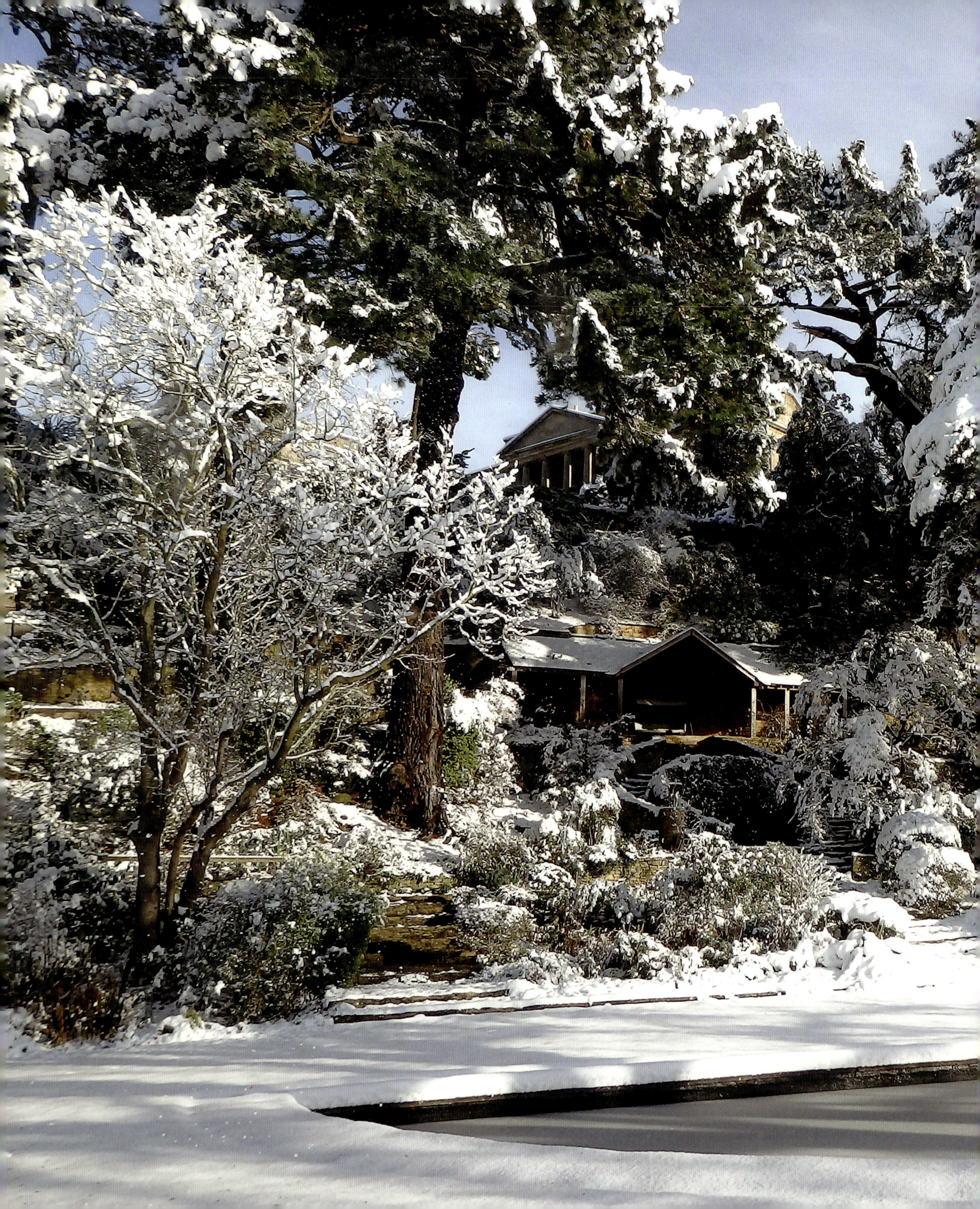

Mediterranean in style in high summer, the Banks are just as remarkable when covered with a heavy fall of snow. This really is a garden for all seasons.

The 'Kiftsgate' Rose

In 1938 Heather Muir bought what she believed was a repeat-flowering, white musk rose, *Rosa moschata*, from the Kent nurseryman and rose breeder Edward Ashdown Bunyard. Bunyard's family fruit-growing business was founded in 1796, and Edward was just seventeen when he became the fourth generation of his family to join it on its centenary. (In the same year, the nursery introduced the Allington Pippin apple.) Four years later, in 1900, Edward was apprenticed to a nursery in the Île-de-France, before returning to become a fellow of the Royal Horticultural Society and to help stage the nursery's exhibits at RHS shows. This largely self-educated nurseryman always showed an academic, as well as a commercial, appreciation of fruit, publishing several books, including *A Handbook of Hardy Fruits More Commonly Grown in Great Britain* (1920) and *The Anatomy of Dessert* (1929).

In 1936 Bunyard published *Old Garden Roses*, for he had diversified the family business into selling roses. He was particularly interested in old roses cultivated for centuries in Britain and Europe, a passion that involved extensive research, not least looking at paintings in the galleries of Europe. Familiar through his RHS work with leading gardeners in Britain, he came to know the super-rich English owners of gardens in the French Riviera while searching there for roses. He enjoyed this lifestyle, spending time on Capri and in Florence in the company of his close friend the writer Norman Douglas.

No doubt, Bunyard met Lawrence Johnston on one of his French Riviera trips, and his fondness for the Mediterranean would also have struck a chord with Heather Muir. Bunyard's book and nursery catalogue were an inspiration to Johnston at Hidcote, to Vita Sackville-West at Sissinghurst, and to Heather at Kiftsgate; she also knew of Bunyard through her head gardener, Ralph Arnold. Not surprisingly, then, Heather turned to Bunyard when she wanted a new rambler to run along the back of her Rose Border.

Rosa moschata, dating from 1824, is likely to grow to a height of 15 feet (4.5 m). Not so the rose that Heather bought from Bunyard, who died in 1939, leaving no records of either its parents or its provenance. The rosarian Graham Stuart Thomas suggested that Bunyard may have found it at the Roseraie de L'Haÿ (now known as Roseraie du Val-de-Marne), near Paris. Thomas, an admirer of Bunyard's work, credited him with introducing another of Heather's roses, 'La Mortola', into Britain (in fact, it had been at Kew for some years before it appeared in Bunyard's 1938–39 catalogue).

Bunyard did not live, therefore, to see the rose grow unchecked through the war years, climbing up into a copper beech and across the fence of the Rose Border. Only in 1951 did Thomas, by then a close friend of both Heather and Diany, correctly identify the rose as a cultivar of the much more vigorous *filipes* (a species native to western China), and he named it after the garden.

Eighty years later, the musk-scented rose remains in the Rose Border, flowering from late June, later than most ramblers. 'Kiftsgate' is hacked back fiercely each year, but nevertheless its clusters of small white flowers cascade over an area of some 60 feet (18 m) high by 60 feet (18 m) wide by 30 feet (9 m) deep. It still rockets up through the beech, with stems like hawsers, crowning the tree for a month with a blanket of white, and producing good hips in autumn.

Visitors flock to see this extraordinary rose, which has become a symbol of the garden. 'Home of Rosa Kiftsgate' proclaim some road signs and travel information leaflets, leading the occasional misguided member of the public to believe that the rose is a member of the family rather than a garden plant. Potted-up grafts can be bought from the plant stand at Kiftsgate, and indeed from such rose growers as David Austin. But because of its extreme vigour, it is recommended only to those with very large gardens and space to let it fly.

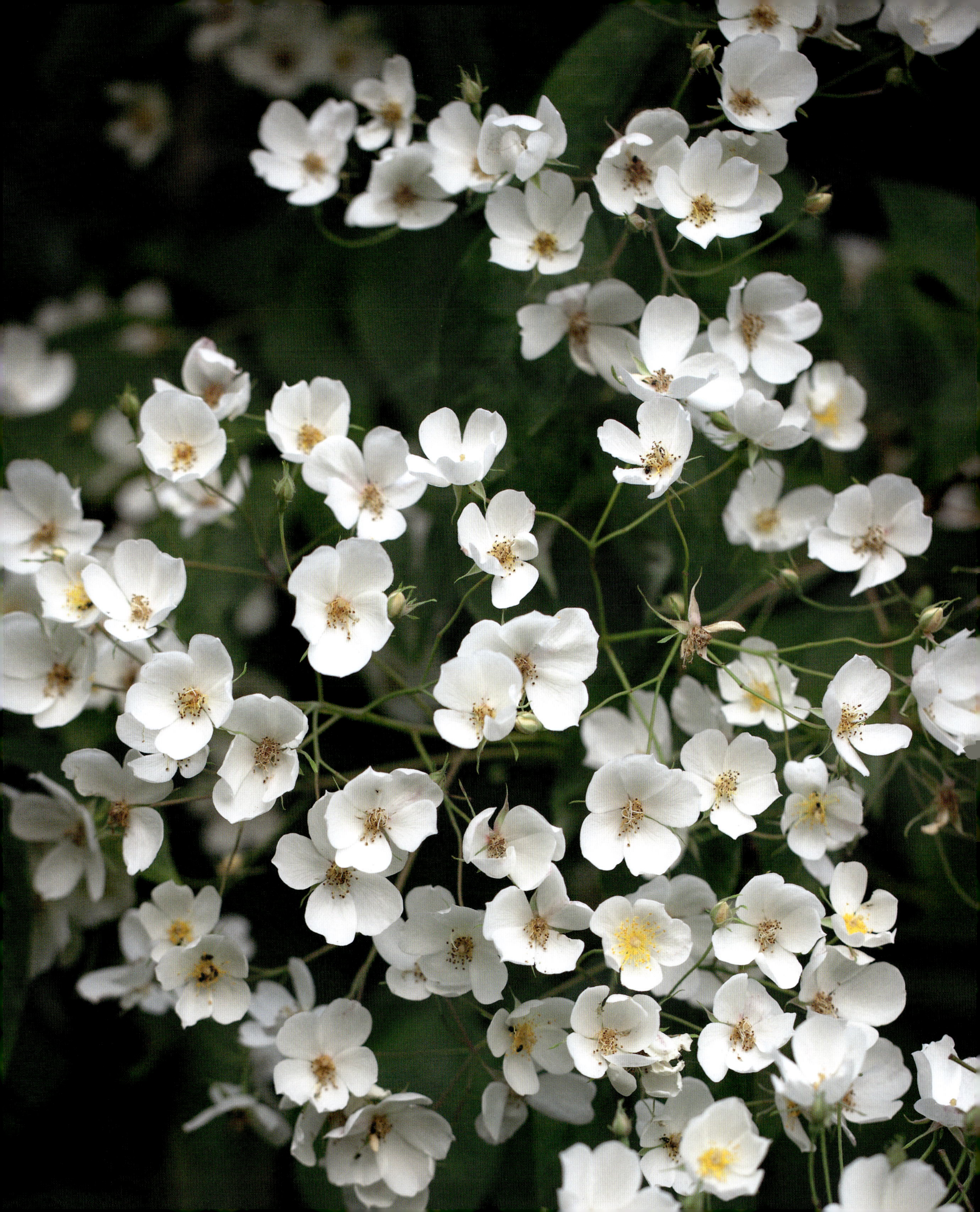

Kiftsgate's Signature Plants

The sharp-eyed visitor to Kiftsgate will notice the restrained but sure repetition of plants throughout the garden. Although she has made new additions to the planting and indeed to the fabric of the garden itself, Anne Chambers has continued to work in the style of her mother and grandmother, husbanding the species and cultivars that previously they tended and loved. Eschewing the current taste for block planting, Anne likes to use plants individually within a border, and then to repeat them in other borders or areas of the garden, often with different companions. This links the various areas of the garden, while making the visitor look at each plant anew for these diverse associations. Some plants have been in the garden for decades, creating a historical thread through the opulent embroidery of the borders.

ABUTILON VITIFOLIUM was first planted by Heather Muir in the Lower Garden in the 1930s as she finished her creation of the Banks. A fast-growing, erect and deciduous shrub, it produces generous quantities of saucer-shaped, mauve-veined flowers with reddish-yellow stamens from late spring to early summer. With sharply denticulated grey-green foliage, this great stand of abutilons is robust in its sunny position, sheltered by the steep bank behind. Hardy but not long-lasting, the abutilons have always seeded themselves around, and all the more profusely in the mostly mild winters of the early 2000s. As a result, the descendants of Heather's original planting still make a major statement today.

CARPENTERIA CALIFORNICA, also known as the tree anemone or Californian anemone bush, is on one of Diany Binny's early plant lists, turned out in the 1960s on a Roneo machine like a parish magazine. This bushy evergreen shrub was planted in both the White Sunk Garden and the Lower Garden, where it remains today, itemized in the latest, rather more smartly printed list drawn up in 2018 by Anne and Johnny Chambers. Originating in California, as the name suggests, *Carpenteria californica* first flowered in the United Kingdom in 1885 in Gertrude Jekyll's garden at Munstead, Surrey. Still something of a rarity, it has glossy, dark foliage, and fragrant white flowers in summer. It is happiest in full sun and in a sheltered position. The Chambers now also grow a more recently bred cultivar, 'Ladhams' Variety', described by the Cornish Burncoose Nurseries as 'the best form of this scarce plant', with slightly larger white flowers and very yellow stamens.

KIFTSGATE COURT GARDENS

Deutzias abound at Kiftsgate, none more than DEUTZIA SETCHUENENSIS VAR. CORYMBIFLORA, which Diany probably first planted in the 1960s: according to her notebooks, she was already taking cuttings from it in 1967. In the spring of 1973, she wrote a note to remind herself to give cuttings of the deutzia, along with white agrostemma and Salvia candelabrum, to Jeryl Smith-Ryland, a gardening friend at Sherbourne Park, a Georgian house at Barford, near Warwick. Originating in China, and slightly tender, the deutzia might not have been expected to survive Cotswold winters. But this neat and versatile deciduous shrub has flourished at Kiftsgate, its fragrant white star-like flowers complementing the floral abundance of the Four Squares and the Wide Border, helping to set the colour theme of the White Sunk Garden, and providing foliage contrast to the Mediterranean-style planting of the Lower Garden. It also flowers with other white shrubs in the North Border.

DICTAMNUS ALBUS VAR. PURPUREUS is mentioned by Diany in the large, early alphabetized notebook in which she listed the plants she was learning about; her notes describe it accurately as 'perennial' and 'pinky purple'. The RHS Gardeners' Encyclopaedia of Plants and Flowers states that this upright perennial 'resents disturbance', which may be why it has remained in the Wide Border for the last fifty years. Such was its success that, in 1968, Diany ticked the item urging herself to 'Get more dictamnus.' Spires of star-shaped, fragrant purplish-pink flowers appear first in early summer above light-green oval leaves. It is combustible: a party trick of the Chambers is to set its oily seed heads alight on a still day in late summer – an act that, surprisingly, does no harm to the plant itself.

Hebes, as useful for their foliage as for their flowers, are also used throughout the borders and banks at Kiftsgate. Some of them, such as Hebe recurva, were grown from cuttings listed by Diany as coming from Betsy Muir's garden at Hidcote Boyce in August 1980. A particular favourite of Diany's was always HEBE HULKEANA, an unusual species from New Zealand. She planted it throughout the Banks, where it thrives on a dry, windy and exposed shelf. An evergreen, upright shrub with a graceful open habit, it reaches a height and spread of no more than 20 inches (50 cm), so does not sprawl out on to the narrow paths of the Banks. It has oval, glossy leaves outlined in red, and produces plentiful lilac-like sprays of pale-mauve flowers in late spring and early summer.

PAEONIA ROCKII, originally planted by Diany in the White Sunk Garden, under the listing 'Tree Paeonia Suffruticosa (Rock's Variety)', now also grows in the Lower Garden. Graham Stuart Thomas, in one letter, acknowledged his gratitude to Diany for being given the peony: he wanted to know whether it had been struck from a cutting or from layering, suggesting that Diany had become a versatile propagator of plants. In 1990 Anne sent the Swiss-based peony expert Sir Peter Smithers a photograph of what she believed to be a Rock's peony, which he confirmed: 'It strikes me as being certainly Rock's var., English form, probably of Highdown origin and perhaps originally a grafted plant. The slight pink flush is typical though not always present, and it varies from season to season according to temperature.' Named after the Austrian-American explorer and botanist Joseph Rock, the tree peony is native to China, and has a large purple blotchy centre in the middle of its papery white flowers.

There is an exception to every rule: ROSA 'FELICIA' is Kiftsgate's only example of mass planting. Diany's Roneoed plant list suggests that this silvery-pink, dwarf hybrid musk was planted by Heather in 1928, shortly after it was bred by the Reverend Joseph Pemberton. An Anglican clergyman for more than forty years, Pemberton joined the Royal National Rose Society not long after it was founded in 1876 and served as its president in 1911. Even before his retirement from the Church, he had turned to rose-breeding to try to re-create the highly scented, cluster-flowering roses that he recalled from childhood. Crossed from the short rambler 'Trier' and the climbing hybrid tea 'Ophelia', 'Felicia' flowers twice, in June and September.

ROSA 'RITA' is now so rare that it has not been listed in recent editions of the *RHS Plant Finder*. It is possible that the pink floribunda rose in the Four Squares is almost the last survivor of a rose given to Diany by her close gardening friend the rose breeder Hilda Murrell before her retirement in 1970. The rose, a cross between a hybrid tea and a polyantha, was bred at the Murrell nursery in Shrewsbury, Shropshire, to have large clusters of flowers, with a high colour over a long season.

KIFTSGATE COURT GARDENS

Afterword
Anne Chambers

Looking back over thirty years of living and gardening at Kiftsgate, I would not want to change a moment. It must be seldom that one is so fortunate as to have had a totally fulfilling and rewarding life doing the thing that gives one most pleasure with the person whom one loves the most.

My childhood memories of growing up at Kiftsgate are happy: my sister, Emma, and I had an old-fashioned and sheltered upbringing, taking our surroundings for granted, as children do. Tea at Front Lodge with my elderly grandmother was a weekly ordeal for me. The garden was part of everyday life but did not seem to dominate our lives. It was only when I had my own tiny patch in London that I began to take an interest in plants, and the gardening seed was sown.

I was never going to be a successful office worker and, by luck and inheritance, I ended up doing the perfect job. When Johnny and I first married, I had imagined that our life would be in London with our three children, weekending at Kiftsgate, but the commuting backwards and forwards to Gloucestershire began to take its toll. When the matter of schools arose, the decision was made to move full-time to Kiftsgate. This meant that Johnny had to give up his job with Morgan Crucible and completely reinvent himself. Also, he was moving into a very female-dominated environment, with my mother, my Aunt Betsy and their cousin Beryl Hobson all a stone's throw away. He charmed them and adapted to his new role with ease.

When I think back to those early days, I am not sure how we managed to fit everything in. Admittedly, I had some help with the children, but there was so much to learn and we were complete novices. Mum was very patient, and we had many an expedition to nurseries to buy countless plants, quite a few of which she said would not live as they were too tender. We also visited other people's gardens, both in the UK and abroad, to get new ideas. Gradually, gardening became our way of life and Kiftsgate the centre of our universe.

I remember the excitement of an article on the garden in *Country Living* when we first moved here. Mum had not courted publicity, but we realized that we had to attract more visitors in order to make the garden financially self-sustaining. Slowly but surely, we have increased visitor numbers and plant sales, recognizing that new challenges come with success. However, the weather still plays a vital part in a prosperous year.

Now there is no inch of the garden that I do not know. We must have planted thousands of plants over the years and, like all gardeners, we have had our failures and losses. We continue to get a thrill from a new discovery and the wonder of the changing seasons. All winter, one waits for spring and then it is over so quickly; the summer months seem to rush by, but we still love to walk slowly round the garden when it is closed, noting new additions and jobs that should be done. Mum instilled in us the importance of observation and also of never walking past a weed or something that should be attended to straight away.

And what of the future? Will there be a fourth generation? Robert, our elder son, has shown an interest in taking up the challenge, but is still working in London and unmarried, so I feel it will be a few years yet before Johnny and I retire happily into Front Lodge and hand over the running of the garden to him. I now recognize the anxiety that my mother must have had over the future of the garden and her relief – and, frankly, her surprise – when Johnny and I made the move to Kiftsgate. My mother never knew that I would want to come and live here until I was well into my thirties: life and plans evolve slowly in our family, rather like the garden projects.

I cannot now imagine life without the garden. It has provided us with enormous interest and given us connections all over the world; through it, we have met many fascinating and knowledgeable people. It has also been wonderful to bring up our family in a place that I know means so much to them. I hope that, in this book on the history and lives of my family members over the past one hundred years, you too can get a glimpse of the magic and love that have gone into making Kiftsgate such a special family home.

Timeline of Kiftsgate's History and Development

1750s

Visits to Morgan and Richard Graves at Mickleton Manor by William Shenstone, and his suggested planting of the Scots pines, and lime and elm avenues.

Late 18th century

Rebuilding of Mickleton Manor as a Georgian house by Walwyn Graves.

1887–91

Building of Kiftsgate Court by Sidney Graves Hamilton and transfer of Georgian façade from Mickleton Manor to Kiftsgate.

1906

Marriage of Sidney Graves Hamilton, who then lets both Mickleton Manor and Kiftsgate Court.

1919

Purchase of Kiftsgate Court by Jack and Heather Muir.

1920s

Tapestry Hedge planted.

Four Squares and White Sunk Garden laid out.

Wide Border, Rose Border and Yellow Border created.

1930s

Yew hedges planted and tennis court laid out.

Banks terraced in Italianate style.

Summer house built.

1936

Death of Judy Muir.

Aubrey Waterfield murals installed at Kiftsgate Court.

1938

Heather Muir buys what she thinks is *Rosa moschata* from E.A. Bunyard.

Kiftsgate Court Gardens open for the first time for the National Garden Scheme.

1951

Rosarian Graham Stuart Thomas identifies Bunyard's rose as a *Rosa filipes* and names it 'Kiftsgate'.

1954

Diany Binny takes over the garden from her mother, Heather Muir, and demolishes the front court of Kiftsgate Court.

1956

Death of Jack Muir.

1960s

Swimming pool and ha-ha built at the bottom of the Banks.

Second path laid down through the Banks.

Shenstone's limes in the avenue gradually replaced by weeping silver limes.

1961

Death of Heather Muir.

1970s

North Border and Fern Border planted.

Sorbus Arch created.

Shenstone's elm avenue felled by Dutch elm disease.

1972–73

White Sunk Garden paved and fountain installed at its centre.

1975

Rosa 'Diany Binny' registered.

Diany Binny moves to the Front Lodge, and Kiftsgate Court is left uninhabited for some years. Diany continues to garden at Kiftsgate.

1978

Simon Verity statues commissioned.

1980s

Transformation of kitchen garden into nursery.

Garden opens to the public more regularly.

Anne Chambers, Diany Binny's daughter, begins her involvement with the garden.

Banks reterraced.

1988

Anne and Johnny Chambers and their three children move permanently to Kiftsgate Court and gradually take on responsibility for the garden.

Early 1990s

Swimming pool painted black.

Grass path through Rose Border paved.

1999–2000

Creation of Water Garden on the site of Heather Muir's tennis court.

2003

Winner of the Historic Houses Association/Christie's Garden of the Year Award.

2005

Death of Betsy (Bettine) Muir, fellow gardener and sister of Diany Binny.

2006

Death of Diany Binny.

2017

Opening of Orchard and Mound to the public.

2018

Magnolia wilsonii planted in the North Border to mark 80 years of opening for the National Garden Scheme.

2019

Centenary of the Muirs buying Kiftsgate Court.

Select Bibliography

MANUSCRIPT SOURCES

Chipping Campden, Gloucestershire, Kiftsgate Court Gardens, Kiftsgate Court Archive

Gloucester, Gloucestershire Archives

PRINTED SOURCES

Beevor, Kinta, *A Tuscan Childhood*, London (Viking) 1993

Brown, Jane, *Vita's Other World: A Gardening Biography of V. Sackville-West*, London (Viking) 1985

———, *The English Garden in Our Time: From Gertrude Jekyll to Geoffrey Jellicoe*, Woodbridge, Suffolk (Antique Collectors' Club) 1986

———, *My Darling Heriott: Henrietta Luxborough, Poetic Gardener and Irrepressible Exile*, London (HarperPress) 2006

Hayward, Allyson, *Norah Lindsay: The Life and Art of a Garden Designer*, London (Frances Lincoln) 2007

Humphreys, A.R., *William Shenstone: An Eighteenth-Century Portrait*, Cambridge (Cambridge University Press) 1937

Hunt, John Dixon (ed.), *The English Landscape Garden*, New York (Garland) 1982

Mickleton Women's Institute, *The Story of Our Village, 1850–1957*, Mickleton, Gloucestershire, 1957

Nicolson, Nigel, *Long Life*, London (Weidenfeld & Nicolson) 1997

Pearson, Graham S., *Hidcote: The Garden and Lawrence Johnston*, rev. edn, London (National Trust) 2013

Richardson, Tim, *The Arcadian Friends: Inventing the English Landscape Garden*, London (Bantam) 2007

Thomas, Graham S., 'Kiftsgate Court: A Garden of Colour', *Journal of the Royal Horticultural Society*, vol. 76, no. 5, May 1951, pp. 159–65

Waterfield, Lina, *Castle in Italy: An Autobiography*, London (John Murray) 1961

Wheeler, David, *Over the Hills from Broadway: Images of Cotswold Gardens*, with paintings and drawings by Simon Dorrell, Stroud, Gloucestershire (Alan Sutton) 1991

Williams, Marjorie, *William Shenstone and His Friends*, English Association pamphlet no. 84, London 1933

Wilson, Edward (ed.), *The Downright Epicure: Essays on Edward Ashdown Bunyard, 1878–1939*, Totnes, Devon (Prospect Books) 2007

ONLINE SOURCES

Abstract of answers for Kiftsgate, 1831 Census of Great Britain, A Vision of Britain through Time, www.visionofbritain.org.uk/census/table/GB1831ABS_M[1]?u_id=10140596&show=DB (accessed March 2018)

'Beauty on the Go: Victorian Vanity Cases', Chiswick Auctions, 1 August 2017, https://chiswickauctions.co.uk/beauty-go-victorian-vanity-cases (accessed March 2018)

Lane Fox, Robin, 'French Leaves', *Financial Times*, 11 September 2010, www.ft.com/content/742507ae-bba0-11df-89b6-00144feab49a (subscription only; accessed May 2018)

Acknowledgements

Writing a book is generally a solitary business. Not so this book, which has been very much a collaboration with Anne and Johnny Chambers. To mark the centenary of Anne's grandparents buying Kiftsgate Court, the Chambers commissioned me to write a history of their house, family and glorious garden, and they have supported and trusted me throughout the process. They have given me exclusive access to their archive, taken me round the garden on countless occasions, vastly extended my plant knowledge, answered endless queries, and given me numerous lunches as I worked through the family's letters and diaries. For me, as I hope for Anne and Johnny, it has been a joyous partnership, and I thank them most sincerely.

Many other people have made an important contribution to the book. Anne's sister, Emma Mackenzie, helped to illuminate for me the lives of Diany Binny and Heather Muir. I am also grateful to two Muir cousins – Helen Younger, daughter of 'Chou' (Margaret) Hayes (née Muir), who was Anne's godmother, and Caroline Meynell, daughter of Beryl Hobson – for their fascinating insights into generations of the family's Scottish history.

Others gave up their time to talk to me about their gardening friendships with Diany Binny. Louisa Arbuthnott at Stone House Cottage Garden, Worcestershire, paid tribute to Diany's generosity in helping her to establish her nursery. Timothy Leese, a friend of Emma, recalled weekends at Kiftsgate with the Binnys and Diany's importance in his changing career from art dealer to garden designer. Gina Price of Pettifers Garden, Oxfordshire, and Victoria Wakefield of Bramdean House, Hampshire, evoked the bracing experience of accompanying Diany and her sister, Betsy, on garden tours and the stringent but constructive advice given by Diany to both about their gardens.

Several people have kindly sourced pictures to supplement Sabina Rüber's beautiful photography: they include Nigel Beevor, grandson of Diany's great friends Aubrey and Lina Waterfield; Graham S. Pearson, Archivist at Hidcote Manor; Chris Charman, General Manager for the National Trust at Hidcote; Judith Ellis, Archive Coordinator at the Chipping Campden History Society; John Rogers at Chiswick Auctions; and Emma House at the Garden Museum, London. Commander Robert Green, nephew of Diany's friend the rosarian and environmental campaigner Hilda Murrell, gave permission for the use of a portrait photograph and checked my short biography of his aunt. Duncan Gilmour, Editor of *Finlays Magazine*, provided the image of Sir John Muir and contributed invaluable background to the Muir family's relationship with the Glasgow importers James Finlay Limited. Supplementary picture research was undertaken by Nick Wheldon.

Although most of my research for the book was carried out at Kiftsgate, I needed library resources as well. In particular, I am thankful to the librarians of the London Library and the RHS Lindley Library, who prepared material for me on my visits and supplied books by post.

I would also like to thank the team at Merrell Publishers: Hugh Merrell for suggesting to the Chambers in the first place that I might be a suitable author; Nicola Bailey for the splendid and responsive way she has laid out the book; and Claire Chandler for her painstaking and detailed editing of the copy. She has saved me from several slips. I am also grateful to the proofreader, Rosanna Fairhead, and the indexer, Hilary Bird, for their work.

As ever, an enormous debt of thanks goes to my husband, Chris Evans, who reads every word I write and remains endlessly patient and encouraging.

Picture Credits

All illustrations copyright © 2019 Sabina Rüber, with the exception of the following (key: l = left, r = right, t = top, b = bottom):

Courtesy of Nigel Beevor, grandson of Aubrey and Lina Waterfield: 34t, 35tl, 35tr

Courtesy of the Garden Museum: 31

Courtesy of Gloucestershire Archives/Chipping Campden History Society: 19, 25t

Courtesy of Gloucestershire Archives/Chipping Campden History Society, Jesse Taylor Photographs: 26

© Robert Green: 39

Courtesy of James Finlay Limited: 21b

Kiftsgate Court Archive: 6, 7, 11, 18, 21t, 22l, 22r, 23b, 24t, 24b, 25b, 27t, 27b, 28t, 33t, 33b, 35b, 36, 37, 38, 40t, 40b, 41, 43t, 43b, 45t, 45b, 46t, 46b, 47, 53, endpapers

© National Portrait Gallery, London: 17, 29

Courtesy of National Trust/Hidcote: 28b

© John Rogers/Chiswick Auctions: 23t

© Tessa Traeger/National Portrait Gallery, London: 42

The map on p. 4 was drawn by Lucy Payne.

The publisher and author have made every effort to trace and contact copyright holders of the illustrations reproduced in this book; they shall be happy to correct in subsequent editions any errors or omissions that are brought to their attention.

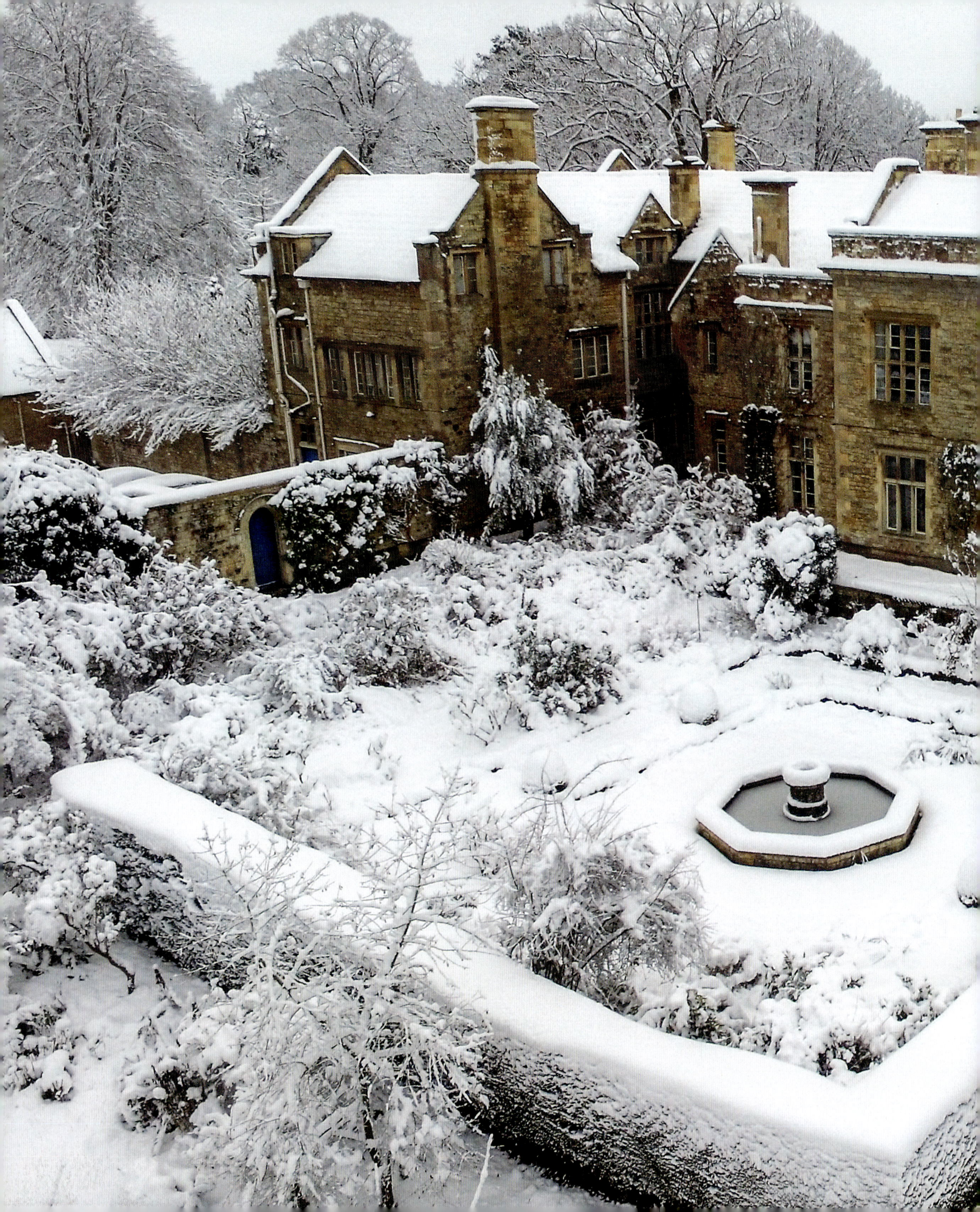

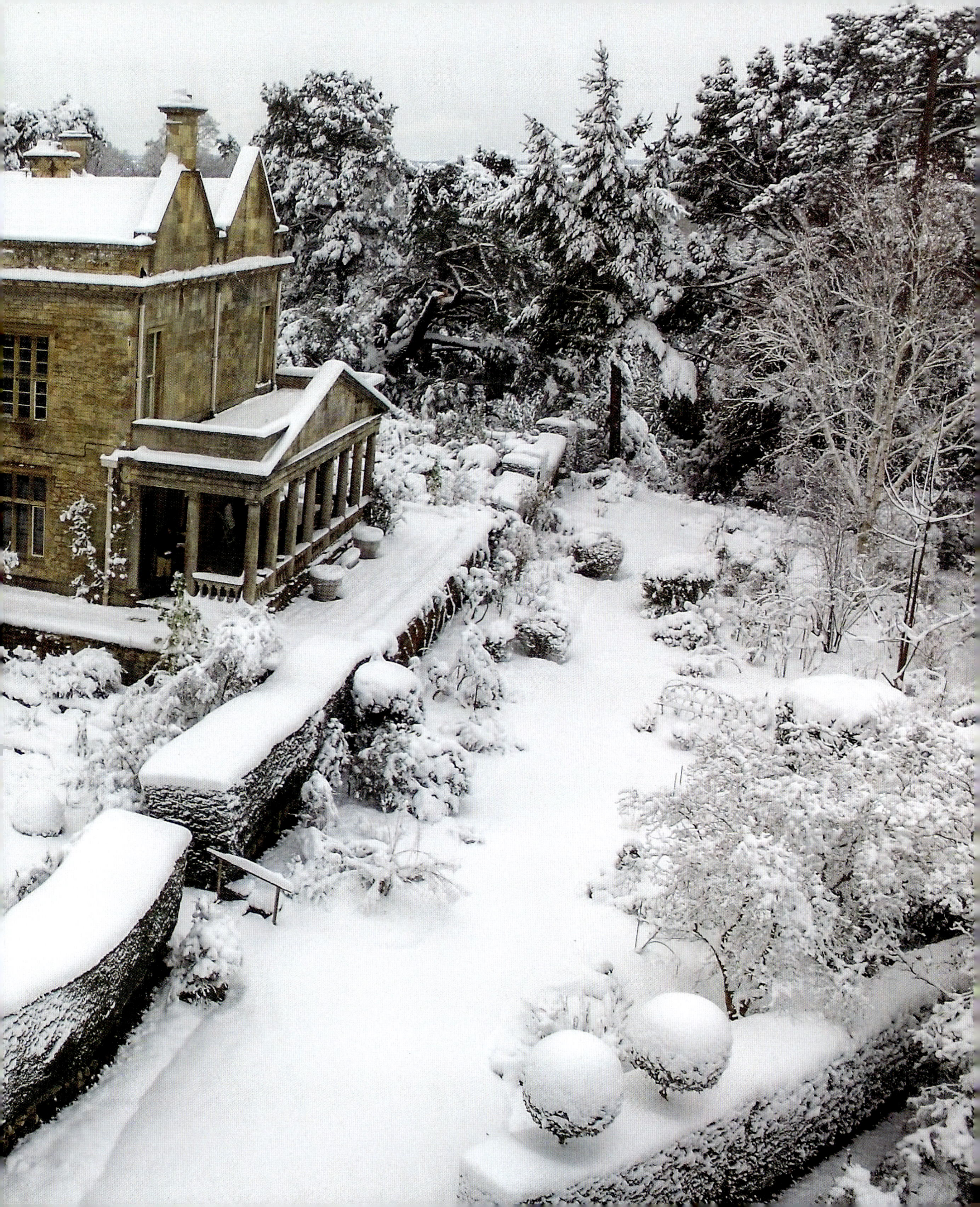

Index

Page numbers in *italic* refer to the illustrations.

A

Abbotswood, nr Stow-on-the-Wold, Gloucestershire 29
Abies 61
Abutilon 48, 50, 92
    A. vitifolium 48, *163*, 174, *174*
Acer 9, 27, 57, 59, 62, 66, *66*, 86, *103*, *140–41*, 142, *143*, 147, *158*, 159, *165*
Achillea 91
Aconitum 114
Actinidia 61, 70, 98
Adiantum 118
Agapanthus 97, *99*, *165*
Agrostemma 175
Alchemilla 61, 118, *119*, 163, 164, *167*
Alcock, Edward 17
Allison, Simon 6, 48, 134–35, *135*
Allium 88–89, 92, 97, *98–99*, *122*, 123, 152
Alstroemeria 97
Amateur Gardening 26–27
Amelanchier 61
Ammi 123
Amory, David Heathcoat 43, 47
Amsonia 88
Anemone 30, 69, *72*, 73, 95, *95*, *96*, 98, *98*, 101, 103, 151
Anglo-Saxons 15
Anthemis 146, 159, 161
Aquilegia 88–89, 97, 146
arboretum 43, 50, *60–61*
Arbuthnott, Louisa 39, 42, 43, 50, 80
Arbutus 48, 163
Argyranthemum 73
Arnold, Ralph 172
Artemisia 73, 88
Arts and Crafts movement 10, 26
Aruncus 121
Asplenium 118, *120*
Aster 42, 80, 91, 101, 113
Astilbe 113, *116–17*
Astor, David 29
Astor, Nancy 29
Astrantia 91, 97, 103, 113, *116–17*, 142, *144–45*, 146

Athyrium 118
Auden, W.H. 35
Austin, David 172
azaleas 103
Azara 161

B

Baccharis 61
Baker's Hill, Gloucestershire *18*, 57
Ballards Nursery, Malvern, Worcestershire 38
Bamford family 51
The Banks 7, 9, 19, 26, 27, 39, 40, 48, 51, 152–61, *152–61*, *165*
Barnsley House, nr Circencester, Gloucestershire 41, 114
Barrells, Warwickshire 17
Barrington, Lord 30
BBC 52
Bearsted, Lady 29
beech trees 25, 57, 95, 103, 108, 118, 142, 152, 172
Beevor, Jack 34
The Belvedere *104*, 148, *148*
Berberis 59, 69, *71*, *77*, *82–83*, 142, 152, 159
Berenson, Bernard 35
Betula 81, 86
Bhutan pine 59
Binny, Diany 6–7, *11*, 30, 33–43, *33*, *35*, *40–41*, *43*, 45, 46, 48, 51
    The Banks 158–59, 161
    early life 25, 27, 28, *28*, 33–36, *36*, *38*
    entrance to Kiftsgate 61
    Fern Border 118
    Four Squares 80
    Front Lodge 41, 57
    House and Side Lawn 69–73
    Lower Garden 39–40, 163–64
    marriage and divorce 37, 41
    North Border 40, 148–51
    nursery 43
    opens garden 43, 49
    and the Oxford Group 34–35
    plant lists 11, 27, 38–39, 88, 146, 174, 176
    Rose Border 108, 113–14
    in Second World War 36
    signature plants 174–76

    swimming pool 39–40, 50
    takes over at Kiftsgate 9–10, 31, 37–39
    White Sunk Garden 10, 40, 92–95, 98, 164
    Wide Border 85, 86, 88–91
    Yellow Border 141, 142–46
Binny, Tony 7, 31, 35–36, 37, *38*, 41, 47, 88
birch trees *81*, 86, 128
Bismarck, Prince Otto von 29
Bluebell Wood 9, *14*, 27, 62–66, *62–67*, 161
Border Lines 53
box hedges 26, 51, 75, *75*, 92, *98*, *101*, 141
Brachyglottis 159
Bramdean House, Hampshire 79
Bredon Hill, Worcestershire 9, 69
Bridge Border 46, 50, *102–107*, 103–106
Bridgeman, Lady Anne 28
Brook Cottage, Banbury, Oxfordshire 167
Brunnera 79, 86
Buchman, Frank 34
Buddleja 80, 86, 91, 161, 163
Bunyard, Edward Ashdown 7, 42, 123, 172
Burlington, Lord 17
Bury Court, Surrey 50

C

Calamagrostis 118
Callicarpa 61
Callistemon 161
Calycanthus 38, 51, 79, 80, 113
Camassia 124, *124*
Camellia 61
Campanula 91, 97
Carex 146
Carpenteria californica 43, 50, *84–85*, 88–91, 164, *167*, 174, *174*
Ceanothus 61, 73, 86, 103, *114*, *153*, 159, *159–61*
Cephalaria 146
Cercidiphyllum 61
Cercis 61
Cerinthe 73, 123
Chaenomeles 41, 57, *57*
Chamaecyparis 66
Chambers, Anne 6–7, *6*, *11*, *11*, 37, 45–53, *45*, *49*, *53*
    The Banks 7, 48, 158–61
    Bluebell Wood 62–66

Bridge Border 106
early life 38, 45–47, *45–47*
entrance to Kiftsgate 57–59
Four Squares 51, 79, 80
House and Side Lawn 51, 69, 70–72
Lower Garden 48, 164, 167
marriage 47
the Mound 49, 124–27
North Border 148–51
opens garden 49, 52
Orchard 49, 124
plants 49–52
Rose Border 48, 108, 113
signature plants 174
takes over at Kiftsgate 10, 45, 47–48
Tresco 48, 161
Tulip Tree Avenue 49
Water Garden 48–49, 124–27, 132–34
White Sunk Garden 51, 95, 97, 98
Wide Border 85, 91
Wild Flower Corner 49, 118–23
Yellow Border 146
Chambers, Clare 47, *53*, 80, 128
Chambers, Jonathan (Johnny) 6, 7, 31, 47–53, *49, 53*
The Banks 7, 48, 152, 158–61
Bluebell Wood 62–66
Bridge Border 106
early life 47
Four Squares 51
House and Side Lawn 51, 69, 72
Lower Garden 48, 164
Mound 124–27, 128
nursery 7, 49, *50*
Orchard 49, 124
Rose Border 48, 108, 113
signature plants 174
takes over at Kiftsgate 45, 47–48
Tresco 48, 161
Water Garden 48–49, 124–27, 132–34
White Sunk Garden 51, 95, 98, 101
Wild Flower Corner 49, 118–23
Chambers, Patrick 47, *53*
Chambers, Robert 7, 47, *53*, 59, 177
Chatto, Beth 11, 38
Chelsea Flower Show 40, 85, 92, 146

chestnut trees 21, 127, 148, 163
Child, David 47
Chiswick, London 17
Cholmeley, Ursula 52, 124
Cholmondeley, Sybil 30
Christie, Agatha 167
Churchill, Sir Winston 22
Cistus 61, 159, 163
Clematis 45, 79, 86, 88, *158*, 159
Le Clos du Peyronnet, Menton, France 53
Cobham, Lord 17
Coke, John 50
Coleman, Tom 51
Coprosma 163
Cornus 52, 61, 96, 98, *104*, 122–23, *123*, 142, 148, *148*, 151, 163
Corylus 142
Cosmos 99
Cotinus *82–83*, 142, 152, 159
Coton Manor, Northamptonshire 10, 52
Cotswold Hills 9, 66, 106, 152
Cotswold Way 15
Council for the Protection of Rural England 39
Country Life 11, 26
Country Living 177
Crambe *84–85*, 85, 88
Crathes, Aberdeenshire 98
Crinodendron 48, 164
Crocosmia 146, 151
Crocus 62
Crûg Farm Plants, North Wales 50, 161
Cyclamen 152, 159
cypress trees 159

D

daffodils 59, *59*, 61
Dahlia *82–83*, *86*, 91
Dalyell, Tam 39
Daphne 38, 151
Daphniphyllum 164, 167
Davidia *60–61*, *61*, 161
Delphinium *144–45*, 146, *147*
Dent-Brocklehurst family 124
Deutzia 51, 79, 85, 92, *111*, 113, *113*
D. setchuenensis var. corymbiflora 43, *78*, 85, 92, 151, *167*, 175, *175*

Dianthus 51, 123
Dicentra *150*, 151
Dictamnus 50
D. albus var. purpureus *84–85*, 91, 175, *175*
Dierama 98, *99*, 161
Digitalis see foxgloves
Dillon, Helen 53, 73
Douglas, Norman 172
Dove Cottage Nursery, Halifax, West Yorkshire 50
Dover's Hill, Gloucestershire 15
Dyck, Anthony van 15

E

Easton Walled Gardens, Lincolnshire 52, 124
Ebrington, Viscount 29
Echium 48, 161, 163
Edward, Prince of Wales 29
Elaeagnus 90, *104*, 148, 159
Eliot, T.S. 35
Elliott, Clarence 42
Embothrium 106, *107*
The English Country Garden (TV series) 52
English landscape movement 16, 17, 18
entrance to Kiftsgate 56–61, *57–61*
Epimedium *142*
Eranthis 69
Erica 61
Erodium 97, *97*
Eryngium 97
Erythronium 86, 95
Escallonia 69, 98, 141
Eucalyptus 148
Eucryphia 57, 61, 92
Euphorbia 51, 70, *70*, *88–89*, 142, 146, 159, *160–61*, 161, 163, *166*
Exochorda 42, *86–88*

F

Fagus 57, 61
see also beech trees
Farrer, Reginald 26
Fenwick, Cicely 29
Fenwick, Mark 29
Fern Border 41, 118, *118–21*
Fibrex Nurseries, Evesham, Worcestershire 38

Financial Times 47
Finlay, James & Co. 21–22
First World War 10, 24–25, 92
Fleming, Richard 28, 37
Florence, Italy 33, *34*, 35, 47
Foley, Lord 23
Forrest, George 26
Fortescue, Daisy 28, 29
Fortescue, Lionel 39, 48
Four Squares *8–9*, 17, 26, *38*, 46, 51, 69, 74–81, *75–80*, 92
foxgloves 66, 73, 103
Francoa 113
Fraxinus 57
Fritillaria 69, *72*, *86*, 124
Front Lodge 31, 37, 39, 41, 45, 57
fruit trees 124, *125*
Fruiterers' Company 123
Fuchsia 151

G

The Garden House, Buckland Monachorum, Devon 39
Gardeners' World (TV programme) 43, 52
Gardner, Bernard 134
Garvin, J.L. 35
Gentiana *144–45*, 146
Geranium 51, 73, *78*, 80, *80*, 84–85, 88, 97, 113, *114–15*, 151, 152, 159, 163, 164
Geum 146
Gilkes, Martin 35
Ginkgo *59*, 61
Gladiolus 84–85, 88, *98*
Gloucestershire Echo 28
Glyde Hill, Gloucestershire 15, 17, 18, 40
grasses 51, 69, 98, *99*, 118, 146
Graves, Morgan 16, 18
Graves, Richard 15–16, 17, 18
Graves, Walwyn 18
Graves family 15–16
Graves Hamilton, Mary 16, 19
Graves Hamilton, Sidney 15, 18–19, 57
Great Dixter, East Sussex 10, 11
Green, Robert 39
greenhouses 19, *50*
Greenway, Dittisham, Devon 167

H

Hacquetia 146
Hakonechloa 146
Halesia 103, *103*, 106
Hamamelis 92
Hamlyn, Paul 37
Hanbury, Sir Thomas 156
Hayes, Margaret 'Chou' *43*
Hebe 41, 85, *165*
 H. hulkeana 43, 159, 175, *175*
Hedychium 161
Helianthemum 97
Helleborus 61, 91, 103, *106*, 159
Hellyer, A.G.L. 26–27
Hemerocallis 142, 146, 151
Heptacodium 59
Hepworth, Barbara 132
Heuchera 79
Hidcote Boyce, Gloucestershire 41, 73, 101, 175
Hidcote Manor, Gloucestershire 7, 10–11, 21, 25, 26, 30–31, 42, 57, 73, 80, 103, 134, 172
Hidcote Vale, Gloucestershire 41
Hillier Nursery 61
Historic Houses Association/Christie's Garden of the Year Award *6*, 49, 123
Hobhouse, Penelope 159–61
Hobson, Beryl 41–42, *43*, 177
Hodges, Nicky 167
Hoheria 42, 92
Holboellia 161
holly 25, 57, 85, 91, *91*, 103, 148
Hopkins, Gerard Manley 35
Hornby, Sir Simon 80
Hortus magazine 10
Hosta 96, 98, 101, 146, 163
Hughes-Hallett, Lucy 47
Humphreys, A.R. 16
Humulus 142
Hydrangea 7, 70, 73, 96, 98–101, 103, *104*, 151, 163
Hydrangea Border 96, 98–101, *99–101*
Hylotelephium see sedums
Hypericum 146

I

Ibsen, Henrik 35
Ilex *152*, 158
 see also holly
Indigofera 27, *78*, 80, 91, 159
Iran 47, 128
Iris 57–59, *58*, 97, *158*, 159, 163
Isola Madre, Lake Maggiore, Italy 59
Italianate gardens 9, 18, 26, 27–28, 35
Italy 33, 35, 47, 156
Itea 73

J

Japan 26
Japanese anemones 96, *98*, 101
Jekyll, Gertrude 10, 42, 75, 174
Jellicoe, Sir Geoffrey 48, 132–34
Johnson, Samuel 17
Johnston, Lawrence 7, 10, 21, 25, 26, *26*, 28, 29, 30–31, 52, 73, 103, 156, 172
Jones, Mr 40, 46
Journal of the Royal Horticultural Society 30, 42
Joyce, James 35
Juglans 61, 163
Juniperus 57, 92

K

Kennedy Memorial, Runnymede, Surrey 132
Kent, William 17
Kenyon, John 43
Kerdalo, Brittany, France 42
Keswick, Emma 97
'Kiftsgate' rose see *Rosa filipes* 'Kiftsgate'
Kiftsgate Stone 15, *15*
Kirengeshoma 80
kitchen garden 19, 29, 40, 43, 46, 49
Knautia 88, 151
Knight, Henrietta, Lady Luxborough 17
Knightshayes, Devon 43
Kniphofia 43, 146
Kreutzberger, Sibylle 50, 53

L

La Mortola, Ventimiglia, Italy 156
Lancaster, Nancy 29

Lancaster, Roy 43
Lane Fox, Robin 47, 53
Lathyrus 86
lavender 69, 159, 164, *167*
Lawrence, D.H. 35
Lawrence, Frieda 35
Le Rougetel, Hazel 53
The Leasowes, Halesowen, Shropshire (West Midlands) 16–17
Lees-Milne, Helen 28
Lees-Milne, James 28, *69*, 73, 85
Leese, Timothy 38, 40–41, 42, 70
leylandii hedge 161, 163–64
Ligularia 146, *150*, 151, 163
Lilium 80, 87, 91, *103*, *142*, 159
lily of the valley 30, 46
lime trees *see Tilia*
Lindsay, Nancy 30
Lindsay, Norah 10, 28–29, *29*, 30
Liriodendron 49, 128, *129*, 163
Lloyd, Christopher 11
Lloyd, Daisy 10
Lobelia 80, *86*
Logan Botanic Garden, Scotland 48, 167
Lomatia 27
Long Barn, Kent 10, 31
Lonicera 80, *86*, 159, 167, *167*
Lothian, Marquess of 29
Lower Garden 39–40, 48, 50, 52, *162–69*, 163–67
Lunaria 163
Lychnis 163

M

MacCarthy, Sir Desmond 29
Mackenzie, Emma 34, 37–38, *38*, 40, 41, 45–47, *45*, *46*, 164, 177
Magnolia 41, 53, 61, 69–70, *70*, 73, 86, *105*, 106, *135*, *149*, 151, *152*, 161, *162–63*, 163, 164, 167
Mahonia 159
Maianthemum see smilacinas
Malus 61, 66
Malva 73
Malvern Hills 9, 69
Marsh, Sir Edward 29

Matteuccia 120
Mawson, Thomas 26
Mediterranean 27, 48
Melianthus 73
Metasequoia 57
Mickleton, Gloucestershire 10, 15–16, *102*, 151, 159, 163
Mickleton Manor, Gloucestershire 15–16, 17, 18, 19, 40
Miscanthus 98, 118, 146
Molinia 118
Moltkia 106
Moncreiffe of that Ilk, Thomas 22
Monterey pines 19, 21, 57, 69, *71*, 73, 80, 152, *153*
Moore, George 35
Moore, Henry 132
Moorhouse, Pete 44, 49, 128, *130–31*
Moraea 146
Morrell, Lady Ottoline 29
Morris, William 10
Mottisfont Abbey, Hampshire 42
The Mound 47, 49, 51, 124, *126–28*, *127–29*, 134
Muir, Alexander Kay 22
Muir, Bettine Clara (Betsy) 37, 40, *40*, 42, *43*, 48–49, 73, 177
  early life 24, *25*, 27, *27*, 28, 29–30, 33, *33*, 36–37, *36*, 124
  garden at Hidcote Boyce 41, 101, 175
  gardening style 80, 85
Muir, Clara Gardiner 23–24, *23*, 25, 37, 124
Muir, Elizabeth 22
Muir, Gillian 25, 36–37, 124
Muir, Heather 6, 9–11, 19, 21–31, *33*, 36–37, 39, *40*, 45, 50, 51
  The Banks 9, 27–28, 40, 152, 156, 158–59, 163
  Bluebell Wood 27, 66
  Bridge Border 103
  buys Kiftsgate 21
  early life *21*, 22–24, *23–25*
  Four Squares 26, 75–79, 80
  Front Lodge 57
  and Hidcote 30–31
  House and Side Lawn 69, 72

Hydrangea Border 98
influences 10–11
'Kiftsgate' rose 7, 29, 42, 172
Lower Garden 163, 167, 174
marriage 24–25
opens garden 29, 49
Rose Border 9, 26, 108, 113
in Second World War 29–30
signature plants 174, 176
Tapestry Hedge 9, 11, 25, 103
use of colour 26–27
White Sunk Garden 92
Wide Border 26, *27*, 85, 86, 91
Yellow Border 26, 142–46
Muir, Ian Kay (Kim) 25, 29, 124
Muir, Jack 9, 19, 21, 22, 24–25, *24*, 30, 31, 37, 40
Muir, James Finlay 22
Muir, Jean 22
Muir, Jessie Agnes Henderson 22–23, *22*
Muir, Sir John 21–22, *21*
Muir, John Gardiner 22–23, *22*, 24
Muir, Judy 24, *25*, *27*, 28–29, *33*, *34*, 37, 106, 124
Muir, Margaret 21, 22
Muir, Matthew 25
Muir, Muriel (Milly) 23
Muir, Nada 24
Muir, Robin 35
Munstead Wood, Godalming, Surrey 42
Munster, Peggy 80
Murphy, Duncan 39
Murrell, Hilda 39, *39*, 79, 176
Muscari 95
Mussolini, Benito 35
Myosotis 38

N

Nandina 165
Narcissus 124, *124*
  see also daffodils
National Garden Scheme 29, 49, 53, 61, 151
National Trust 6, 9, 11, 26, 30, 42, 73
Navarro, Mary Anderson de 30
Navarro, 'Toty' de 30
Nectaroscordum *143*, 146

Nesfield, William Andrews 6, 23, 24
Newport House, Almeley, Herefordshire 23–24
Nicholson, Ben 132
Nicolson, Harold 29, 31
Nicolson, Nigel 28
Noailles, Vicomte de 31
North Border 40, 53, 148–51, *148–51*
Nothofagus 66
nursery 7, 49–50, *50*, 51, 57

O

oak trees 21, 27, 57, 152, 163
The Observer 11, 31, 35
Oldcastle, Sir John 23
Olearia 79, 86, 95, 161, 163, *166*, 167
Ophiopogon 118
Orchard 49, 52, 124–27, *124–26*
Osmanthus 43, 57, *59*, 61, 86, 92, 148, 159, 161
Osmunda 118
Oudolf, Piet 97
Oxford Botanic Garden 38, 135
Oxford Group 34–35
Ozothamnus 41

P

Paeonia (peonies) 26, 41, 52, 61, 75, 79, 88, 97, *140–41*, 146, 151, 161, *164*
    P. rockii 52, 79, *166*, 167, 176, *176*
    see also tree peonies
Pan-Global Plants, Frampton-on-Severn, Gloucestershire 50, 51, 91
Panicum 146
Papaver 151
Parahebe 97
Pasley-Tyler, Ian and Susie 52
Paulownia *84–85*, 86
pear trees 27
pelargoniums 73
Pemberton, Rev. Joseph 92, 176
Pennisetum 68, 69, 98, *99*
Penstemon 80, *82–83*, 91, 151
peonies see *Paeonia*; tree peonies
Persian gardens 128
Pettifers Garden, nr Banbury, Oxfordshire 42

Philadelphus 31, 51, 61, 91, 92, *113*, *115*, 151, *151*, 167
Phillyrea 70
Philodendron 48, *133*, 135, *135*
Phlomis 91, 142, 146, *166*, 167
Phlox 97, *99*, 101
Phormium 152, *160–61*
Photinia 86, *90*
Phygelius 42, 151
Pidgeon, Rosa Leah 19
pine trees 129
    Bhutan pine 59
    Monterey pines 19, 21, 57, 69, *71*, 73, 80, 152, *153*
    Scots pines 9, 16, 17, *18*, 21, 71, *130–31*, 151, 152, *158–59*
Pittosporum 152, 159, 163, *166*
Pivoines Rivière, France 52
Poggio Gherardo, Florence, Italy 27, 28, 33, *34*, 35
Pope, Alexander 17
Populus 66
Porter, Sir Endymion 15–16
Potentilla 142, 146
Powis Castle, Powys, Wales 52
Price, Gina 42
Primula 79, *95*
Prostanthera 164
Proust, Marcel 35
Prunus 7, 9, 66, 69, *72*
Pterocarya 161
Pterostyrax 7, 61
Pulmonaria 97
Pyrus 27

Q

Queen magazine 31
Quercus 57, 66
    see also oak trees

R

Raven, Sarah 73
Red Cross Society 36
Repton, Humphry 50
Rhaphiolepis 42, *160–61*
Rhodochiton *132*, 134

Rhododendron 27, 57, *66*, 67, 103, 106, *107*
Richardson, Tim 16
Robinia 57, 142
Robinson, Henry 108
Robinson, William 10
Rock, Joseph 176
Rockcliffe House, Upper Slaughter, Gloucestershire 97
Rodgersia *75*, 80, 101, 146
Roper, Lanning 30–31
Rose, Graham 43
roses (*Rosa*) 48, 51
    The Banks 152
    entrance to Kiftsgate 57
    Four Squares *75*–79, 80, *81–83*
    Lower Garden *166*, 167
    the Mound 127, *127*
    North Border *150*, 151
    in the Orchard *124*
    Rose Border 9, *20*, 25–26, 29, 41, 48, 51, 108–14, *108–17*
    Tresco 161
    White Sunk Garden 92, 95, *97*, 98
    Wide Border *84–85*, 85–86, *88–89*
    Yellow Border 141, 142, *144–46*
    R. 'Albertine' 69, *71*
    R. *banksiae* 'Lutea' 41, 72, 75
    R. 'Blanche Double de Coubert' 49, 108, 127, *127*
    R. Bonica 108
    R. 'Charles de Mills' 108
    R. 'Cooperi' 72–73
    R. 'Dentelle de Bruges' 61
    R. 'Diany Binny' 141
    R. Eyes For You *75*, 79
    R. 'Fantin-Latour' 86, 108
    R. 'Felicia' 80, 176, *176*
    R. *filipes* 'Kiftsgate' 7, 9, 29, 31, 41, 42, 43, 108, *108*, 112–13, 141, 172, *172–73*
    R. 'François Juranville' 70, 75
    R. 'Fritz Nobis' *115*
    R. *gallica* var. *officinalis* 108, 113
    R. *gallica* 'Versicolor' *20*, 26, 108, *108–109*, 114, 115
    R. Gertrude Jekyll 108
    R. 'Magenta' *75*, 79

R. moschata 29, 42, 172
R. × odorata 'Mutabilis' 43, 72
R. 'Pax' 92, 108
R. 'Penelope' *114*
R. 'Prince Charles' 86, 108
R. 'Rita' *78*, 79, 176, *176*
R. 'Roseraie de l'Haÿ' 49, 127, *127*
R. Scarlet Fire 50
R. sericea 'Heather Muir' 92, *92*
R. 'Tuscany Superb' 108, *114–15*
R. 'Una' 108
R. 'Veilchenblau' *57*, 108
Ross, Janet 35
Royal Horticultural Society (RHS) 31, 80, 132
Royal National Rose Society 39, 141, 176
Russell, Jim 42

S

Sackville-West, Vita 10, 11, 16, 29, 30, 31, *31*, 39, 92, 172
Salvia 52, 73, *78*, 80, 91, 96, 146, 159, 164, *166*, 175
Sambucus 152
Sanguinaria 95
Santolina 152
Schizophragma 50, 61, 98
schizostylis 50
Schwerdt, Pamela 50, 53
Scilla 69, 70, 159
Scilly Isles 48, 161
Scots pines 9, 16, 17, *18*, 21, *71*, *130–31*, 151, 152, *158–59*
Second World War 29, 35–36, 37
sedums 90, 91, 151
Serre de la Madone, Menton, France 25, 26, 31, 52, 156
Sezincote, Moreton-in-Marsh, Gloucestershire 50–52
Shenstone, William 9, 16–18, *17*, 40, 57, 151, 152
Sherbourne Park, Barford, Warwickshire 175
Shute House, Dorset 132
Side Lawn *68–73*, 69–73
Sir Henry at Rawlinson End (film) 43
Sissinghurst Castle Garden, nr Cranbrook, Kent 10, 11, 28, 29, 30, 31, 39, 50, 92, 97, 172
Sisyrinchium 97
Six Hills Nursery, Stevenage, Hertfordshire 42
Skelmersdale, Christine 53
Skimmia 161
smilacinas 70–72, 86, 97, 103, 151, 161
Smith-Ryland, Jeryl 175
Smithers, Sir Peter 52, 79, 167, 176
snowdrops 62, *62–63*, 69
Soil Association 39
Sophora 27
Sorbus 141
Sorbus Arch 41, *111*, 113–14, 118, *118*
Southcote, Philip 16, 17
Spender, Stephen 35
Spetchley Park, Worcestershire 38
Stachys 84–85, 95, *97*, 161
Staphylea 90, 92
Stein, Gertrude 35
Stone House Cottage Nursery, Kidderminster, Worcestershire 38, 39, 42, 43, 50, 80
Stowe, Buckinghamshire 17
Strangman, Elizabeth 88
Strong, Sir Roy 90, 91
Styphnolobium 57
Sudeley Castle, Winchcombe, Gloucestershire 124
Sunningdale Nurseries 42
Sutton Courtenay, Oxfordshire 29
Sutton Place, Surrey 48, 132–34
swimming pool 7, 39, 48, 50, *157*, 159, *160–63*, 164, *168–71*
Syringa 61, 80, 85, 86

T

Tanacetum 95
Tapestry Hedge 9, 11, *20*, 25, 26, *27*, 103–106, *108–109*
tennis court 27, 30, 48, 132
Teucrium 159
Thalictrum 88, 113, 151, 163
Thomas, Graham Stuart 30, 42, *42*, 50, 142, 167, 172, 176
Thomson, James 17
Thrower, Percy 39
Thyssen, Baron 51
Tilia (lime trees) 17, 40, 57, *59*, 61

Tollemache, Xa 85
Top Banks 41, 48, 51, 151, 152
Trachelospermum 48
Trachycarpus 80
tree peonies 7, 41, 52, 61, 79, 88, 97, *97*, 113, *150*, 161, *164*, *166*, 167
see also *Paeonia rockii*
Tresco 48, 51, 161
Tricyrtis 7, 101
Trillium 43, 52, *94*, 95
Tropaeolum 118
Tulip Tree Avenue 9, *44*, 47, 49, 124, 128–29, *129–31*
tulips 43, 73, 79, *88*, 103, *103*, *110–11*, 113, 124, *140–41*, 146, *150*, 151, 152
Twain, Mark 35
Twickenham, Middlesex 17

U

Upton House, Warwickshire 29

V

Veitch, Robert & Son 27
Veratrum 86
Verbascum 165
Verey, Rosemary 11, 41, 52, 114
Verity, Simon 41, *41*, 114, 118, *119*, *154–55*, 158
Veronica 88, *97*
Viburnum 57, 61, 92, 103, *107*, 151, 159, 161
Villa Boccanegra, Ventimiglia, Italy 156
Vincent, Philip 51, *51*
Viola 86

W

Wakefield, Victoria 42, 79
Water Garden 6, *7*, 48–49, 51, 124–27, 132–35, *132–39*
Waterfield, Aubrey 27–28, *28*, 33–35, *34–35*, 53, 156
Waterfield, Kinta 33–34, 53
Waterfield, Lina 27, 33–35, *35*, 37, 53
Watt, James 23
Watts, G.F. 35
Weigela 49, *90*
Weller, David 43
Wellingtonias 21

Welsh poppies *88–89*, 164
Whately, Thomas 17
Wheeler, David 10
White Sunk Garden 10, *32*, 40, *40*, 50, 51, 92–101, *92–101*, 132, 164
Wide Border 26, *27*, 39, 40, 41, 49, 51, 80, *84–91*, 85–91, 151
Wild Flower Corner 49, 118–23, *121–23*
William IV, King 15
Williams, Evan 37
Willmott, Ellen 156

Wilson, Ernest Henry 26, 53
Winthrop, Gertrude 26, 28
Wisley, Surrey 132
Wisteria 70, *74*, 75
Woburn Farm, Surrey 16, 17
Wolkonsky, Prince Peter 42, 48
Wollerton Old Hall Garden, Shropshire 52
Woodfield brothers 146
Wormesley, Mr 40
Wynn-Jones, Bleddyn and Sue 50

X
Xanthoceras 70

Y
Yeats, W.B. 35
Yellow Border 26, 39, 52, *140–47*, 141–46
yew 25, 51, *74*, 75, 80, 85, 91, *91*, 92, 103, *111*, 113, *119*, 129, 134, *134*

Z
Zanthoxylum 51, 152

First published 2019 by Merrell Publishers,
London and New York

Merrell Publishers Limited
70 Cowcross Street
London EC1M 6EJ

merrellpublishers.com

Text copyright © 2019 the authors
Illustrations copyright © 2019 the copyright
 holders; see p. 181
Design and layout copyright © 2019 Merrell
 Publishers Limited

All rights reserved. No part of this publication may be reproduced, stored in a retrieval system or transmitted, in any form or by any means, electronic, mechanical, photocopying, recording or otherwise, without the prior written permission of the publisher.

British Library Cataloguing in Publication Data.
A catalogue record for this book is available from the British Library.

ISBN 978-1-8589-4669-6

Produced by Merrell Publishers Limited
Designed by Nicola Bailey
Project-managed by Claire Chandler
Additional picture research by Nick Wheldon
Proofread by Rosanna Fairhead
Indexed by Hilary Bird

Printed and bound in China

JACKET, FRONT: View of the Georgian portico of Kiftsgate Court from the Four Squares.

JACKET, BACK, FROM TOP: Hydrangea Border in the White Sunk Garden; Yellow Border; Water Garden.

ENDPAPERS: Detail of an image of the 'Kiftsgate' rose from the Kiftsgate Court Archive.

FRONTISPIECE: The Hydrangea Border along the top edge of the White Sunk Garden.

PAGES 12–13: An aerial view of Kiftsgate shows the dense tapestry of planting through the formal flower garden.

PAGES 54–55: The planting at Kiftsgate is as remarkable for its shapes and textures as for its flowers, as can be seen from this aerial view.

PAGES 182–83: Under a deep blanket of snow, the strong structure laid down by Heather Muir at Kiftsgate is all the more apparent.

OVERLEAF: *Dahlia* 'Bishop of Llandaff' on the terrace beside the Four Squares.

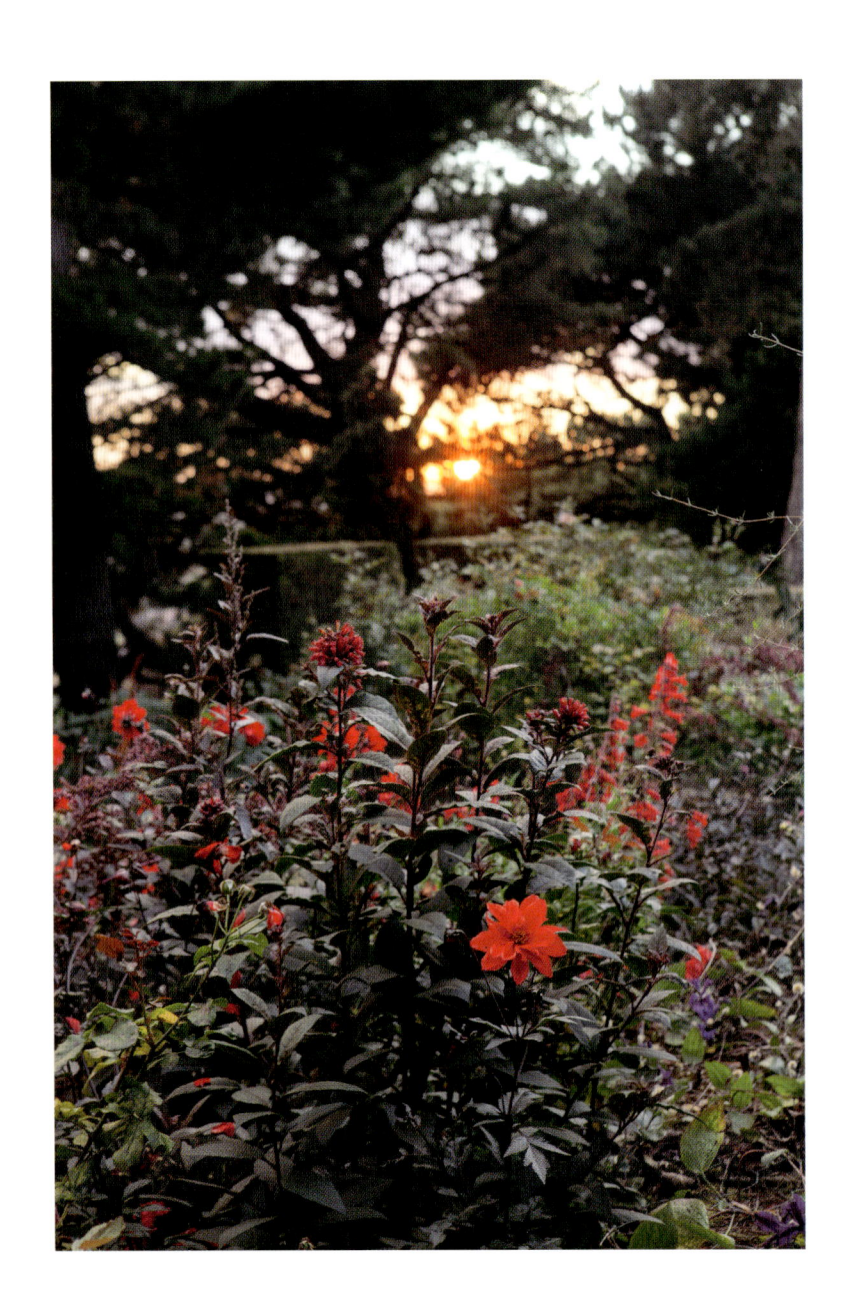

For the Kiftsgate gardeners – past, present and future